GREAT SMOKY MOUNTAINS
NATIONAL PARK

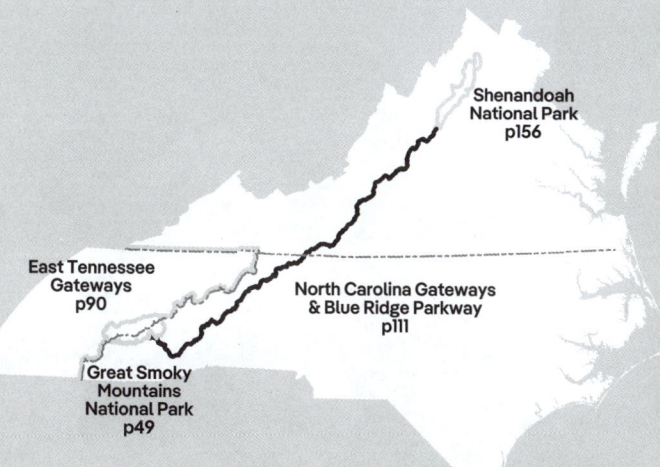

Shenandoah National Park p156

East Tennessee Gateways p90

North Carolina Gateways & Blue Ridge Parkway p111

Great Smoky Mountains National Park p49

Amy C Balfour, Gregor Clark

Dragon's Tooth (p131)

CONTENTS

Plan Your Trip

Great Smoky Mountains National Park: The Journey Begins Here 4

Map 6

Our Picks 8

Regions & National Parks 18

Itineraries 20

When to Go 26

Get Prepared for the Smokies 28

Wildlife 30

A Land of Ancient Mountains 32

The Food Scene 34

Multiday Hikes 38

Mountain Music 40

The Outdoors 42

Collard greens and bacon (p35)

The Guide

Great Smoky Mountains National Park 49
- Find Your Way 50
- Plan Your Time 52
- Sugarlands, Elkmont & the Northern Park 54
- Oconaluftee & the Southern Park 62
- Cades Cove & the Western Park 68
- Cataloochee & the Eastern Park 76
- High Country 84

East Tennessee Gateways 90
- Find Your Way 92
- Plan Your Time 93
- Knoxville 94
- Gatlinburg & Pigeon Forge 101

North Carolina Gateways & Blue Ridge Parkway 111
- Find Your Way 112
- Plan Your Time 114
- Charlottesville 116
- Staunton & Lexington 122
- Roanoke 129
- Beyond Roanoke 134
- North Carolina High Country 139
- Asheville 144
- Beyond Asheville 150

Shenandoah National Park 156
- Find Your Way 158
- Plan Your Time 159
- Skyland & Big Meadows 160
- Beyond Skyland & Big Meadows 164

Woodpecker

Toolkit

Arriving 170

Getting Around 171

Money 172

Accommodations 173

Family Travel 174

Health & Safe Travel 175

Food, Drink & Nightlife 176

Responsible Travel 178

Accessible Travel 180

Nuts & Bolts 181

Storybook

A History of the Great Smokies & Beyond in 15 Places 184

Meet the Ranger 188

Parks under Pressure 190

GREAT SMOKY MOUNTAINS NATIONAL PARK
THE JOURNEY BEGINS HERE

Like my great-grandfather, who grew up at the base of the Peaks of Otter and guided hikes to the summit of Sharp Top in the 1890s, I have a deep love for the southern Appalachians, especially Great Smoky Mountains National Park. There's something about the gentle beauty here – ancient mountains, fertile valleys and mighty rivers – that's good for the soul. The park is linked to Shenandoah National Park by a federal roadway in the Blue Ridge Mountains called the Blue Ridge Parkway, and together, these parks from a gorgeous trio of national recreation areas.

Complementing the natural beauty here is Appalachian culture and food, from Asheville's Chow Chow Festival to the delicacies at Mama Jean's in Roanoke. Opportunities for outdoor adventure keep hikers, mountain bikers and paddlers busy. And the best part? Dolly Parton, paragon of Appalachian friendliness, and the patron saint of the Smokies.

Amy C Balfour

@amycbalfour

Amy writes about travel, culture and outdoor adventure, and she's always up for a hike with a view.

My favourite experience is camping in the Great Smokies (p72). The setting is spectacular and the campsites, from Cades Cove to the Appalachian Trail shelters, share a welcoming and festive vibe.

WHO GOES WHERE

Our second writer and expert chooses the place which, for them, defines Great Smoky Mountains National Park.

While researching this guidebook, I fell in love with the primeval splendor of **Cades Cove** (pictured; p68). Walking or cycling this vast mountain-fringed valley at dawn on a traffic-free Wednesday, with bears and wild turkeys roaming the meadows and morning mist shrouding the trees, was a step back into an earlier century, and a reminder of the importance of leaving some places untamed.

Gregor Clark

@thewideopenroad

A Lonely Planet author since 2000, Gregor is a lifelong polyglot and outdoors enthusiast whose passion for languages, world cultures and the Earth's wild places has taken him to over 50 countries on five continents.

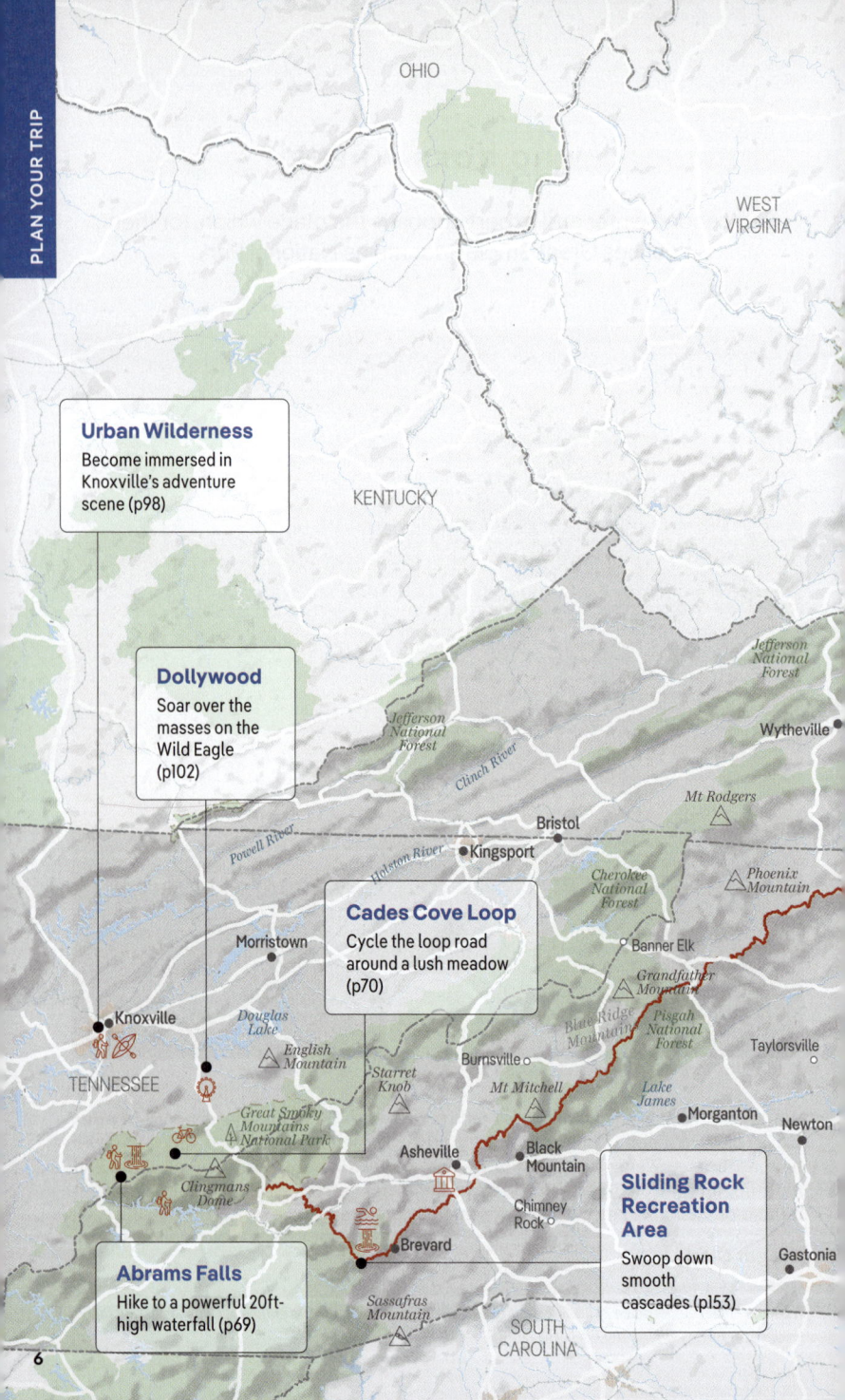

Old Rag Mountain
Scramble up boulders to a vertiginous summit (p166)

McAfee Knob
Pose on a photogenic ledge of the Appalachian Trail (p131)

EPIC HIKES

A hike with a scenic payoff usually qualifies as a good one. But what elevates a hike from good to epic? It's usually a wander with some 'oomph' along the way, where the journey is just as important as the destination. With boulder climbs, rock scrambling and towering wooden ladders, these trails across Great Smoky Mountains National Park, Shenandoah and the Blue Ridge Parkway deliver plenty of epic.

Permits

To hike up Old Rag, you'll need to buy a $1 day-use ticket. Before hiking the Grandfather Mountain Trail (pictured above), fill out a permit at the trailhead.

Trail Etiquette

Greet those you meet on the trail and provide assistance if necessary. Remember: those hiking uphill have right of way. Don't feed wild animals or leave food unattended.

Hiking Safety

Allow plenty of time to finish a hike before dark. Leave details of your intended route with someone, and let them know when you return.

Alum Cave Trail (p88)

PLAN YOUR TRIP OUR PICKS

BEST EPIC HIKE EXPERIENCES

Scramble up, over and through a boulder playground on the last mile to the summit of ❶ **Old Rag Mountain** in Shenandoah National Park. (p166)

Scale the wooden ladders and steel cables of the mountain slopes on ❷ **Grandfather Mountain Trail** near Blowing Rock. (p142)

Climb past wild rock formations on the steep ❸ **Alum Cave Trail** in this lush stretch of forest in the Great Smokies. (p88)

Take the trail 1600ft to ❹ **Rainbow Falls**, one of the Smokies' highest waterfalls, cascading 90ft down a cliff immersed in forest. (p56)

High on the ridge above Cades Cove is famous ❺ **Gregory Bald**, a grassy high-altitude clearing replete with flame azealas and spectacular views. (p73)

9

Abrams Falls (p69)

WATERFALL WONDERS

Thanks to abundant rainfall and steep elevation, waterfalls flourish in the Great Smokies. The national park is dotted with thundering cascades, and trails often follow creeks upstream to reach them. You'll also find an enchanting concentration of falls near Big Meadows in Shenandoah National Park and along the Blue Ridge Parkway.

What Goes Down...

Most waterfall hikes in Shenandoah drop from the parkway to the base of the falls – so reserve any extra energy for the hike back up.

Slippery Rocks

Rocks along the sides of the waterfalls can be deceptively slippery, leading to bad falls. Don't try to climb up the waterfalls either – the paths alongside them can be treacherous.

BEST WATERFALL EXPERIENCES

Picnic near the base of ❶ **Abrams Falls**, the most voluminous falls in Great Smoky Mountains National Park. (p69)

Wander a beautifully engineered but strenuous trail through old-growth trees to the 100ft-tall ❷ **Ramsey Cascades** in the Smokies. (p61)

Make the mile-long journey to the impressive 67ft-high ❸ **Rose River Falls** in Shenandoah National Park; continue to Deep Hollow Falls for a longer loop. (p162)

Snap some great photos and walk directly under the falling water at ❹ **Grotto Falls**, just south of Gatlinburg. (p56)

Pull over your car, step out and say 'wow!' at ❺ **Looking Glass Falls**, a true stunner with a wheelchair-accessible overlook. (p153)

MOUNTAIN BEERS

Craft breweries in the southern Appalachians are often flanked by mountains that provide a picture-perfect backdrop after a hard day on the trails. In Asheville, aka 'Beer City USA,' enjoy a cold one amid the city's many murals. In this region, the brewers are innovative, often showcasing the best of local and seasonal ingredients.

Field Guides

The field guide published by the Asheville Ale Trail has a comprehensive list of more than 100 regional breweries. Download its digital passport for swag (ashevillealetrail.com).

Shuttles

Climb aboard Hop On C'ville ($75 per person) to safely visit some of the breweries on Virginia's Brew Ridge Trail near Charlottesville, such as Three Notch'd Brewing (pictured above).

Unexpected Locations

Craft beer bars can be found in unexpected places these days, from bike shops in Roanoke to outdoor stores in the Smokies.

BEST MOUNTAIN BEER EXPERIENCES

Scramble up Devil's Marbleyard and reward yourself with a light Hibiscus Wit beer and Blue Ridge mountain views at ❶ **Great Valley Farm Brewery & Winery** in Lexington. (p125)

Visit the eight breweries in ❷ **South Slope** in downtown Asheville for quality and quantity, and a very sudsy afternoon. (p147)

Revel in the hospitality, the good beer and the family-friendly digs at ❸ **Booneshine**, just outside Boone. (p142)

Sample a crazy flavor or two at ❹ **Innovation Brewing** in Sylva, also known for its sweet creek-side setting and delicious meatball pizza slices. (p153)

Treat yourself when in Knoxville to ❺ **Pretentious Beer**, which serves a constantly changing mix of brews in artsy handblown glasses from the shop next door. (p96)

APPALACHIAN CULTURE

Settled by Scots-Irish and German settlers in the mid 1700s, the Appalachian mountains make an appearance in 14 US states. Generations of Appalachian families have lived on farms and homesteads in small communities in the region's foothills and valleys. Customs aren't uniform across the vast area, but there are rich, often-shared traditions in crafts, music and food that unite these communities, particularly across the southern reaches of the range.

Pronunciation

Some travelers may be surprised to hear locals say Appa-LATCH-a instead of Appa-LAY-cha. You'll hear both versions, but you may cross paths with those who insist on the former.

Southern Highlands Crafts Guild

Managing two shops on the Blue Ridge Parkway and two in Asheville, the Southern Highland Crafts Guild (pictured above) is a reliable purveyor of quality Appalachian arts and crafts.

The Appalachian Voice

For well-informed, up-to-the-minute news about environmental issues in the mountains, as well as insights on culture and the outdoors, read the *Appalachian Voice*.

Museum of East Tennessee History (p96)

BEST APPALACHIAN CULTURAL EXPERIENCES

Get insight into early ❶ **Cades Cove** residents, their homes and their lifestyles with a self-guided auto tour. (p70)

Explore cultural topics at the ❷ **Museum of East Tennessee History** in Knoxville, including mountain music and the impacts of mountain tourism. (p96)

Take a pottery-making or woodworking class at ❸ **Arrowmont School of Arts and Crafts** in Gatlinburg and watch local artisans at work in their studios. (p108)

Gather among mountain-music fans, both young and old, for an evening of community, old-time music and dancing during the ❹ **Friday Night Jamboree** in Floyd. (p135)

Step into ❺ **Ole Smoky Moonshine** and other distilleries in Gatlinburg for samples and a good time. After all, you can't talk about the best of Appalachia without mentioning moonshine! (p187)

Rafting on the Nantahala River (p153)

WILD OUTDOORS

Hiking, we love ya, but with swift rivers, bumpy singletrack, slick rockslides and swinging bridges, there is a ton of additional options for outdoor fun here. While a horseback ride may not be wild, it's not sitting in your desk chair, either. And for one adventure the whole family can enjoy, try tubing – a specialty of the region.

River Floating

Tubing and kayaking are easy and affordable adventures. Numerous companies will rent you the necessary gear and shuttle you to the starting point a few miles upriver.

Gravel Riding

Gravel riding has exploded in popularity in recent years and encompasses a range of bike-riding surfaces, with a focus on fire roads, forest service roads and unmaintained paved roads.

BEST OUTDOOR EXPERIENCES

Kayak, canoe or tube the James River in the foothills of Virginia's Blue Ridge with ❶ **Twin River Outfitters**, where paddling routes follow a scenic 'blueway.' (p125)

Pedal around a lake in the second-largest municipal park in the US on these mountain biking trails at ❷ **Carvins Cove** in Roanoke. (p133)

Enjoy intense white-water rafting on the Nantahala River near Bryson City, where you can join a guided trip at the ❸ **Nantahala Outdoor Center**. (p153)

Slide down a 60ft-long all natural rockslide powered by a mountain stream at ❹ **Sliding Rock Recreation Area** near Brevard. (p153)

Saddle up for a horseback ride to a waterfall with ❺ **Smokemont Riding Stables**, or let someone else take the reins on a wagon ride. (p65)

PLAN YOUR TRIP   OUR PICKS

BEST ICONIC SITES EXPERIENCES

Explore the main house and delve into slavery and archaeology at ❶ **Monticello**, the mountaintop home of Thomas Jefferson. (p118)

Mimic an eagle in flight on the Wild Eagle at ❷ **Dollywood**, dropping 135ft and reaching speeds of 61mph. (p102)

Soak up the grandeur of the ❸ **Biltmore**, where the azaleas in spring and the sunflowers in summer are something to behold. (p145)

Pass near the ❹ **Appalachian Trail** and take a short detour to appreciate the tell-tale blazes of the flame azaleas. (p73)

Listen out in the depths of ❺ **Luray Caverns** for the Stalactite Organ, which taps against stalactites throughout the caves, making it the largest musical instrument in the world. (p165)

Monticello (p118)

ICONIC SITES

Founding Fathers and wealthy industrialists built grand homes with beautiful gardens in the southern Appalachian foothills that are today open for tours. Seekers of beauty will also love the grandeur of the Appalachian Mountains, with guaranteed immersion in their natural wonders – on long-distance trails, underground tours and the Wild Eagle roller coaster.

Specialty Tours

Historic homes like Monticello and the Biltmore have standard tours, but reserve early for one of the smaller specialty tours that dig into unique historic perspectives.

Holiday Events

Grand homes celebrate the season with holiday lights, festive decor and Christmas trees, plus workshops and evening tours. More than 6000 lights illuminate Dollywood.

TOP OF THE WORLD

Skyline Drive, the Blue Ridge Parkway and Newfound Gap Rd swoop along ridges that hug the tallest mountains on the East Coast. These mountains formed when sedimentary rocks pushed skyward after a continental collision hundreds of millions of years ago. Today, eroded by wind and rain, many of these once fierce peaks – and their views – can be accessed by foot, and often by car. Effort? Minimal. Rewards? Profound.

Misplaced Rocks

How did all those boulders end up in the streams and mountain slopes? Ice sheets from the Pleiostocene Epoch froze and thawed here, breaking rocks from cliffs and crags.

Photo Etiquette

When looking for that perfect photo spot, be cognizant of fellow visitors taking photographs. Stay out of their frame and don't hog the best spot.

Selfie Safety

Be mindful of your surroundings – crumbly ledges, steep drops – when taking selfies. The number of fatal accidents while attempting that perfect shot is surprisingly high.

Clingmans Dome (p89)

BEST TOP-OF-THE-WORLD EXPERIENCES

See up to 85 miles on a clear day from the top of ❶ **Mt Mitchell** (6684ft), the highest peak east of the Mississippi. (p147)

Breathe it all in from the observation tower with its 375ft-long ramp atop ❷ **Clingmans Dome**, the highest point in Great Smoky Mountains National Park. (p89)

Watch the southern Appalachians unfurl magnificently in every direction from ❸ **Gregory Bald**, framed by fiery flaming azaleas in late June. (p73)

You might not be quite on top of the world, but photogenic ❹ **McAfee Knob** – which juts over the Catawba Valley near Roanoke – sure looks like it might be. (pictured second from left; p131)

Climb 1½ miles to the rocky summit of ❺ **Sharp Top** at the Peaks of Otter for a quick workout ending with high-elevation views. (p127)

REGIONS & NATIONAL PARKS

Find the places that tick all your boxes.

East Tennessee Gateways

SPRINGBOARDS TO SMOKY ADVENTURES

In this largely rural region of small towns, rolling hills, thick forests and river valleys, opportunities for adventure – rafting, tubing and hiking – are plentiful. Knoxville is a bastion of culture and cuisine, with a vibrant student population and great city parks, while Gatlinburg and Pigeon Forge keep families busy with pancake houses and Dollywood.

p90

East Tennessee Gateways
p90

Great Smoky Mountains National Park
p49

Great Smoky Mountains National Park

APPALACHIAN ROOTS AND EXUBERANT NATURE

Waterfalls, wild animals and leafy trails are hallmarks of this park of 500,000 acres, which sprawl across Tennessee and North Carolina. Cades Cove teems with wildlife, while grassy balds dazzle with summer blooms. Fontana Lake is water-sports central, remote Cataloochee is a haven for elk, and lofty Clingmans Dome presides over it all.

p49

Shenandoah National Park

ADVENTURE BECKONS AT EVERY BEND

This lofty park ribbons across the high-elevation ridges of the Blue Ridge Mountains for 100 miles. Its centerpiece – Skyline Drive – serves up a scenic buffet for drivers looking for a quick nature escape near northern Virginia. History, wondrous caverns and good eats await in the small towns that dot the Shenandoah Valley.

p156

Shenandoah National Park
p156

VIRGINIA

North Carolina Gateways & Blue Ridge Parkway
p111

NORTH CAROLINA

North Carolina Gateways & Blue Ridge Parkway

WATERFALLS, SCENIC VISTAS AND APPALACHIAN CULTURE

The most visited national parkland in the US, the mountain-top Blue Ridge Parkway swoops past college towns, the Appalachian Trail and mountain-music venues in Virginia. It then curves through North Carolina High Country, where it passes the East Coast's highest peak before careening past sudsy Asheville and ending at the doorstep of the Smokies.

p111

Ripley's Moving Theater (p106), Gatlinburg

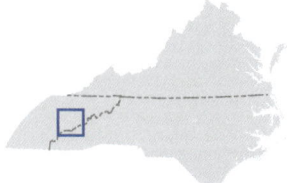

ITINERARIES

Tennessee Family Fun

Allow: 6 ½ days   **Distance:** 100 miles

Families, put down your smartphones and hold on tight: this trip is a wild ride through East Tennessee, where you'll bounce over rapids, take sky lifts to mountaintops and plunge down coaster tracks. And there's even quality campfire time to balance out all those thrills.

❶ KNOXVILLE ⏱ 1 DAY

Knoxville (p94) is home to an extensive park system known as the Urban Wilderness. Here, you can swing through the trees on a canopy tour, look for wildlife on a riverside boardwalk and test your bike skills at the Baker Creek Preserve. Explore the city's many fascinating museums, and end with a stroll through Market Square and a sunset tipple at one of its many rooftop bars.

❷ TOWNSEND ⏱ ½ DAY

Just 9 miles from the Cades Cove Loop, **Townsend** (p73) is a blast for a half-day pit stop. Get comfortable in inner tubes for a splashy float down the Little River, then dig into burgers and shakes at a local drive-in. Families can also learn about Appalachian culture at the Great Smoky Mountains Heritage Center (pictured).

❸ CADES COVE ⏱ 2 DAYS

If you can, time your camping reservation for a Tuesday night so you can pedal the 11-mile loop road around the meadows at **Cades Cove** (p70) on car-free Wednesdays. The abundant wildlife here lives, loves and maybe even laughs in the adjacent meadows. Horseback rides and hayrides are available, too, and hiking trails follow creeks and climb mountain slopes. This is the place to roast those s'mores over a campfire.

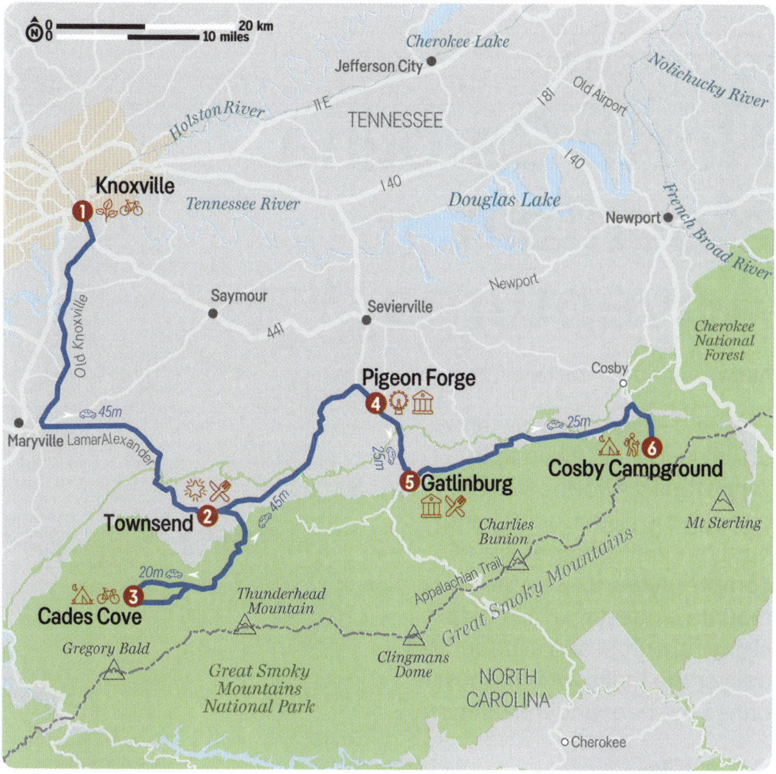

④
PIGEON FORGE ⏱1 DAY

Next up is **Pigeon Forge** (p101), which, at first glance, is a little dispiriting. Maybe after the second glance, too. But behind the bling and billboards are gobs of fun attractions. Amenities at hotels and motels – like free evening popcorn – keep families in mind. Quirky museums, mini-golf courses, mountain coasters and, of course, Dollywood, might be the setting for your favorite East Tennessee memories.

⑤
GATLINBURG ⏱1 DAY

If you're traveling with teens, your best bet is letting them go feral in downtown **Gatlinburg** (p106), where the walkable Gatlinburg Strip is lined with Ripley's Believe It or Not Museums and gondolas that swoop riders up to mountaintops loaded with more attractions – like summer ice-skating. Hotels and pancakes houses are thick on the ground. And parents, several moonshine distilleries await.

⑥
COSBY CAMPGROUND ⏱1 DAY

Wrap up this wild ride with a calm day and overnight at **Cosby Campground** (p82), a large but less frenetic campground beautifully set in the forest in the far eastern reaches of the park. If your kids are up for long hikes, tackle the 5.2-mile round-trip hike to the Mt Cammemer Lookout Tower (pictured) and its 360-degree views.

ITINERARIES

North Carolina Mountain Adventures

Allow: 6 days **Distance:** 210 miles

The Blue Ridge Parkway throws up its hands and gives a big 'whoot!' as it swoops south through the High Country and hurtles – well, plugs along, at 45mph – toward Asheville. A mountain coaster, a mile-high swinging bridge and a ladder trail deliver the thrills, while Asheville brings the beer and the Biltmore.

❶ BOONE & BLOWING ROCK ⏱ 1 DAY

Kick off this trip with a great dinner in **Boone** (p142) followed by a craft beer in **Blowing Rock** (p140), the small urban anchors of the High Country. A college town, Boone has a compact but energetic core stocked with good restaurants, festive watering holes and an awesome statue of Doc Watson. Blowing Rock hugs the parkway and keeps families happy with a scenic train and a gravity-defying mystery house.

❷ HIGH COUNTRY: BLUE RIDGE PARKWAY ⏱ 1 DAY

Between Blowing Rock and Asheville, the **Blue Ridge Parkway** (p111) has some fun to offer. Pull over for trails leading to waterfalls, wildflowers and the highest peak east of the Mississippi. A beautiful viaduct swoops around **Grandfather Mountain** (p141) and its many attractions. To unwind while immersing in the regional beauty, pitch a tent at the Linville Falls Campground.

❸ ASHEVILLE ⏱ 2 DAYS

After your camping, this cultural and culinary beacon in the western North Carolina mountains will delight. **Asheville** (p144) is a magnet for hikers, artists, craft-beer enthusiasts, hippies and those who love them all. The Biltmore and the Grove Park Inn (pictured) have impressed travelers for decades, while the River Arts District and West Asheville are delivering contemporary cool.

FROM LEFT: DANAFOREMAN/SHUTTERSTOCK ©, PGIAM/GETTY IMAGES ©, IRINA MOS/SHUTTERSTOCK ©

❹ FOREST HERITAGE SCENIC BYWAY ⏱ ½ DAY

Next is the national forest, which gets its due along the **Forest Heritage Scenic Byway** (p152), a leafy playground just off the parkway that glows an otherworldly green in late spring and summer. Brake for waterfalls and one really cool rock slide, which all sit beside the road. Beside the byway, a museum examines the origins of forestry, and lots of trails shoot off toward adventure.

❺ SYLVA ⏱ ½ DAY

The multi-block Main Street may look old-fashioned, but behind those low-key storefronts you'll find experimental breweries, fantastic restaurants and the City Light Bookstore, which throws out great staff picks and serves tasty crepes in its cafe. **Sylva** (p154) is a welcoming spot for dinner and maybe even an overnight stay.

🚗 *Detour: Drive north to Cherokee (p151) to learn more about the Cherokee Nation and the Trail of Tears.* 🚗 *2 hours*

❻ BRYSON CITY ⏱ 1 DAY

All aboard for the last stop! A scenic train chugs from **Bryson City** (p153) into the mountains beside the Nantahala Gorge, just east of Great Smoky Mountains National Park. The train brings family crowds while the adventure-central location brings hikers, paddlers and cyclists.

🚗 *Detour: Drive west to the Nantahala Outdoor Center (p153) for white-water rafting and zip-lining.* 🚗 *20 minutes*

ITINERARIES

Blue Ridge Mountain Reverie

Allow: 5 days **Distance:** 225 miles

Skyline Drive and the Blue Ridge Parkway roll along the spine of the Blue Ridge Mountains, with lush farmland views unfurling to the east and west far below. College towns bring fascinating history – and youthful energy – to all the beauty.

Big Meadows (p160)

① WINCHESTER ½ DAY

For an engaging introduction to the region, pull into the Museum of the Shenandoah Valley in lovely **Winchester** (p165), where apple blossoms bloom along the streets in spring. Enjoy the good food and craft beer, and stroll the historic downtown. The 10-day Apple Blossom Festival in May brings celebrities and a parade.

② SKYLAND ½ DAY

From Winchester, pull into **Skyland** (p160) in the Central District of the park, then climb for big views at the Stony Man Overlook – the kids can handle this short climb. Take a guided horseback ride into the woods with Skyland Stables, then sip a sunset libation from the terrace at the nearby Skyland Lodge.

*Detour: Drive to **Luray Caverns** (p165) to tour the surprisingly beautiful underground formations. 3 hours*

③ BIG MEADOWS 1 DAY

If you're not base-camping at Skyland, head to **Big Meadows** (p160) and check into your room at Big Meadows Lodge, then take your pick of waterfall trails, which are easily accessed from the lodge and the adjacent campground. Learn about the creation of the park at the visitor center museum, then stroll the game trails through the namesake meadows. After dinner at the lodge, attend the evening ranger talk.

④ CHARLOTTESVILLE ⏱1 DAY

The culturally rich city of **Charlottesville** (p116) is home to the architecturally resplendent University of Virginia. Its grounds, Main St and the pedestrian downtown mall overflow with students, professors and tourists, endowing 'C-ville' with a lively and diverse atmosphere that's fun to explore. Drive into the countryside to tour Thomas Jefferson's Monticello, then explore breweries, wineries and the Blue Ridge Tunnel Trail.

⑤ STAUNTON ⏱1 DAY

Next on the list is **Staunton** (p122). More than 200 of Staunton's buildings were designed by noted Victorian architect TJ Collins, hence the attractive uniformity. Home to Mary Baldwin College, the city is anchored by pedestrian friendly Beverley St and the wonderful Blackfriars Playhouse at the American Shakespeare Center.

⑥ LEXINGTON ⏱1 DAY

If you like to clean up nice after a day on the trail to prepare for cocktails, a fine meal and a bit of collegial good cheer, **Lexington** (p112) has got you covered. A two-college town with a historic downtown and a thriving restaurant and brewery scene, 'LexVegas' is a great launchpad for exploring the Blue Ridge. It's close to Natural Bridge and Devil's Marbleyard, too.

WHEN TO GO

Great Smoky Mountains National Park and the surrounding region serve up fun in every season, but fall and late spring really shine bright.

For seekers of waterfalls and wildflowers, the Great Smokies, the Blue Ridge and Shenandoah are the places to be in spring. High-altitude shrubs bloom atop mountains in late June and early July – a prime time for leg-stretching hikes. Campgrounds fill in summer with families enjoying the long break from school. Higher elevations bring relief from lowland heat and humidity, while mountain music often drifts across the foothills.

Book a few weeks ahead for lodging during the fall foliage season, particularly on weekends. Adorned with holiday lights, a new Christmas tree soars 35ft every year on the front lawn of the Biltmore Estate in Asheville come Holiday Season.

Camping in National Parks

Don't immediately say no to camping. Spending the night with friends or family in a national park campground is typically a convivial experience with an authentic sense of community – and an amazing backdrop. Solo campers will feel welcome, too.

Catawba rhododendrons, Blue Ridge Parkway

 I LIVE HERE

FROZEN WATERFALLS

District manager and hiking guru at Walkabout Outfitter, Vince Mier is an all-seasons hiker along the Blue Ridge Parkway.
@walkaboutlexington

Head to Apple Orchard Falls; that's Milepost 78.4. It's fun to go in the wintertime and see if it's frozen. It's not an incredibly rugged hike, but the payoff is really nice. I like to go on the off season because the leaves are off the trees and there's an immaculate 360-degree view. Typically January and February would be a cool time to experience it.

SPECTACULAR WILDFLOWERS

The Great Smokies wins Best in Show when it comes to wildflowers, with more than 1500 types of flowering plants – more than any other national park in the US. Thriving at elevations above 3500ft, the Catawba rhododendron blooms in June, and you can hike to colorful explosions of flaming azaleas atop the park's balds in early July.

Weather Through the Year (Low/High Elevations)

JANUARY	FEBRUARY	MARCH	 APRIL	MAY	JUNE
Avg. daytime max: **51/35°F**	Avg. daytime max: **54/35°F**	Avg. daytime max: **61/39°F**	Avg. daytime max: **71/49°F**	Avg. daytime max: **79/57°F**	Avg. daytime max: **86/63°F**
Days of rainfall: **9/12**	Days of rainfall: **9/12**	Days of rainfall: **8/12**	Days of rainfall: **8/10**	Days of rainfall: **9/10**	Days of rainfall: **9/11**

GREAT SMOKIES RAINFALL

The lower regions of the park average 55in of rain per year, which is above the 33in annual average for the contiguous US. Higher elevations can see about 85in. July is typically the wettest month, when afternoon rains and storms are common.

The Big Festivals

A must for nature lovers, the four-day **Spring Wildflower Pilgrimage** (p72) in the Great Smokies features more than 160 events, including guided hikes, wildlife photography and bird-watching. **April**

Thousands converge on Winchester for the **Shenandoah Apple Blossom Festival** (p165), a 10-day celebration of spring with a parade, carnival and music. **April to May**

Immerse yourself in mountain music at **Shindig on the Green** (p149), an outdoor concert series in Pack Square Park in Asheville most Saturday nights. **June to September**

The streets of Bristol, which straddles the Virginia–Tennessee state line, fill with music for the **Bristol Rhythm & Roots Festival** (p135), which honors the region as the birthplace of country music. It's replete with Appalachian roots music and a lineup of dynamic emerging acts and well-established favorites. **September**

⊙ I LIVE HERE

MAGICAL NANTAHALA

Lawyer and biker Rob Saunooke lives in Cherokee and has completed the long-distance Hoka Hey Motorcycle Challenge.

Riding through the Nantahala Gorge on US 74 from Cherokee, then heading east on Wayah Road, with a quick stop at a few of the waterfalls and lunch at Lakes End Cafe, then continuing to Franklin and back north on US 23... the view of the lake and the winding roads through old growth forests is beautiful. In the fall, the colors of the changing leaves provide a backdrop that is hard to duplicate.

Quirky Local Festivals

The **Big Ears Festival** (p95) in Knoxville is an avant-garde and experiential party showcasing music, art and film and the connections between them. Performances are held at various music venues across downtown. **March**

For two weeks every year, you can see the incredible display of **synchronous fireflies** (p55), when thousands of fireflies blink in perfect harmony in the Great Smokies. Lottery held in late April. Elkmont Campground is the best place to see it. **May to June**

More than 200 booths showcase the handmade work of the nation's top artists and craftspeople during the **Gatlinburg Craftsmen's Fair**. **July**

During the **National Gingerbread House Competition** (p156), ornate – and tasty-looking – gingerbread houses are displayed at the Omni Grove Park Inn in Asheville. **November to January**

FALL FOLIAGE

Peak foliage time in the Great Smokies is typically mid-October through early November, with the colors kicking off at higher elevations, then dropping to lower elevations. Fall is the busiest time of year at Shenandoah National Park, with the peak color time varying annually. Check Shenandoah's social media feeds for foliage updates.

JULY	AUGUST	SEPTEMBER	OCTOBER	NOVEMBER	DECEMBER
Avg. daytime max: **88/65°F**	Avg. daytime max: **87/64°F**	Avg. daytime max: **83/60°F**	Avg. daytime max: **73/53°F**	Avg. daytime max: **61/42°F**	Avg. daytime max: **52/37°F**
Days of rainfall: **10/13**	Days of rainfall: **10/12**	Days of rainfall: **5/8**	Days of rainfall: **6/8**	Days of rainfall: **7/9**	Days of rainfall: **8/10**

GET PREPARED FOR THE SMOKIES

Useful things to load in your bag, your ears and your brain

Clothes

Layers To cope with changing temperatures and exertion, layer your clothing. Choose garments that are moisture-wicking, breathable, waterproof, windproof, insulating and comfortable.

Synthetic fabrics Modern outdoor garments made from synthetic fabrics (which are breathable and actively wick moisture away from your skin) are best for hiking. Cotton T-shirts are particularly ill-suited to outdoor activities, as cotton holds water – as you sweat, you'll feel chilly if the weather turns cold and wet.

Waterproof apparel Hikers should carry a windproof, waterproof rain jacket, headwear and, in the cooler months, pants.

Hiking boots Waterproof hiking boots are essential given the wet weather and abundant stream-crossing trails.

River sandals Many hikers carry waterproof sandals with straps to wear when crossing creeks and streams. Sandals are also handy for rafting and tubing trips, and wearing around camp.

Manners

It's best to avoid bringing up hot-button **political issues** – eg abortion, gun control – with people you've just met. Cities tend to be more liberal than rural areas, but it can be hard to guess political views, and feathers can get easily ruffled.

Respond to basic pleasantries with a **smile** or **quick hello**.

In the South and on hiking trails, hospitality norms bend toward friendliness.

📖 READ

Our Southern Highlanders
(Horace Kephart; 1913)
A fascinating and at times comical portrait of Appalachian people.

Cataloochee
(Wayne Caldwell; 2007)
An epic story following three generations of mountain people.

Bear in the Back Seat
(Carolyn Jourdan and Kim DeLozier; 2013)
Accounts of wildlife work with bears and other park creatures.

Dopesick
(Beth Lacy; 2018)
Spotlights the devastating impact of opioid addition across Appalachia.

Words

You may come across a few words and sayings that are popular in the Appalachian region and the American South but not across the wider US. Here are a few you may encounter in the Smokies:

Bald means a treeless area on top of a mountain, typically surrounded by forest.

Britches refers to pants or trousers. Usually heard in the idiom 'Their getting a little big for their britches' (i.e. undeservedly proud).

Clogging, flatfooting and **buck dancing** are styles of Appalachian dance, often with tap shoes. Clogging is more showy, with choreographed steps often performed with a group. Flatfooting is a solo endeavor marked by quick footwork, or shuffling, that matches the rhythm of the band. Buck dancing, often used interchangeably with flatfooting, tends to have slightly higher steps.

Cove refers to a small and level valley surrounded by mountains (e.g. Cades Cove).

Fixin' means getting ready to, as in 'I'm fixin' to go to the Smokies.'

Gap refers to a mountain pass.

Holler is a derivation of the word 'hollow' – a small valley deep in the mountains.

Hooch refers to moonshine, which is un-aged corn whiskey. Also known as mountain dew and white lightning.

Y'all is a contraction of 'you all' – used when addressing a small group. 'All ya'll' tends to refer to a bigger group but can be used for emphasis when addressing a small group: 'All ya'll better get this room cleaned up before I get back!' Do not disobey this order when coming from an annoyed mother. She means everyone within earshot.

📺 WATCH

A Walk in the Spring Rain
(Guy Green; 1970) A romantic drama starring Ingrid Bergman (pictured) and Anthony Quinn, filmed partly in Cades Cove.

Dirty Dancing (Emile Ardolino; 1987) Outdoor scenes, including the iconic 'lake lift,' were filmed around (and in!) Lake Lure.

Christy (Michael Ray Rhodes; 1994–95) Captivating TV series about a young teacher from the city charged with running a rural school in the Smoky Mountains in the early 1900s.

A Walk in the Woods
(Ken Kwapis; 2014) A rollicking man-vs-nature tale of two aging friends tackling the Appalachian Trail.

🎧 LISTEN

On Top of Old Smoky
(Norman Blake et al; 2016) A collection of classic, old-time mountain music featuring more than a dozen new performers.

My Tennessee Mountain Home
(Dolly Parton; 1973) One of the legends of country music reminisces on her rural upbringing.

Volunteer (Old Crow Medicine Show; 2018) Latest album by this feel-good folk and bluegrass band who celebrate the southern landscapes.

Down the Road on the Blue Ridge Music Trails
(Kevin Washington; 2023) Podcast about the musicians and history of mountain music in western North Carolina.

Black bear

TRIP PLANNER

WILDLIFE

Southern Appalachia's vast wildlands shelter an extraordinary variety of creatures, including dozens of species of mammals, fish, reptiles and amphibians, and more than 200 different birds. So slow down, get out your field guide and take time to experience this remarkable biodiversity, from the tiny fireflies that light up the summer skies to the iconic black bears that roam the region.

Mammals

The full spectrum of common North American mammals is represented in southern Appalachia, including white-tailed deer, gray squirrels, chipmunks, cottontail rabbits, skunks, raccoons, opossums, woodchucks and mice. Also present but more rarely seen are coyotes, red and gray foxes, bats and bobcats.

BEARS

At the top of the food chain, the American black bear *(Ursus americanus)* holds a special fascination for visitors. Great Smoky Mountains National Park has the highest concentration of black bears in North America, with 2.6 per sq mile (close to 2000 bears in total). Shenandoah National Park estimates its population to range from 200 to 1000, while thousands more roam the surrounding southern Appalachians. Bears thrive here in large part because of the parks' vast contiguous forest habitat and the abundance of mast crops – woody plants bearing nuts, seeds and fruit. Sightings of bears, both adults and juveniles, are frequent throughout the region, especially in open areas such Cades Cove in the Smokies. Maintain a distance of 50 yards or more from bears – for the bears' sake, as well as your own.

ELK

The region's largest mammal, once prevalent throughout southern Appalachia, was reintroduced to Great Smoky Mountains

SALAMANDER CAPITAL OF THE WORLD

The southern Appalachians hold the world's greatest diversity of salamanders. Whether they are fully aquatic or live mostly underground, they require constant moisture. The region's plentiful rainfall, clear-running streams, mist-covered mountaintops and moist forest bottoms provide this essential condition. Some salamanders breathe through gills for all or part of their lives; some develop lungs. Some are gill-less and lungless and breathe through their skin. All are carnivores, eating anything from bugs to worms to crayfish. The endangered Shenandoah salamander is found only in Shenandoah National Park, and only on three mountaintops. But all are threatened by air and water pollution, habitat degradation, habitat loss and climate change.

National Park in the early 2000s. The population has swelled from two dozen to roughly 200 in recent decades, and elk are frequently spotted in the park's Cataloochee and Oconaluftee valleys, especially around dawn and dusk.

Reptiles, Amphibians & Birds

Among the parks' reptiles are several species of turtles, lizards and snakes, including the venomous timber rattlesnake and northern copperhead. Salamanders thrive here like nowhere else on Earth, alongside Eastern American toads and several species of frogs. Northern cardinals, American goldfinches and indigo buntings light up the fields and forests with flashes of primary color; hawks and vultures soar overhead, and woodpeckers provide a distinctive soundtrack for walks in the woods. Wild turkeys are also commonly seen in the Great Smoky Mountains. Native brook trout abound in southern Appalachian streams, though they have suffered from competition with the rainbow and brown trout introduced for sport fishing.

Salamander

PEREGRINE RESTORATION: TWO STEPS FORWARD, ONE STEP BACK

By the late 1960s, DDT (an insecticide used in agriculture) had driven peregrine falcons to the brink of extinction. People took action. They banned DDT in the US and passed the Endangered Species Act. Wildlife experts hand-raised falcons in special cliff-side nesting boxes – a painstaking process known as 'hacking' – so the juveniles would imprint on historic sites and return to nest as adults.

Peregrines were removed from the Federal Endangered Species List in 1999. However, they remain state-listed as threatened or endangered across most of their range in the Appalachians. In Virginia, peregrines have rebounded in coastal areas but have been slow to return to their homes in the mountains. At Shenandoah, rangers are still hacking.

Peregrines mate for life and can return to the same nest site for up to 20 years. They require high cliff ledges where their young are safe from predators like eagles and raccoons, and from which adults can easily hunt. But the real threat is humans. Any human intrusion can drive off nesting falcons and cause the nest to fail, as the mating pair simply abandons it. At Devils Courthouse on the Blue Ridge Parkway, peregrines nested successfully between 2000 and 2007, and again in 2016, but have not since then. Why? Too many people ignoring park-posted signage and clambering near the cliff edges to take selfies.

Newfound Gap (p86)

TRIP PLANNER

A LAND OF ANCIENT MOUNTAINS

Running roughly 600 miles north to south, the southern Appalachians encompass over four million acres of public land, including Great Smoky Mountains National Park, the Blue Ridge Parkway and Shenandoah National Park. These protected areas cradle a diversity of complex ecosystems.

Undergirding It All

Images from NASA's Earth Observatory show the southern Appalachians as a gently curved arc extending south of Great Smoky Mountains National Park, all the way along the Blue Ridge Parkway to Shenandoah National Park; their ridges running southwest to northeast like the deeply grooved bark on an unimaginably massive felled tree. The ranges of southern Appalachia – the Blacks, Unakas, Great Smokies, Great Balsams, Great Craggies and others – are, for geologists, part of what's called the Blue Ridge physiographic province, a bed of rock almost as old as Earth itself.

The Appalachians – sometimes called 'the Backbone of the East' – stretch from Alabama to Maine and into Canada. The southern Appalachians are much taller than their northern counterparts, having somewhere between 30 and 60 peaks taller than 6000ft, depending on how you count. The tallest mountains in Maine, Vermont and Pennsylvania, by contrast, come in at 5269ft, 4393ft and 3213ft, respectively.

During the last ice age, glaciers ground down the mountains of northern and central Appalachia, but stopped somewhere along what is now the Ohio River. Flora and fauna fled south, making southern Appalachia a kind of Noah's Ark for the northern ecosystems as the glaciers receded.

A PARADE OF BLOOMS

From spring ephemerals to witch hazel blooming in snow and from rare orchids to showy shrubs, the southern Appalachians are home to some 1500 native species of flowering plants. Bloom times vary by latitude, elevation and sunlight, so plan accordingly.

Early to Mid-Spring
- Spring beauty
- Hepatica
- Squirrel corn
- Trout lily
- Dwarf crested iris
- Serviceberry

Late Spring
- Phacelia
- Wild ginger
- May apple
- Lady's slipper
- Mountain laurel
- Tulip tree

Summer
- Flame azalea
- Catawba rhododendron
- Butterfly weed
- Sourwood
- Rosebay rhododendron
- Turk's cap lily

Fall
- Virgin's bower
- Aster
- White Snakeroot
- Mountain Gentian
- Goldenrod
- Witch hazel

An Abundance of Life

The southern Appalachians support greater biodiversity than any other part of North America. The jewel in this crown, Great Smoky Mountains National Park, supports 19,000 plant and animal species.

Fueling this abundance are the southern Appalachians' ice-age legacy: dramatic variations in elevation, the relative temperateness of southern latitudes, and abundant water. Many species pushed here by the glaciers remained. Lowest to highest elevations within a single mountain range can be over a mile, and each 1000ft shift upwards or downwards mimics a move 250 miles north or south.

Winters are milder than further north, so even on the highest peaks there is no true treeline. There is more precipitation here than anywhere else in the US, except the Pacific Northwest and Alaska, and water abounds, starting from the headlands as springs and trickling downhill in ever-growing rivulets, creeks and rivers toward the Atlantic or the Mississippi.

> ### THE FORESTS OF SOUTHERN APPALACHIA
>
> Ninety-five per cent of the national parks of Shenandoah and Great Smoky Mountains is forested, as is 85% of the Blue Ridge Parkway. Different forest communities make their homes across these spectacular public lands, responding to elevation, moisture, drainage, orientation to the sun and soil type. Below are some of the most important forest ecosystems.
>
> **Spruce-fir forest** caps the high peaks in dark green, at elevations of 4500ft to 6500ft. Red spruce and fraser fir dominate, and the climate resembles that of Quebec or Nova Scotia.
>
> The **northern hardwood forest**, found at around 4500–5500ft, is dominated by yellow birch and American beech. These forests – remnants, like the spruce-fir, of when the glaciers pushed trees south – are reminiscent of New England's.
>
> Trees in the **cove hardwood forest** prefer elevations below 4500ft, rich soils and moist, sheltered valleys. This is the richest and most ecologically diverse of all southern Appalachian forests; trees can grow to a tremendous girth here.
>
> The **pine-oak forest** is found on dry, exposed south- and west-facing slopes below 4000ft. Tree species here are adapted to poor soils and fire. Bears, squirrels and turkeys rely on acorns in fall.
>
> **Oak-hickory forest** is found below 3500ft in ravines, coves and more sheltered areas. The American chestnut formerly dominated. Bears and other wildlife feed on acorns and hickory nuts here.

Trout lily

BBQ at 12 Bones Smokehouse (p146), Asheville

THE FOOD SCENE

From morels to moonshine, the southern Appalachians hide intriguing and elusive treasures while the nearby cities and towns show off an award-winning collection of culinary must-trys.

Native Americans and subsequent European settlers relied on wild game and freshwater fish for survival, and you'll find both on the menus of farm-to-table restaurants throughout the southern Appalachians. Fresh, locally grown food is also a specialty of the region, where fertile valleys fed by mountain streams produce lots of fruit and vegetables. For generations, families preserved their summer surpluses to survive the hard mountain winters, and traditions of canning, smoking and curing remain strong.

The agricultural riches of Appalachia are evidenced in the colorful displays of bounty at farmers markets across the foothills. Innovative restaurant menus incorporate numerous aspects of Appalachian cooking in their dishes, and you'll find everything from Italian pizzas to Indian street food and Spanish tapas, all made with regional ingredients. Chef-driven restaurants in Knoxville, Asheville and Charlottesville are earning national acclaim and magazine spreads, but mom-and-pop joints and food trucks draw comparable lines with their passion-driven endeavors – we're looking at you, Woodruff's Cafe and Pie Shop (p128) and Mama Jean's (p132).

Moonshine

What is moonshine? If you take away the outlaw reputation, moonshine is nothing more than un-aged whiskey, often made

---

Best Appalachian Dishes

BEANS WITH CORNBREAD
Pork-flavored pinto beans with cornmeal-based bread.

APPLE STACK CAKE
Five or more layers of crisp cake separated by an apple filling.

PEPPERONI ROLLS
Soft bread rolls stuffed with cured meat.

SHUCK BEANS
Green beans that have been hung up and dried.

from corn. Its origins trace back to the Scots-Irish settlers who followed the Great Wagon Road south from Pennsylvania in the mid-1700s. These hardy pioneers built small farms and distilled spirits for medicinal purposes. And yes, sometimes 'medicine' was just a euphemism for whiskey.

Moonshine earned its modern reputation during Prohibition, when the production and consumption of alcohol in the US was banned by constitutional amendment in 1920. Enforcement, however, was difficult, and illegal whiskey production became a source of extra income for Appalachian home distillers. To hide the smoke from their stills, the distillers made their corn liquor at night, under the light of the moon, hence the name 'moonshine.' This primitive un-aged whiskey earned a reputation for its rough taste and its burn.

Asheville's BBQ Smackdown

BBQ fans have a tough choice in Asheville. Perched beside the French Broad River in the River Arts District, 12 Bones (p147) is beloved for its slow-cooked smoky meats and its mouthwatering sides. Buxton Hall prepares its pork Eastern-Carolina style, infusing a whole hog with a peppery vinegar sauce, then slow-cooking it over hardwood coals. With James Beard nominee Elliott Moss as pitmaster, this is the place to eat before exploring the South Slope breweries.

FOOD & WINE FESTIVALS

Asheville Bread Festival *(ashevillebreadfestival.com)* Workshops, lectures and breads – including pastries – take the stage at this two-day festival in Asheville in April.

Strawberry Festival *(strawberryfestivalroanoke.org)* Strawberries are served atop shortcakes and dipped in chocolate at this two-day strawberry celebration (pictured) in downtown Roanoke in May.

Knox Food Fest *(knoxfoodfest.com)* The dishes are international, vegetarian and vegan at this relatively new food festival in Knoxville in August.

Chow Chow Food & Culture Festival *(chowchowasheville.com)* Chow chow and other traditional Appalachian favorites – and their modern interpretations – get their due in Asheville in September.

High Country Beer Fest *(hcbeefest.com)* Come for the 35 mountain brewers who bring their best beers to this sudsy party in Boone in August.

Pepperoni roll

COLLARD GREENS	**COUNTRY HAM**	**RED EYE GRAVY**	**APPLE PIE MOONSHINE**
Boiled collards fried in grease and sprinkled with bacon.	Heavily salted cured ham. Benton's Country Hams has been a must since 1947.	Sauce of fried ham drippings and coffee; best over biscuits or grits.	Whiskey flavored with apple juice, cinnamon and sugar.

35

Specialties

Read on for a selection of Appalachia's culinary classics and best homegrown comfort dishes.

In the Wild

Paw paws This is the largest edible native fruit in the US and tastes like a blend of banana, pineapple and mango. Was very popular with Native Americans and early settlers.

Ramps These leafy vegetables grow in the mountains and are similar to leeks, but with more of a garlicky flavor.

Morels Renowned for their earthy, nutty taste and meaty texture, these are mushrooms that grow – elusively – in the mountain forests of the region.

Comfort Food

Buttermilk biscuits Whether smothered in peppered sausage gravy or slathered with honey, these billowy bits of buttery bliss always hit the spot.

Grits This thick porridge of boiled, milled corn is often offered as a breakfast side. In truth, it may just be a conduit for ingesting mounds of butter and/or cheese.

Paw paw

Memorable Preserves

Apple butter No actual butter is used in this treat. Instead, it's a thick spread of preserved apples typically flavored with cinnamon, cloves and nutmeg, and is generally much thicker than applesauce.

Chow chow This is a pickled vegetable relish – typically with bell peppers, onions and tomatoes – that can be drizzled onto hot dogs, burgers, bean dishes and deviled eggs – whatever you like!

MEALS OF A LIFETIME

The Gamekeeper (p141) Soak up views of the forest from the patio while dining on innovative game dishes and delicious local veggies near Boone.

The Shack (p124) Caviar with local potato chips? Yes please. The prix fixe menu brings delicious surprises at Ian Boden's 'shack' in Staunton.

Cúrate (p148) Spanish tapas with innovative Southern twists at Katie Button's convivial hot spot in Asheville.

The Appalachian (p108) High-end American regional cuisine serving wood-grilled meats and reimagined Southern classics.

Woodruff's Cafe and Pie Shop (p128) Two sisters bake delicious pies in a former gas station a few miles off the Blue Ride Parkway east of Glasgow, VA.

THE YEAR IN FOOD

SPRING

It's strawberry season from late April through June in Virginia and North Carolina. The Roanoke Strawberry Festival occurs in May. Look for fresh beets and radishes, too.

SUMMER

Farmers markets have colorful berries, peppers, squash, watermelons and more on weekly display. Pick wild blueberries at Craggy Gardens and Graveyard Fields along the Blue Ridge Parkway from August through early fall.

FALL

Hey, pumpkins! September and October are your months to shine – or maybe scare. Apples and corn are doing their best work, too. Warm up with regional spirits at the Grains & Grits Festival in Townsend come November.

WINTER

Apples are still in season, as are year-round stalwarts peanuts and kale. It's also time to dig into fruit preserves and smoked meats. To celebrate the holidays Appalachian-style, carve into a country ham for Christmas dinner.

BBQ ribs, Buxton Hall Barbecue (p35)

Backcountry shelter, Shenandoah National Park

TRIP PLANNER

MULTIDAY HIKES

With a combined 1350 miles of hiking trails, Great Smoky Mountains and Shenandoah National Parks are prime territory for long-distance trekking. Whether you're out for a night or a month, sleeping in the backcountry will immerse you in the natural beauty of these parks in ways most visitors never experience. Here are some tips to help you plan.

Backcountry Permits, Campsites & Shelters

A backcountry permit is required for overnight stays in Great Smoky Mountains and Shenandoah National Parks.

In the Smokies, there are nearly 100 designated backcountry sites and 15 backcountry shelters, which must be reserved in advance. Each site accommodates between four and 20 campers, and the popular ones fill fast (see smokiespermits.nps.gov for the backcountry sites). Check availability and book online; a permit will be issued upon payment; print this and bring it with you. Last-minute planners can reserve sites and collect permits at Sugarlands Visitor Center.

In Shenandoah, there are no designated backcountry campsites. To obtain the required permit, campers must fill out a form (nps.gov/shen/planyourvisit/bc-permit.htm) documenting their planned itinerary. Once on the trail, you're free to choose whichever campsite meets specifications (nps.gov/shen/planyourvisit/backcountry-regulations.htm). If you'd prefer a roof over your head, the Potomac Appalachian Trail Club operates six cabins within Shenandoah (reserve ahead at patc.net). Shenandoah is also home to nine shelters along the Appalachian Trail, available on a first-come, first-served basis.

BEAR SAFETY

Bear safety is serious business here. The combined black bear population of the

ONE-NIGHT BACKCOUNTRY ADVENTURES

There are plenty of wonderful one-night adventures suitable for those seeking a brief taste of the wild. The following trails get you into the Great Smokies' backcountry with minimal effort.

Big Creek Trail to Campsites 36 and 37 This gently ascending old logging road leads 5 miles past waterfalls and boulder-fringed pools to a pair of tree-shaded campsites near the banks of Big Creek. Site 37 is for hikers only; site 36 also accommodates horses.

Appalachian Trail to Icewater Spring Shelter A scenic 3-mile jaunt along the Appalachian Trail that climbs from Newfound Gap parking area to the beautifully sited Icewater Spring Shelter.

Smokies and Shenandoah is estimated at 3000, raising the odds of a backcountry encounter. In the Smokies, backcountry campers are required to hang all food and scented items (toothpaste, etc.) using the bear cable system provided. In Shenandoah, campers must store scented items in a bear-resistant food container or hang them in a rope-suspended waterproof bag at least 12ft off the ground and 6ft from the nearest tree trunk or branch.

Food hung out of reach of bears

PREPARE FOR PRIMITIVE LIVING

Backcountry camping is a back-to-nature experience. In the Smokies, campgrounds are marked with a numbered post. Within each numbered area are bear cables for food, fire rings and areas for tents. Sites are generally close to water, but you'll need to boil or otherwise purify all water before drinking. Outhouses are scant, so prepare to 'go natural' and bury all feces and toilet paper at least 6in deep. Camping in Shenandoah's backcountry is even more rustic, as there are no designated campsites, and campfires are forbidden.

PACKING FOR THE TRAIL

Getting prepared for the backcountry means packing sufficient gear, food and water. Use the following list as a guide.

- Water is the single most important necessity for a successful backcountry experience; bring enough for the hike in, and prepare to boil or purify any water obtained from creeks or springs in the backcountry.

- Matches or lighters are needed for campfires (in Great Smoky Mountains National Park only), and for camp stoves.

- Hat and sunscreen are necessary to ensure protection from the sun and avoid sunburn, heat stroke and other maladies.

- Repellent is essential to ward off biting insects on the trails.

- Tents must have a dependable rain fly.

- Sleeping bags should preferably have a quick-drying synthetic fill.

- Sleeping mats and camping pillows will help to amp up the cushiness factor.

- Rain gear is essential for the thunderstorms and sudden downpours that are common in the southern Appalachians; be prepared and protect yourself from hypothermia by getting the best rain gear you can afford.

- Layers of clothing will keep you warm; aim for a mix of lightweight garments that wick moisture away from your skin, along with a windbreaker, a warm coat and hat, and wool socks for chillier nights at high altitudes.

TRIP PLANNER

MOUNTAIN MUSIC

Music is a cultural cornerstone of southern Appalachia, a living tradition that still resonates throughout the mountains of Virginia, North Carolina and Tennessee. Many legendary performers hail from these hills – including the Carter Family, Doc Watson and Dolly Parton – but travelers here will find equal delight in discovering lesser-known musicians at the region's many concerts and festivals.

Origins of Appalachian Mountain Music

Musical influences in southern Appalachia can be traced back to the Scots-Irish immigrants who arrived here in the 18th century, bringing with them fiddle playing and ballad singing. During the 19th century, the banjo, which had evolved from instruments brought here by enslaved West Africans, joined the fiddle as a mountain-music mainstay. Around the turn of the 20th century, other instruments, including the guitar and mandolin, became more available, adding richness and complexity to the mix. Other distinctly Appalachian sounds include the hauntingly spare vocals of *a cappella* ballads and church music, and the melody of the Appalachian dulcimer.

Musical Genres

Even as southern Appalachia's traditional sounds have given rise to new forms, such as bluegrass and country, much of the mountain music you'll hear today remains true to its earliest roots.

OLD-TIME

The term 'old-time' is used to describe a more traditional, less ornamented style that hearkens back to when fiddle-focused bands served primarily as accompaniment for dances, emphasizing rhythm, continuity and unity of sound rather than showy

Rhiannon Giddens

AFRICAN AMERICAN INFLUENCES IN APPALACHIAN MUSIC

African American roots run deep in Appalachian music, from the banjo to the 19th-century evolution of the string band. Techniques such as 'Travis-style' thumb picking and the 'Carter scratch,' commonly attributed to white guitarists Merle Travis and Maybelle Carter, were actually inspired by the Black musicians Arnold Shultz and Lesley Riddle. Riddle played a pivotal role in the Carter Family's commercial success, accompanying family patriarch AP Carter on 'song-catching' journeys, while bluegrass legend Bill Monroe and guitar-pickers Chet Atkins and Doc Watson were heavily influenced by Shultz' virtuosity. In recent years, contemporary artists such as Rhiannon Giddens have revived awareness of these unsung contributions.

Merlefest

improvisation. It's a style still heard at fiddler's conventions throughout southern Appalachia.

BLUEGRASS

Blending high-pitched vocal harmonies with a frenetic virtuosity, bluegrass is a later derivative of traditional Appalachian music that incorporates gospel, blues and jazz influences. The key instruments are the acoustic guitar, resonator banjo, fiddle, mandolin and double bass. Players take turns strutting their stuff, trading solo riffs between verses. The genre's name is derived from the Blue Grass Boys, formed in the late 1930s by Kentucky-born mandolinist Bill Monroe, joined later by Tennessee guitarist Lester Flatt and North Carolina's Earl Scruggs, who replaced the traditional clawhammer banjo technique with his own more dynamic three-finger style.

COUNTRY

Bristol, Tennessee is widely credited as the birthplace of modern country music, thanks to recording sessions held here in 1927 by music producer Ralph Peer, who enticed the Carter Family and other old-time Appalachian musicians to the studio with offers of generous royalties. Peer recorded their songs and introduced them to a wider audience. While modern country music has since strayed with the adoption of drums, electric guitar and pop, the Appalachian influences are present, both in the use of traditional instruments and the vocal styles.

FESTIVALS & LIVE MUSIC VENUES

Festivals
Music festivals abound in southern Appalachia, from old-time fiddler's conventions to celebrations of the new.

Merlefest, Wilkesboro, NC (April; merlefest.org) Four-day event honoring the legacy of Doc Watson's son Merle; billed as 'traditional music of the Appalachian region, plus whatever else we're in the mood to play.'

Old Fiddler's Convention, Galax, VA (August; oldfiddlersconvention.com) Aficionados flock to Appalachia's oldest and largest fiddlers' convention, dating to 1935 and spanning six days.

Mountain Dance and Folk Festival, Asheville, NC (August; folkheritage.org/asheville-events/mountain-dance-and-folk-festival) Ballad singing, bluegrass, clogging, storytelling and other Appalachian traditions.

Bristol Rhythm & Roots Reunion, Bristol, TN–VA (September; bristolrhythm.com) Three-day festival synthesizing musical influences past and present, held in the renowned birthplace of country music.

Earl Scruggs Music Festival, Mill Spring, NC (September; earlscruggs musicfest.com) A celebration of bluegrass, Americana and roots music, honoring North Carolina banjo virtuoso Earl Scruggs.

Venues
Memorable venues for hearing live music include the following:

WDVX Blue Plate Special, Knoxville, TN (wdvx.com/program/blue-plate-special) Public radio station WDVX hosts free midday music performances Monday to Thursday, plus a Saturday performance live from Knoxville's visitor center.

Shindig on the Green, Asheville, NC (romanticasheville.com/shindig.htm) This free mountain-music and dance event is held most Saturday nights in summer.

Horseback riding, Great Smoky Mountains National Park

THE OUTDOORS

Waves of magnificent mountains, free-flowing rivers and rolling green meadows abound in the national parklands of North Carolina, Virginia and Tennessee. Get out and explore them!

The call of the outdoors is irresistible in the Great Smoky Mountains and Shenandoah National Parks, and the Blue Ridge Parkway. Cascading creeks, dramatic mountain vistas, exuberant wildflowers and abundant wildlife beg you to leave your car behind and explore by foot, bike, horseback or boat. Whether you're pausing for a pony ride at Shenandoah's Skyland Stables, camping by the creekside at Cataloochee, or thru-hiking the Appalachian Trail from Georgia to Maine, the time spent in nature will be a highlight of any visit to this beautiful region.

Hiking

The southern Appalachians are a hiker's paradise, with hundreds of miles of signposted trails spread across Great Smoky Mountains National Park, Shenandoah National Park, the Blue Ridge Parkway and neighboring national forests.

In the Great Smokies, there are roughly 150 named trails of varying length and difficulty. These range from self-guided nature trails and 'Quiet Walkways' less than a mile in length to the 71-mile section of the Appalachian Trail (AT) that traverses the park's high ridge lines. In total, 800 miles of trail crisscross the Smokies, served by dozens of backcountry campsites and shelters (p173), making it possible to reach almost any part of the park on foot. Favorite day-hiking destinations include the dramatic rock formations of Charlies Bunion (p85), Chimney Tops (p88) and Alum Cave (p88), waterfalls such as Abrams Falls (p69) and Ramsey Cascades (p61), and the high mountain meadows of Gregory Bald (p73). Indispensable hikers'

More in the Outdoors

ROAD BIKING
Set off at dawn to ride the **Cades Cove Loop** (p70), rolling through Eastern Tennessee's open fields and misty mountains.

CAVING
Admire the stone columns and draperies, underground lake and massive Stalacpipe Organ at dazzling **Luray Caverns** (p165).

MOUNTAIN BIKING
Explore the 60-mile network of trails in **Carvins Cove** (p133) just outside Roanoke, Virginia.

FAMILY ADVENTURES

Plunge into the refreshing waters of **Deep Creek** (p65) and tube downstream to **Moon Goddess** (p66) for milkshakes at the national park's edge.

Enjoy a family-friendly scramble over boulders to reach 360-degree mountain-and-valley views on the 1.2-mile loop to **Bearfence Mountain** (p162).

Set out picnic blankets and lawn chairs by the trailside and watch as synchronous fireflies light up the night skies near **Elkmont** (p55).

Clippety-clop through fields and forest on a wagon ride at **Smokemont Riding Stables** (p65) near Oconaluftee.

Embark on a family rafting adventure through the rapids of the **Upper Pigeon River** (p83), or float serenely downstream on the kid-friendly Lower Pigeon.

Frolic by the dock between dips at **Mead's Quarry Lake** (p100), a favorite swimming spot in Knoxville's Urban Wilderness.

---

resources include the guidebook *Hiking in the Smokies,* the National Park Service's (NPS) *Great Smoky Mountains Trail Map* and National Geographic's excellent topographic map series.

Shenandoah National Park has over 500 miles of hiking trails, including 101 miles of the AT. Favorite hikes in Shenandoah include Big Meadows' waterfall trails (p162) and the loop trail to the summit of Old Rag Mountain (p166). Near Roanoke, hikers challenge themselves to the Virginia Triple Crown, a trio of cool rock formations that includes Dragon's Tooth, Tinker Cliffs and McAfee Knob (p131), the latter renowned as the AT's most photogenic overlook. Further south, off the Blue Ridge Parkway in North Carolina, hikers love navigating the adventurous trail to the summit of Grandfather Mountain (p141), complete with steel cables and wooden ladders.

Horseback Riding

Horseback riding is popular in both Great Smoky Mountains and Shenandoah National Parks. Four riding stables – Smokemont (p65), Cades Cove and Sugarlands in the Smokies, and Skyland (p162) in Shenandoah – lead one-hour guided rides. Smokemont also offers horse-drawn hayrides and longer excursions into the park (two to four hours), while Sugarlands provides horse-drawn carriage rides.

In the Smokies, horse owners have a wealth of other options. The NPS operates five frontcountry horse camps (Anthony Creek, Big Creek, Cataloochee, Round Bottom and Tow String) with hitch racks and 550 miles of trails open to equestrians. There are almost three dozen horse-friendly backcountry campsites here (marked in green on the NPS's *Great Smoky Mountains Trail Map*). In Shenandoah, nearly 200 miles of trail are open to horses, but horse camping is discouraged; riders are instead asked to overnight in the adjacent Rapidan Wildlife Management Area.

MORE HIKING
See our guide to multiday hikes on p38.

Tinker Cliffs (p131)

FISHING
Pitch your tent by the creekside and fish for native brook trout in North Carolina's remote **Cataloochee Valley** (p76).

KAYAKING
Paddle to a backcountry campsite on the shores of **Fontana Lake** (p67) in Great Smoky Mountains National Park.

CANOEING
Spend a day, or several, padding along the scenic **Upper James River Water Trail** (p125) near Buchanan, Virginia.

WILDLIFE WATCHING
Settle into a back porch rocking-chair at **Oconaluftee Visitor Center** (p63) and watch the elk descending to the meadows at dusk.

ACTION AREAS

Where to find the best outdoor adventures.

Cycling & Mountain Biking
1. Baker Creek Preserve (p100)
2. Cades Cove Loop (p70)
3. Nantahala Outdoor Center (p153)
4. Roanoke's mountains, greenways and gravel (p132)
5. Virginia Creeper National Recreation Trail (p138)

Wildlife
1. Big Meadows' deer (p163)
2. Cades Cove Loop's bears (p69)
3. Cataloochee Valley's wildlife (p77)
4. Elkmont's fireflies (p55)
5. The Smokies' birds (p58)

Walking & Hiking
1. Abrams Falls (p69)
2. Alum Cave Trail (p88)
3. Grandfather Trail to MacCrae Peak (p142)
4. Little River Trail (p60)
5. Old Rag Mountain (p166)
6. Ramsey Cascades (p61)

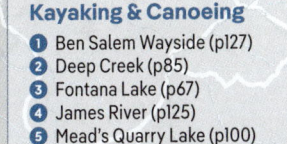

Scenic Overlooks

1. Charlies Bunion (p85)
2. Gregory Bald (p73)
3. Hawksbill (p161)
4. Humpback Rocks (p121)
5. LeConte Lodge (p89)
6. McAfee Knob (p131)
7. Newfound Gap Rd (p86)

Kayaking & Canoeing

1. Ben Salem Wayside (p127)
2. Deep Creek (p85)
3. Fontana Lake (p67)
4. James River (p125)
5. Mead's Quarry Lake (p100)
6. Nantahala Outdoor Center (p153)
7. Pigeon River (p81)

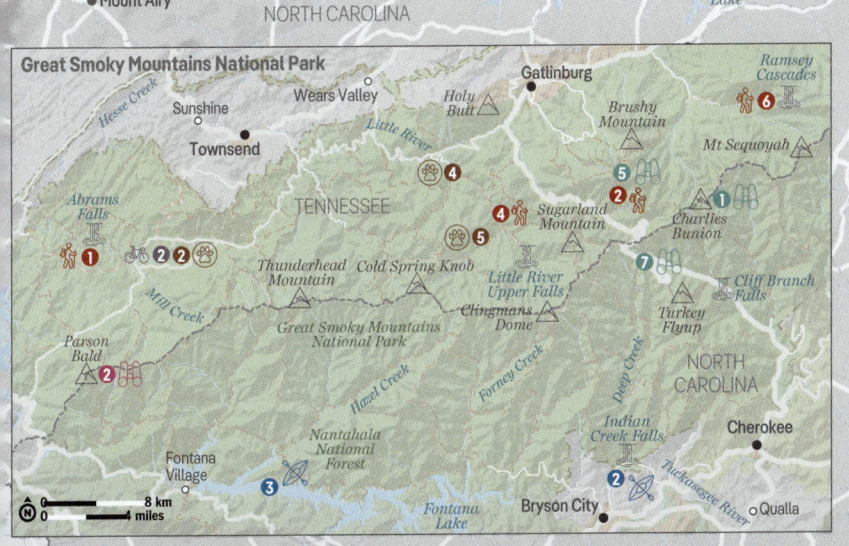

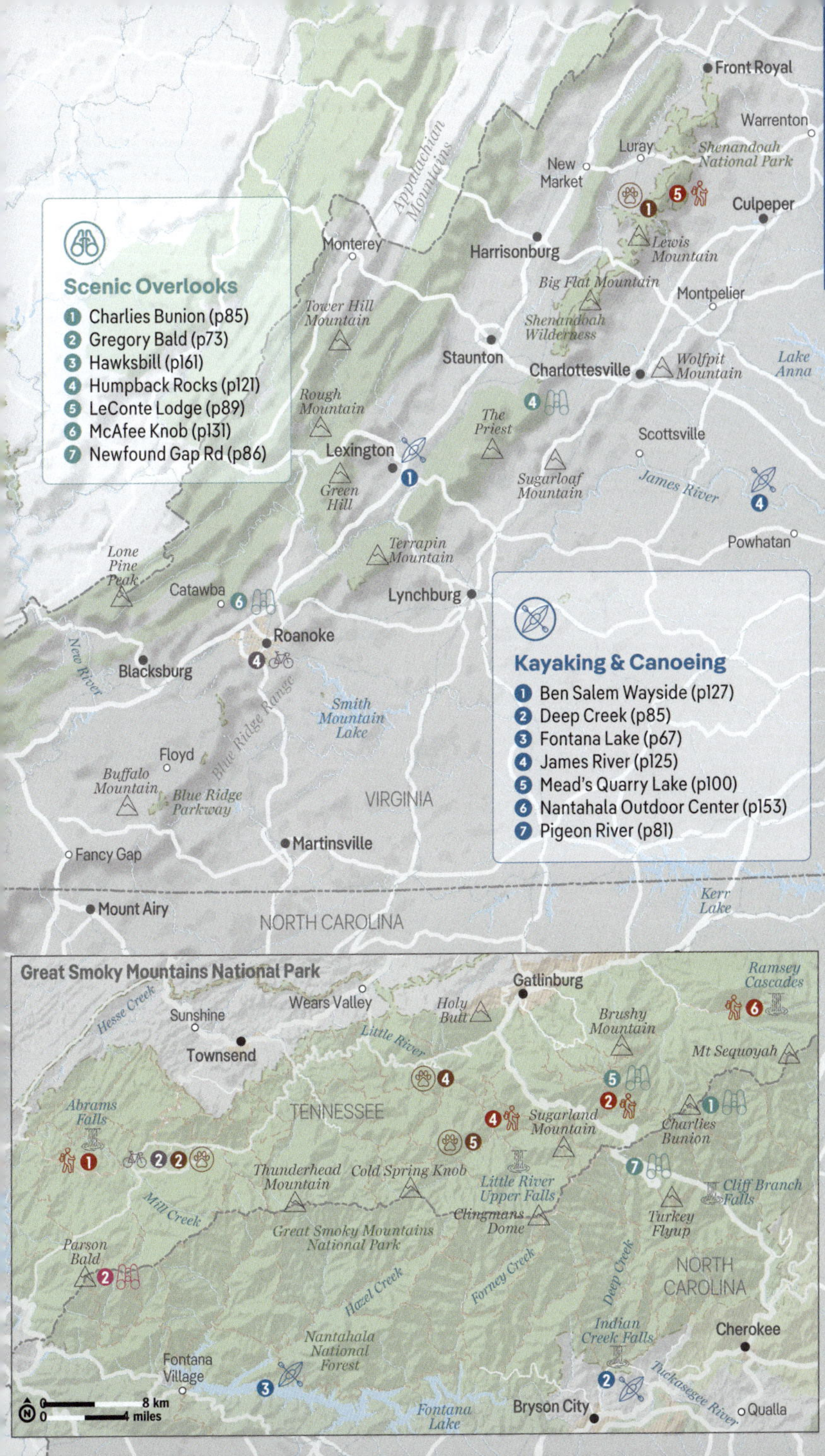

PLAN YOUR TRIP THE OUTDOORS

THE GUIDE

GREAT SMOKY MOUNTAINS NATIONAL PARK

THE GUIDE

Shenandoah
National Park
p156

North Carolina Gateways
& Blue Ridge Parkway
p111

East Tennessee
Gateways
p90

Great Smoky
Mountains
National Park
p49

Chapters in this section are organized by hubs and their surrounding areas. We see the hub as your base in the destination, where you'll find unique experiences, local insights, insider tips and expert recommendations. It's also your gateway to the surrounding area, where you'll see what and how much you can do from there.

Hikers near Clingmans Dome (p89)
KATIE DOBIES/GETTY IMAGES ©

Above: Oconaluftee River Valley, Newfound Gap Rd (p86). Right: Cable Mill (p71), Cades Cove

GREAT SMOKY MOUNTAINS NATIONAL PARK

APPALACHIAN ROOTS & EXUBERANT NATURE

America's favorite national park abounds in fast-flowing streams, glorious wildflowers, venerable wildlife, massive old-growth trees, fascinating human history and wave upon wave of misty mountains.

Recognized as a Unesco World Heritage Site and International Biosphere Reserve, Great Smoky Mountains National Park is the most biologically diverse in the US, with over 19,000 plant and animal species and the densest concentration of black bears in North America. Its 522,427 acres feature some of the East Coast's highest peaks and most gorgeous river valleys, traversed by 850 miles of hiking trails.

The Cherokee called these mountains 'Shaconage,' or 'Place of Blue Smoke,' a phrase later adapted by white settlers. If you're watching elk graze in the gauzy dawn light of Oconaluftee or hiking the slopes of Mt LeConte with wisps of mist hanging in the valleys below, it will be hard to think of a more fitting name.

The Smokies long served as hunting grounds and spiritual sustenance for First Nations people. In the early 1800s, white settlers began carving out a hardscrabble existence, building log cabins, gristmills, churches and schools, many of which remain preserved today. In the 1830s, the Cherokee were rounded up and forcibly relocated. A century later, in 1934, the Smokies' pioneering farmers were themselves bought out and evicted to establish the national park.

Great Smoky Mountains National Park is America's most visited national park, but also one of its most chronically underfunded. Don't forget to buy your parking pass – the park's survival depends on it!

THE MAIN AREAS

SUGARLANDS, ELKMONT & THE NORTHERN PARK
Waterfalls, camping and logging history. p54

OCONALUFTEE & THE SOUTHERN PARK
Mountain history and family fun. p62

CADES COVE & THE WESTERN PARK
Bears, homesteads and sublime meadows. p68

CATALOOCHEE & THE EASTERN PARK
Elk, serene nature and rafting. p76

HIGH COUNTRY
Mountain hikes and endless vistas. p84

Find Your Way

Encompassing more than 500,000 acres and spanning two states, the park is large but easily accessible thanks to modern highways that traverse the heart of the High Country, and hundreds of miles of trails.

Cades Cove & the Western Park, p68

With sublime open meadows set against a mountain backdrop, Cades Cove is the park's favorite bear-watching spot, with a treasure trove of historic structures.

Sugarlands, Elkmont & the Northern Park, p54

On the Tennessee side, the Great Smokies' most visited corner has famous waterfall hikes, synchronous fireflies and a beloved riverside family campground.

High Country, p84

Admire vast mountain panoramas from scenic overlooks on Newfound Gap Rd, or explore the backcountry on the Appalachian Trail and other classic hikes.

Cataloochee & the Eastern Park, p76

Escape the crowds in the park's quietest corner, famous for its natural tranquility, rushing rivers, abundant wildlife and abandoned 19th-century settlements.

Oconaluftee & the Southern Park, p62

The park's North Carolina gateway, which adjoins Cherokee lands, offers the park's best visitor center, prime elk-watching, horseback riding, fishing, river tubing and boating on Fontana Lake.

CAR
Most visitors explore the park by car. State and national highways, including I-40, grant easy access to the park's perimeter. Once inside, prepare to move more slowly on a mix of well-maintained but often crowded scenic drives and off-the-beaten-track dirt roads.

HIKING
The Smokies' exceptional network of hiking trails makes it possible to reach even remote corners of the park on foot, whether you're a casual day hiker seeking out a scenic waterfall or a long-distance backpacker roaming ridge lines and high-altitude meadows along the Appalachian Trail.

SHUTTLE
A network of private shuttle operators (p59) offers rides to trailheads and other points of interest, freeing you up to admire the views, and easing pressure on the park's overcrowded areas.

Plan Your Time

Each corner of the Smokies has its own character, with riveting natural beauty and fascinating human history throughout. Your experience here can be wild or tame, from rugged backcountry adventures to easy walks near well-serviced gateway towns.

Newfound Gap Rd (p86)

If You Only Do One Thing

● Zero in on a single section of the park and take time to enjoy its natural beauty and cultural history.

● If you love long views and scenic overlooks, spend the day exploring **Newfound Gap Rd** (p86), pausing to picnic and hike at least one of the wonderful trails en route.

● If slow-paced solitude is your thing, head for remote **Cataloochee Valley** (p76) to mingle with elk and wander among the historic homes. Or immerse yourself in one of America's most sublime pastoral landscapes while discovering 19th-century settler life on a cycling or driving circuit of the **Cades Cove Loop** (p70).

Seasonal Highlights

The Smokies are gorgeous year-round, whether bursting with spring and summer blooms, glowing with vivid fall foliage or blanketed in new-fallen snow. Crowds are largest from June through October.

JANUARY
Cross-country skiers revel in the Smokies' winter solitude. Snug in their dens, bears give birth to tiny cubs.

APRIL
The annual **Spring Wildflower Pilgrimage** (p72) brings nature lovers and experts together for a four-day exploration of the Smokies.

MAY
Delicate pink-and-white laurels bloom throughout the park, then synchronous fireflies begin lighting up the forests around Elkmont.

Three Days to Explore

● Start on the park's less-visited North Carolina side at **Oconaluftee Visitor Center** (p63), strolling riverbanks and meadows on the **Oconaluftee River Trail** (p64), touring historic **Mingus Mill** (p67) and **Mountain Farm Museum** (p63), and exploring the park at an equestrian pace at **Smokemont Riding Stables** (p65).

● On day two, climb **Newfound Gap Rd** (p86) for vistas at **Clingmans Dome** (p89), the Smokies' highest summit, then descend into Tennessee to see waterfalls along **Roaring Fork Motor Nature Trail** (p57) before overnighting at **Elkmont Campground** (p58).

● Rise on day three for a morning tour of the **Cades Cove Loop** (p70) and an afternoon hike to **Abrams Falls** (p69).

If You Have More Time

● Delve into some of the park's lesser-known corners to escape the crowds. Start in Bryson City, NC, a perfect base for tubing at **Deep Creek** (p65) or kayaking **Fontana Lake** (p67).

● Next, follow our three-day itinerary (left), taking extra time for classic high-country hikes like **Charlies Bunion** (p85), **Chimney Tops** (p88) and **Alum Cave Trail** (p88), or an overnight at **LeConte Lodge** (p89).

● End with two or three days on the park's quieter eastern side. Hike to **Ramsey Cascades** (p61), camp at **Cosby** (p82), raft the **Pigeon River** (p81) and experience the wild solitude of historic **Cataloochee** (p78).

JUNE
Flame azaleas explode on the high-country 'balds,' and rhododendrons reach peak bloom across the park.

JULY
Nature-focused summer camps for kids, families and adults take place at the **Great Smoky Mountains Institute at Tremont** near Cades Cove.

OCTOBER
Join the **Smokies Harvest Celebration** at the Mountain Farm Museum, hear elk bugle their mating call and enjoy stunning fall foliage.

DECEMBER
Sugarlands Visitor Center celebrates its Festival of Christmas Past with children's activities, old-time music, storytelling and craft demonstrations.

KELLY VANDELLEN/SHUTTERSTOCK ©, DIONYSIUS/SHUTTERSTOCK ©, KELLY VANDELLEN/SHUTTERSTOCK ©, JENNLSHOOTS/SHUTTERSTOCK ©

SUGARLANDS, ELKMONT & THE NORTHERN PARK

Of the park's 13-million-plus annual visitors, over 90% enter from Gatlinburg and Pigeon Forge via the Sugarlands Visitor Center. With this steady flood of humanity, many popular spots in the northern park – most notably Laurel Falls and the Roaring Fork Motor Nature Trail – get heavily overused, creating parking headaches and ecological stress. Even so, the Sugarlands area is home to many deservedly beloved attractions, including Elkmont Campground, where dozens of family-friendly campsites line the banks of the Little River. Sugarlands is the northern terminus of Newfound Gap Rd, offering easy access to the park's high country. It's also intriguing for history buffs, with its vestiges of early 20th-century logging camps, 19th-century settler cabins and turn-of-the-century vacation cottages. To the west, the rushing waters of Little River Gorge make a delightful backdrop for picnics and family outings. For something wilder and more remote, head east of Gatlinburg to the park's Greenbrier entrance.

TOP TIP

Roads and parking lots near Sugarlands are among the park's most congested due to the high volume of visitors entering from Gatlinburg. Consider visiting top attractions early or late in the day – or taking a shuttle to the trailhead (p59). Support the park's well-being by purchasing your parking tag and park only in designated spaces.

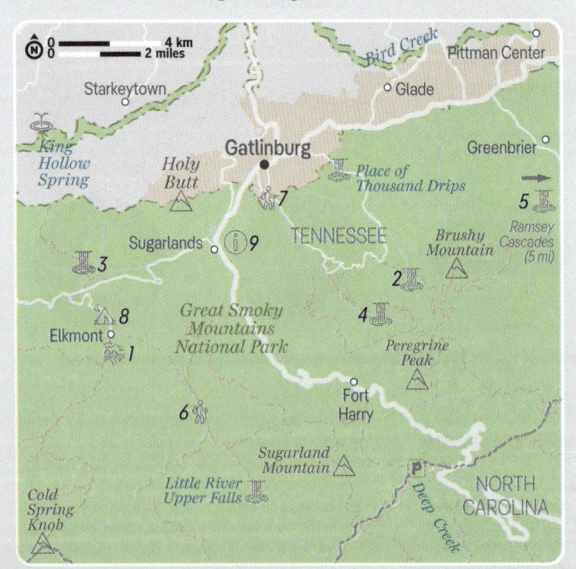

SIGHTS
1 Daisy Town
2 Grotto Falls
3 Laurel Falls
4 Rainbow Falls
5 Ramsey Cascades

ACTIVITIES
6 Little River Trail
7 Roaring Fork Motor Nature Trail

SLEEPING
8 Elkmont Campground

INFORMATION
9 Sugarlands Visitor Center

Fireflies

Watch Fireflies at Elkmont

NATURE'S MESMERIZING LIGHT SHOW

Every year in late May/early June, *Photinus carolinus* fireflies light up the forests around **Elkmont** in a rare display of entomological magic. Also known as the synchronous firefly, *P carolinus* males synchronize their flashing as part of a mating display. For several seconds at a time, the fireflies fill the forest with pulsating light, then go dark, then begin again. The pattern builds as each firefly joins the cloud of twinkling light, and the effect is eerie and stunningly beautiful. The synchronized twinkling begins at nightfall and continues till around midnight.

The human pilgrimage to join the festivities begins just before dusk. A parade of campers armed with red headlamps (white light disrupts the fireflies) walk south from their campsites toward the Little River and Jakes Creek trails. The anticipation is palpable as folks scope out the best spots, towing drowsy toddlers in wagons, laying out picnic blankets and setting up folding chairs. The low murmur of voices is replaced by reverent whispers as the fireflies begin their nightly dance.

PARK LOVERS, PARK IT FORWARD!

With visitation at over 13 million people a year, Great Smoky Mountains National Park sees more tourists than the Grand Canyon, Yosemite and Yellowstone combined. Yet while these parks charge entrance fees that generate over $1 million per park per year, this park cannot – for reasons historic and legal. The result? 'As the park keeps giving to more and more people every year,' says park superintendent Cassius Cash, 'it's putting a strain on the Smokies.'

Starting in March 2023, the park began requiring parking tags on all vehicles. This new initiative, dubbed **Park It Forward**, provides a means to raise much-needed funds. Visit nps.gov/grsm/planyourvisit/fees.htm to find prices and details on where to purchase your pass.

WHERE TO PICNIC NEAR SUGARLANDS

Mynatt Park
Picnic by LeConte Creek in this unexpected patch of Gatlinburg greenery near Roaring Fork Motor Nature Trail.

Chimneys Picnic Area
Dozens of picnic tables, including many creekside options, east of Sugarlands on Newfound Gap Rd.

Metcalf Bottoms
The perfect riverside picnic spot to break your journey between Sugarlands or Elkmont and Cades Cove.

Grotto Falls

BEARS NEED PRIVACY, TOO!

Even the toilets provide teachable moments in the Smokies. The park's hilarious **'Bears need privacy, too!'** poster – found on many a toilet door – reminds visitors to keep their distance while watching wildlife, both for their own and for the bears' safety. The 'Did You Kill This Bear?' poster reminds campers and visitors to store all food in their cars and place trash in bear-proof bins only. At the park's backcountry campsites and shelters, backpackers must use a cable system to dangle food beyond the reach of bear paws.

Since switching its focus to educating humans, the park has seen a significant reduction in bears gone bad. Help protect these magnificent creatures: keep your distance and handle food and trash responsibly.

Great Smoky Mountains National Park is one of the few places in the US – and the world – to witness this spectacle. The easiest way to participate is to snag a campsite at Elkmont Campground (p58). Savvy campers reserve months in advance, but you can sometimes get in on a last-minute cancellation or join the annual Firefly Viewing Lottery in late April (recreation.gov/ticket/facility/233374).

Waterfall Hikes near Sugarlands

THE SMOKIES' MOST POPULAR FALLS

The Sugarlands–Gatlinburg area is home to three of the park's most famous waterfalls.

Picturesque **Grotto Falls** is most easily accessed from the Roaring Fork Motor Nature Trail via a 1.4-mile section of the Trillium Gap Trail. Beyond the scenic beauty of the falls themselves, this trail offers two unique features: the chance to walk behind the 25ft cascades (a classic Smokies photo op!) and the rare opportunity to cross paths with llamas carrying supplies to and from LeConte Lodge (p89) on Mondays, Wednesdays and Fridays.

Rainbow Falls is the most dramatic of the three, and the most challenging to reach. From the Rainbow Falls trailhead,

WHERE TO SLEEP NEAR SUGARLANDS

Elkmont Campground
The soothing sounds of Little Creek are omnipresent at this delightful, family-friendly campground (p58). **$**

Ely's Mill Cabins
These two kitchen-equipped cabins are adjacent to a mill near the end of Roaring Fork Motor Nature Trail. **$$**

Bearskin Lodge
Enjoy the pool and prime location at this river-facing Gatlinburg hotel on the park's doorstep. **$$**

near the start of the Roaring Fork Motor Nature Trail, it's a 2.8-mile uphill trek with 1600ft of elevation gain. Your reward is one of the Smokies' highest waterfalls, cascading 90ft down a cliff immersed in forest. The nifty stone-slab bridge over LeConte Creek makes for a delightful place to soak up the view.

Multi-tiered **Laurel Falls** is the most popular of the three, thanks to its privileged location halfway between Sugarlands and Elkmont Campground. The 1.3-mile out-and-back trail climbs moderately through a laurel-dotted forest, reaching a bridge that crosses the falls near the midpoint of their 75ft drop. At the time of research, the asphalt path to the falls was severely degraded due to overuse, making it useless for strollers and wheelchairs; however, plans have called for its imminent renovation. There are multiple parking lots for Laurel Falls, some more than half a mile from the trailhead. Make sure you park only in designated spaces.

To avoid the crowds, arrive as close to dawn as possible; otherwise, allow extra time to find a parking space, and expect a longer walk to the trailhead.

Traverse the Roaring Fork Motor Nature Trail

A SLOW-PACED SMOKIES SAMPLER

This short one-way **driving loop** just south of Gatlinburg provides an excellent introduction to the Great Smokies' natural and historic attractions, especially for visitors with limited mobility. Designed to be taken slowly (the speed limit is 10mph, so allow at least an hour), the undulating route weaves along rushing creeks, and rises and dips through gorgeous green forest. Parking spots and pull-ins offer plenty of opportunities to exit your vehicle and explore on foot, with short trails leading to historic homesteads and longer paths climbing to some of the park's most beloved waterfalls. The road can get crowded, so for maximum enjoyment, consider visiting midweek or early in the day.

The Motor Nature Trail begins about 5 miles outside Gatlinburg; follow Cherokee Orchard Rd south from town. After passing turnoffs for the Bud Ogle Cabin and the Rainbow Falls trailhead, you'll reach the official entrance to the narrow one-way section. Worthwhile stops over the next 5 miles include the Grotto Falls trail, the 19th-century **Ephraim Bales Cabin**, the brightly painted **Alfred Reagan Homestead** – complete with its 'tub mill' (a primitive gristmill) across the road – and the **Place of a Thousand Drips** (an intermittent waterfall). Pick up a handy booklet covering these and several other stops at one of the park's visitor centers.

PARK-APPROVED FIREWOOD

The American chestnut tree was once so plentiful in the park it's said that a squirrel could hop from Maine to Georgia on its boughs. The chestnut fed bears, birds, deer, squirrels and humans, and was used to build everything from coffins to cradles. Then, in 1904, a forester noticed a fungus attacking it. By 1950, the chestnuts were all but gone: a 40-million-year-old species devastated.

We can't undo the damage done by the invasive chestnut blight, but we *can* prevent similar devastation. Non-native pests again threaten the eastern forests, and these 'critters' travel easily on firewood. Tree-loving campers can do their part by using only heat-treated, park-approved firewood. Your best bet? Buy it within the park itself.

WHERE TO EAT BREAKFAST NEAR ELKMONT

Crockett's Breakfast Camp
Challenge yourself to the world's largest cinnamon roll at Gatlinburg's favorite breakfast spot. $

Elvira's
Hearty Southern breakfast fare served on a wraparound porch in Wears Valley. $

Hillbilly's
Convenient option for breakfast without the Gatlinburg crowds, 20 minutes from Elkmont in Wears Valley. $

Camping at Elkmont

COZY AND CONVIVIAL RIVERSIDE CAMPING

Despite Elkmont being the park's largest **campground**, it feels so cozy. At night, you'll hear the murmurs of fellow campers gathered around their campfires, while kids run around and families of all shapes and sizes have fun together. Large portions of the campground are generator free (loops A–B and L–M–N), and there are two walk-in areas for tent campers (with one in a grassy open space). Some 44 of Elkmont's 215 sites are along Little River or Jakes Creek, and you can hear the river from most places. Elkmont is also home to Daisy Town, a cluster of getaway cabins from the early 1900s that is fun to prowl.

From your campsite, you can set off for a gorgeous walk along the Little River and other trails. In late May or early June, Elkmont campers can gawk in wonder at the park's fabled synchronous fireflies (p55). Elkmont has 11 Americans with Disabilities Act–approved campsites, and three with electrical outlets for medical machinery. A small outpost sells ice, firewood, and limited food and supplies, and the closest towns are Wears Valley and Gatlinburg, each about 20 minutes away.

Birding in the Smokies with Merlin

THE MAGICAL BIRD-IDENTIFICATION APP

What do you do when the incessant call of what you think is a whip-poor-will wakes you up in your tent at 5am? Grab your phone and start up **Merlin**! How about when you're out hiking and want to know just who it is you can hear but not see up in those trees? Merlin. How about when taking a quiet moment at your campsite to do your own mini-bird BioBlitz? Merlin.

Developed by the Cornell Lab of Ornithology – with many contributors from elsewhere – the Merlin bird-recognition app is like having the world's greatest bird-watching coach in your pocket. The Sound ID feature is pure magic: press the microphone icon, and Merlin will record and process the nearest bird sounds before spitting out a list of potential matches. Then you can click on a bird to hear its calls, discover its range, see a photo of it and read a description. Of course, Merlin also does way more than this.

Using Merlin in the Smokies, with its 240 bird species, is a delight. Just make sure you download the 'US: Southeast' bird pack while you still have internet. Inside the park, Merlin works without cell coverage or wi-fi.

GET ORIENTED AT SUGARLANDS VISITOR CENTER

Sugarlands is one of Great Smoky Mountains National Park's two main visitor centers, and the best place to get oriented if you're entering the park from Tennessee. The other large visitor center is Oconaluftee (p63), on the North Carolina side.

Inside, you'll find helpful staff, a park-focused bookstore and gift shop, resources to help plan your trip, a small museum dedicated to the park's plant and animal communities, and the park's lone Backcountry Office. From late May through October, there are daily ranger programs. Buy your parking tag in the bookstore or from vending machines outside. Behind the visitor center, short trails lead to **Cataract Falls** and the historic **John Ownby Cabin**.

WHERE TO BUY GROCERIES NEAR ELKMONT

Dollar General, Wears Valley
Budget chain offering mostly packaged food, but it's the closest option at 10.6 miles from Elkmont.

Food City, Gatlinburg
Large, locally owned and operated supermarket; 13.5 miles from Elkmont via the Gatlinburg Bypass.

Kroger, Pigeon Forge
A large chain supermarket; 18 miles from Elkmont on the more scenic Wears Valley Rd.

Appalachian Clubhouse (p60), Daisy Town

Discover Daisy Town
A VACATION COMMUNITY RECREATED

In 1908, the Little River Lumber Company built a railway from Townsend to Elkmont to support its burgeoning lumber operations in the region. Soon thereafter, the company began marketing the train ride to vacationers, and the western Smokies' tourism industry was born. Business and civic leaders from Knoxville flocked to Elkmont to hunt and fish, while the prestigious Appalachian Club served three meals a day to members and hosted dances on Saturday nights. By 1925, the lumber company had moved on to greener pastures at Tremont, and the railway was replaced by a gravel road, drawing even more visitors.

During this period, numerous vacation homes sprang up in Elkmont, many embracing the 'craftsman' style of architecture, sporting large porches, bold colors and plenty of natural wood details. Today, you can experience a remnant of the whimsical world they created a century ago with a visit to **Daisy Town**, a painstakingly restored cluster of structures at the far end of Elkmont Campground. Highly skilled artisans have contributed their talents in restoring the buildings, incorporating original architectural features and colors – as

SHUTTLES FOR VISTA-SEEKERS & HIKERS

Unless you hike at sunrise or in the dead of winter, you might get skunked if you try parking at the park's most popular trailheads – Alum Cave (p88), Chimney Tops (p88), Grotto Falls (p56), Laurel Falls (p57), Rainbow Falls (p56), Newfound Gap overlook (p87) or Clingmans Dome (p89). Save yourself the hassle and use one of the park's authorized shuttle providers.

On the Tennessee side, companies offering custom transportation to and from the trailhead include AAA Hiker Shuttle (aaahikerservice.com), A Walk in the Woods (awalkinthewoods.com), Great Smoky Mountains Eco Tours (greatsmokymountainecotours.com/shuttle-services), RockyTop Tours (rockytoptours.com) and Smoky Mountain Rides (smokyrides.com).

In North Carolina, try Bryson City Outdoors (brysoncityoutdoors.com/hikershuttle) or Carolina Bound (carolinaboundadventures.com).

OTHER RESOURCES FOR ELKMONT CAMPERS

Elkmont Store
Twenty-four-hour vending machines and daytime kiosk selling firewood, ice, s'more makings and other essentials.

Maloney Point
The nearest cell service, 3 miles east of Elkmont at the first parking lot beyond Laurel Falls.

Well Wishing
A 24-hour laundromat on East Parkway in Gatlinburg.

REIMAGINING THE PAST

Many of the historic homes throughout the park are unfurnished, and more stand alone, with their former outbuildings long-since demolished. For a fuller recreation of what a 19th-century farmstead might have looked like, visit the **Mountain Farm Museum** (p63) at Oconaluftee and the **Great Smoky Mountains Heritage Center** (p73) in Townsend.

Little River

BEST WATERFALL HIKES WITHOUT THE CROWDS

Prefer to avoid the crowds at Laurel, Rainbow and Grotto Falls? These less-visited waterfalls make fine alternatives.

Baskins Creek Falls Accessed via the Roaring Fork Motor Nature Trail (p57), this 5.6-mile hike leads to a double-tiered 40ft waterfall.

Ramsey Cascades Old growth forest adds intrigue to this 8-mile out-and-back hike to the park's tallest waterfall.

Three Waterfalls Loop On the park's southern edge, this 3-mile loop (p67) is one of the park's most rewarding short hikes.

you can see from the 'before and after' photos displayed on plaques along Daisy Town's main street. At the end of the street, rocking chairs on the porch of the **Appalachian Clubhouse** offer a contemplative vantage point.

Walk the Little River Trail

RIVERSIDE RAMBLING FOR ALL AGES

You'll see everyone from toddlers to octogenarians on the easygoing **Little River Trail** near Elkmont Campground (p58). 'Trail' is actually a misnomer for the broad, well-graded gravel road that ambles along the banks of the Little River for miles, with minimal elevation gain. Chimneys of old vacation homes poke out of the trees in the early stages, but as you move upstream it's all about the river, framed by soaring trees, giant boulders and showy sweeps of rhododendrons. Small side trails lead down to rocky pools, while the rushing waters provide a delightful soundtrack. Watch for herons scanning the banks for their next meal or soaring gracefully from rock to rock. Many people do this as an out-and-back walk, turning around whenever they're ready, but you can expand this into a 5-mile loop by turning right at the 2.3-mile mark onto **Cucumber Gap Trail** (2.4 miles), which

OTHER RESOURCES FOR ELKMONT CAMPERS

Heavenly Roast	**Wears Valley Social Food Truck Park**	**Four Daughters Farm, Walland**
Wi-fi, cell service and top-notch coffee including espresso, 1 mile north of the park in Wears Valley.	Great solution for a quick bite, 20 minutes north of Elkmont in Wears Valley.	Fresh organic produce; go to the farm stand Sunday 4pm to 6pm, or order online for Monday delivery to your campsite.

crosses over a small ridge and returns you to your starting point via **Jakes Creek Trail**. Campers can easily access the trailhead by walking across the bridge near campsite F8; if you're driving in from outside the campground, turn left just before the camper registration station and follow the signs.

Climb to Ramsey Cascades

TOWERING TREES AND THUNDERING WATERS

For those with the stamina to tackle it, this beautiful climb to **Ramsey Cascades**, the park's highest waterfall, is one of the Smokies' most rewarding hikes. Ascending 2280ft over 4 miles, the Ramsey Cascades Trail starts in the remote Greenbrier section of the park, 11 miles east of Gatlinburg via the mostly unpaved Greenbrier and Ramsey Prong roads.

The trail initially climbs parallel to the Middle Prong of the Little Pigeon River on a wide, old logging road. It's steep and rocky in places, but three log benches offer opportunities for a rest. After 1.5 miles, the road merges into a much narrower trail, entering a glowing green world of moss-covered boulders, ferns and trees springing from islands in midstream. Despite the steady uphill slog, it's difficult not to marvel at the gorgeous scenery and the trail builders' expertise in navigating the challenging terrain. Just beyond the 2.5-mile mark, you'll pass a trio of massive (and old) tulip poplars; the first two rise majestically on either side of the trail, while the third measures more than 6ft across at its base.

The trail soon emerges at another lovely spot where flagstones have been laid to create a walkable surface alongside the boulder-filled creek. Cross the creek on a recently constructed log bridge around the 3-mile mark and begin the final ascent. Near the top, the sense of adventure is enhanced by graceful wood and stone staircases that traverse tight passages between mossy trees and giant rocks, with rhododendrons towering overhead. You'll hear the falls before you see them, cascading 100ft down the cliff at trail's end – a dramatic place to pause for a picnic before returning downhill.

BEST EASY HIKES FOR FAMILIES

Metcalf Bottoms Trail
Kids can splash in the river, then hike to a 19th-century schoolhouse on this easy 0.7-mile trail from Metcalf Bottoms picnic area.

Big Creek Trail to Midnight Hole & Mouse Creek Falls
Follow the boulder-strewn banks of Big Creek to a sunny swimming hole and a pretty waterfall.

Oconaluftee River Trail
Watch for elk and see nature through the eyes of Cherokee storytellers on this interpretive nature trail near the Oconaluftee Visitor Center.

GETTING AROUND

Gatlinburg, TN, is the main gateway into the park's northern section. It's an easy 2-mile drive south from Gatlinburg to the Sugarlands Visitor Center via Hwy 441; pedestrians can cover this same distance in about 45 minutes via the Gatlinburg Trail (p109). From Sugarlands, two main thoroughfares lead into the national park. Newfound Gap Rd (Hwy 441) heads south over Newfound Gap to Cherokee, NC, while Fighting Gap Creek Rd and Little River Gorge Rd head west to Elkmont Campground, Cades Cove and Townsend, TN. If traveling from Sugarlands or Elkmont to destinations east of Gatlinburg, such as Roaring Fork Motor Nature Trail or the Ramsey Cascades Trail, expect slowdowns along Gatlinburg's main street, which is often congested with pedestrians and traffic.

OCONALUFTEE & THE SOUTHERN PARK

For a less crowded experience, head to the North Carolina side of the Smokies. In the park's southern reaches, you'll find three campgrounds, hiking, horseback riding, fishing, wildlife watching, kayaking and tubing. A half-hour drive northwest from Oconaluftee brings you to the summit of Newfound Gap Rd, while to the east, less visited Balsam Mountain boasts equally compelling vistas.

Immediately outside the Oconaluftee entrance, the town of Cherokee offers multiple ways to explore the art, culture and traditions of the region's First People. Further west, near the park's Deep Creek entrance, walkable Bryson City is the Smokies' most inviting gateway town, with taprooms, restaurants, cafes and shops.

TOP TIP

Oconaluftee is one of the park's top spots for observing wildlife, but timing is important. Arrive at the visitor center near dawn or dusk for the best chance of finding elk peacefully grazing in the surrounding meadows or along the lower reaches of Newfound Gap Rd.

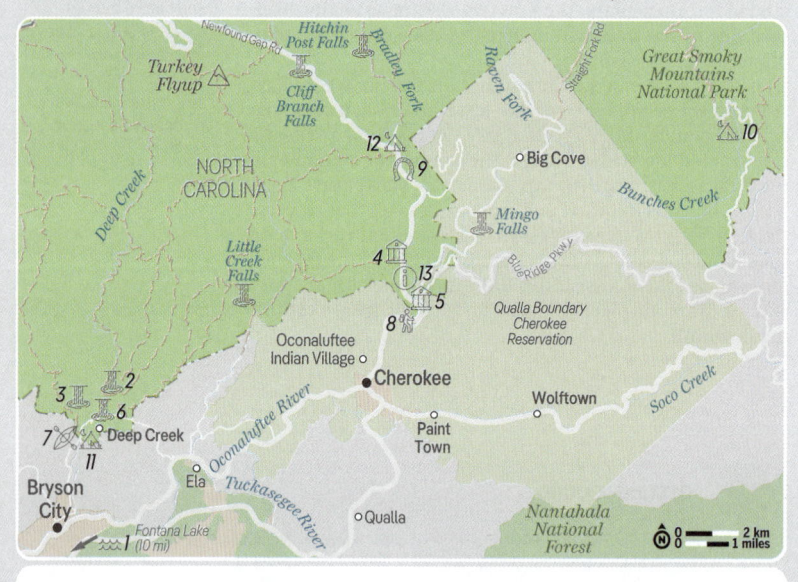

SIGHTS
1 Fontana Lake
2 Indian Creek Falls
3 Juney Whank Falls
4 Mingus Mill
5 Mountain Farm Museum
6 Tom Branch Falls

ACTIVITIES
7 Deep Creek
8 Oconaluftee River Trail
9 Smokemont Riding Stables

SLEEPING
10 Balsam Mountain
11 Deep Creek Campground
12 Smokemont Campground

INFORMATION
13 Oconaluftee Visitor Center

Oconaluftee Visitor Center

The Southern Gateway to the Smokies

THE SMOKIES' SOUTHERN GATEWAY

Set just 2 miles north of Cherokee, NC, the inviting, modern **Oconaluftee Visitor Center** straddles a vast open meadow by the Oconaluftee River. Inside, interpretive displays, a well-stocked bookstore and a scale model of the park help orient visitors to the area's attractions, including several off-the-beaten-track options. Where Oconaluftee really excels is in its well-conceived museum focused on Appalachian culture; don't miss the audio recordings of older local residents describing scenes of traditional life. As you exit, the rocking chairs on the back porch make a perfect perch to watch for elk and contemplate the bucolic setting.

An Older World at the Mountain Farm Museum

EXPLORE A SMOKIES' FARMSTEAD

Just behind the Oconaluftee Visitor Center, the open-air **Mountain Farm Museum** is a recreation of a Great Smokies farmstead, providing a glimpse into the everyday lives

FISHING THE SMOKIES

The park boasts hundreds of miles of trout streams; for a comprehensive map, pick up the National Park Service's free **Great Smoky Mountains Fishing Regulations** brochure. However, you'll need a license before casting your line on either side of the park.

To fish at Cataloochee, Oconaluftee, Big Creek, Deep Creek or elsewhere in North Carolina, apply online at eregulations.com/northcarolina/fishing. Alternatively, get your license in person at a local outlet like Tuckaseegee Fly Shop in Bryson City, which also offers supplies, advice and guided fishing trips. Get your Tennessee license at gooutdoors tennessee.com. For supplies and full-day fly-fishing classes, check out Little River Outfitters in Townsend.

WHERE TO EAT NEAR THE SOUTHERN PARK

Everett Street Diner
The line goes down the street at this friendly diner serving breakfast, lunch and homemade pies.

River's End Restaurant
Dine with spectacular Nantahala River views, southwest of Bryson City at the Nantahala Outdoor Center.

The Bistro at the Everett Hotel
Elegant ambience for a special meal, but seating for non-hotel guests is limited; call for a reservation.

BEST PICNIC SPOTS IN THE PARK

Chimneys Picnic Area
Picnic at this tree-shaded beauty 5 miles southeast of Sugarlands.

Balsam Mountain/ Heintooga
Eat on massive stone tables near Balsam Mountain Campground, with soaring mountain vistas just below.

Big Creek
Watch the river roar past from the picnic tables at Big Creek Campground's day-use area.

Metcalf Bottoms
Dozens of picnic tables line this quiet, shallow stretch of the Little River, 6 miles west of Elkmont.

Cades Cove
Picnic and frolic on the banks of Anthony Creek, adjacent to Cades Cove Campground.

---

of hardworking mountain people in the 19th and early 20th centuries. Each building here came from someone's farm, somewhere else inside the park. For example, the central farmhouse, where John E Davis and his wife 'Creasy' raised their seven children, is an exquisite, irreplaceable example of a 'matched chestnut' log cabin with half dovetail notches at the corners, moved from north of Bryson City.

A more powerful appreciation happens when you see this not as a collection of buildings but as a single farmstead, with each structure needed to keep a family sheltered or fed. This was a largely self-sufficient world in which you ate what you raised and you raised what you ate. Period. As you walk the grounds, you can imagine daily chores: gathering eggs; chopping, stacking and bringing wood inside the home for cooking and heating; storing wood ash in the ash hopper for making soap or hominy; and bringing butter and other perishables to the spring house, where running water kept them cool.

Other features speak to seasonal tasks in the yearly cycle of agriculture: spring planting, summer vegetable gardening, fall harvesting and processing crops for the winter. There were plenty of chores in fall: making sorghum into molasses; picking and storing apples; harvesting and shucking the all-important corn to be ground into meal or flour; rounding up the hogs from the forests and fattening them on corn in the hog pen, then slaughtering and smoking them to be stored in the meathouse. Winters were for working with your hands and making quilts, or hollowing out blackgum trunks for beehives.

Stroll the Oconaluftee River Trail

FOLLOW THE RIVER INTO CHEROKEE

Few walks in the Smokies are as delightfully flat and easy to access as this 1.5-mile **riverside stroll** between the Oconaluftee Visitor Center (p63) and Cherokee. Not only is the scenery gorgeous, but the entire route is also signposted at regular intervals, with plaques delving into Cherokee spirituality, artwork, traditions and lore, with all text written in English and in the beautifully flowing Cherokee script. If you only have time to hike part way, start from the visitor center end, where the trail threads its way through an open meadow before joining the leafy green banks of the broad, tranquil Oconaluftee River. Note that this is one of only three trails in the park that is also open to cyclists.

WHERE TO SLEEP NEAR THE SOUTHERN PARK

River's Edge Motel, Cherokee
Sleep by the Oconaluftee River, less than 3 miles south of the Oconaluftee Visitor Center.

Everett Hotel, Bryson City
Stylish boutique hotel in the heart of Bryson City, complete with an acclaimed in-house bistro (p63).

Fryemont Inn, Bryson City
Dating to 1923, this hilltop classic boasts atmospheric chestnut- and stone-accented common spaces.

Ride Horses at Smokemont Stables

EXPLORE THE PARK ON HORSEBACK

Great Smoky Mountains National Park is an equestrian's paradise, with a huge network of campsites and trails catering specifically to those traveling on horseback. For visitors who don't happen to be traveling with their personal steed, the next best thing is to rent horses from one of the park's three official concessionaires. In business since the 1950s, friendly **Smokemont Riding Stables**, 2 miles north of the Oconaluftee Visitor Center (p63), is the oldest horseback outfit in the park and the only one that's family-run. Activities here run the gamut from half-hour wagon rides to a four-hour jaunt into the national park. Especially popular is the 2½-hour horseback excursion to **Chasteen Creek Waterfall**. Like other local stables, the folks in Smokemont are unable to offer overnight trips into the park due to various legal and logistical challenges, but the knowledgeable staff have roamed every corner and can recommend an endless variety of itineraries, trails and backcountry campsites for serious equestrians with their own horses.

Go Tubing at Deep Creek

FLOATY FUN FOR THE FAMILY

For family fun on a modest budget, you can't beat a day tubing on beautiful **Deep Creek**, near the eponymous ranger station and campground just 2 miles north of Bryson City. Several tubing outfits line Deep Creek Rd, the main conduit leading north from town into the national park. Rentals are generally less than $10 per person and are good for the whole day. Grab your tubes, drive up to the day-use parking area just inside the park boundary, and walk up the Deep Creek Trail as far as you like before plunging into the creek.

Camping in the Southern Park

THREE DISTINCT CAMPING EXPERIENCES

An easy five-minute drive north of Bryson City, NC, family-friendly **Deep Creek Campground** is beloved for its large tent-only walk-in loop, with 42 sites scattered across a grassy creekside expanse where kids can play without worrying about traffic. There's a separate loop serving tents and RVs on the adjacent hillside. Nearby trailheads invite campers to explore the easy Three Waterfalls Loop (p67) or the surrounding backcountry. Tubing down Deep Creek is a major delight

TAKE A WILDFLOWER HIKE!

Throughout the warmer months, wildflowers enliven the trails of Great Smoky Mountains National Park. For spring wildflowers (March through May), experts recommend the Noah 'Bud' Ogle Place Nature Trail, as well as the Bradley Fork, Porters Creek, Chestnut Top and Schoolhouse Gap trails. In May, mountain laurel can be seen on almost all hikes.

From mid- to late June, stunning displays of flame azaleas bloom at Gregory Bald (p73), and at Andrews Bald below Clingmans Dome (p89). June and July are the best months to see rhododendrons. For prime Catawba rhododendron-viewing, try the Alum Cave (p88) and Chimney Tops (p88) trails. The more common rosebay rhododendrons prefer lower elevations and can be found throughout the park.

WHERE TO DRINK NEAR THE SOUTHERN PARK

Mountain Layers
Enjoy the view from the rooftop patio while sipping a microbrew; there's live music on weekends.

Mountain Perks
Start your day well with great coffee, freshly baked goods, local art and wi-fi.

Bryson City Outdoors Taproom
Friendly service, local brews and ciders, rotating food trucks and a patio, all on historic Main Street.

Juney Whank Falls

THE ROAD TO NOWHERE

For a quirky experience, take a spin on the **Road to Nowhere**. Originally designed to extend 30 miles from Bryson City to Fontana Lake, this highway project was abandoned after only 6 miles of roadway had been constructed. The pavement dead-ends abruptly northwest of Bryson City, at an elegant stone tunnel. Barriers block cars from proceeding, but the tunnel remains easily accessible to pedestrians (bring a flashlight).

Emerging on the far side is a through-the-looking-glass experience, as you're suddenly immersed in a deep green forest of chirping birds and footpaths. For an up-close look at Fontana Lake, take the Goldmine Loop Trail and then circle back to the parking lot on the Tunnel Bypass Trail.

in hot weather. Tube rentals, ice, firewood and a burger shack are just a 10-minute walk from the campground.

Twenty miles east of Oconaluftee Visitor Center (p63), lofty **Balsam Mountain Campground** (5310ft) enjoys relatively cool temperatures, even in summer. The long, winding approach via the Blue Ridge Parkway affords outstanding 'top of the world' vistas. Balsam Mountain's 43 campsites include a small grassy patch with six tent-only walk-in sites. Trailers, RVs and buses are prohibited on Balsam Mountain Rd.

Smokemont Campground sits just 2 miles north of Oconaluftee Visitor Center, at the base of scenic Newfound Gap Rd. Despite its convenient location, only 12 of its 141 sites (in the RV-only loop F) are actually on the river, and several are unpleasantly close to toilet facilities. The campground is open year-round and has a handful of Americans with Disabilities Act–approved sites. Ice and park-approved firewood are available on site; other services are a 10-minute drive away in Cherokee, NC.

RESOURCES FOR DEEP CREEK CAMPERS

Moon Goddess Burgers & Shakes
So close you can walk from your campsite; sit by the river and enjoy! $

Darnell Farms
This farmstand offers seasonal produce, ice cream, pick-your-own strawberries, a petting zoo and a riverside playground.

Bryson City Outfitters
Maps, camping supplies and outdoor gear, plus friendly, knowledgeable advice and an on-site brewpub.

Paddle to a Backcountry Campsite
LEAVE THE LANDLUBBERS BEHIND

Adventurous souls adept with an oar can discover one of the Smokies' rare pleasures on the shores of **Fontana Lake**. Here, in the park's southwestern corner, the National Park Service has designated five backcountry campsites (numbers 66, 72, 73, 78 and 87) for people arriving by boat. One of the most appealing and convenient options is to rent a kayak at **Fontana Village Resort & Marina** and paddle out past the houseboats to campsite 87 (Jerry Hollow) on an island just across the lake. It's less than 2 miles away but feels like a world apart: it's perched on a tree-shaded bluff with lovely views of the lakeshore. As with all 'paddlers only' sites, spaces are limited (maximum six people per night), so make sure you reserve ahead at smokiespermits.nps.gov.

Walk the Three Waterfalls Loop
SEE A SCENIC TRIO OF CASCADES

Mile for mile, there's no better trail for waterfall viewing than this 3-mile loop starting from the Deep Creek Campground (p65) near Bryson City. From the parking lot, a short but steep ascent on the Juney Whank Loop Trail brings you to **Juney Whank Falls** (0.3 miles), a 90ft cascade traversed by a bridge that provides a perfect vantage point. Just beyond the bridge, go left at the 'Y' to follow the Deep Creek Horse Trail uphill. You'll climb through second growth forest for about a mile before descending moderately to a junction with Deep Creek Trail. Go downhill (right) and cross a pair of bridges. After the second bridge, follow the Indian Creek Trail 200ft and descend the steps to **Indian Creek Falls**. Afterwards, rejoin Deep Creek Trail, following the rushing creek downstream 0.5 miles to **Tom Branch Falls**, where you can sit on a log bench and soak up the views. From here, it's an easy stroll back to the parking lot.

For a shorter, easier hike, skip the first two falls, following the wide, flat Deep Creek Trail directly from the parking lot to Tom Branch Falls and back (0.4 miles round trip).

MINGUS MILL

Dating to 1886, this beautiful two-story wooden structure was once the Smokies' largest **gristmill**, grinding grain for the local community for roughly half a century. The National Park Service kept the mill fully operational until 2022, when structural problems forced it to shut down indefinitely. Even in its non-operational state, the mill is a delightful and evocative place to wander. Historic mill stones grace the gravel path in front, while water still courses through the 200ft-long wooden flume out back, cascading down the sides of the rough-hewn log spillway and into the creek below. Part of the mill's charm is its peaceful creekside setting just half a mile from the Oconaluftee Visitor Center (p63).

GETTING AROUND

Cherokee, NC, just 3 miles south of the Oconaluftee Visitor Center, is the main gateway into the southern section of the park. From Cherokee and Oconaluftee, US 441 continues 35 miles northwest to Gatlinburg, TN, crossing through the national park's high country via Newfound Gap.

Other important thoroughfares along the park's southern edge include US 19, which connects Cherokee with Bryson City, and NC 28, which continues west to Fontana Lake and the southwestern corner of the park. East of Cherokee and Oconaluftee, the Blue Ridge Parkway and Balsam Mountain Rd grant access to Balsam Mountain, home to the park's highest campground and picnic area. From Bryson City, Deep Creek Rd leads 2 miles north to the park's Deep Creek entrance.

CADES COVE & THE WESTERN PARK

Cades Cove is one of the Smokies' most bewitching landscapes, a vast open valley encircled by mountains, dotted with historic structures and roamed by bears, wild turkeys and deer. At dawn, as the sun's rays pierce the fog and the cove's lush verdancy comes into focus, you feel you've unexpectedly entered another time, another place. With its abundant wildlife, the cove is believed to have been inhabited as early as 8000 BCE, and long served as hunting grounds for the Cherokee.

White settlers began arriving around 1820, building log cabins, churches and gristmills, clearing forests and farming; modern-day visitors traveling the Cades Cove Loop see the preserved remains of this bygone culture. The nearest town to Cades Cove is small but serviceable Townsend; further west, the scenic Foothills Parkway skirts the park's outer perimeter, granting access to the less-visited Abrams Creek and Look Rock entrances.

TOP TIP

Driving the Cades Cove Loop can be a dream come true – or an exasperating nightmare. Bear sightings, combined with high visitor numbers, can freeze up traffic, even on weekdays outside of peak season. The best strategy is to walk or cycle the loop on one of the park's vehicle-free Wednesdays (May–September). Otherwise, arrive as close to sunrise as possible.

Wild turkeys, Cades Cove

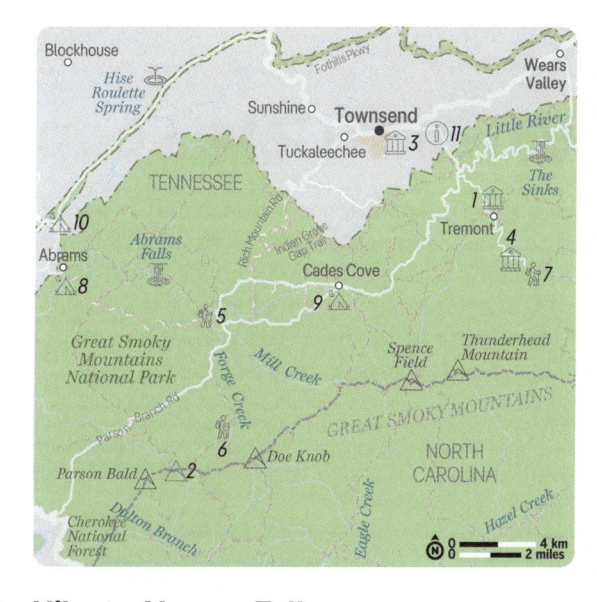

SIGHTS
1 Great Smoky Mountains Institute at Tremont
2 Gregory Bald
3 Little River Railroad and Lumber Company Museum
4 Tremont

ACTIVITIES
5 Abrams Falls Trail
6 Gregory Ridge Trail
7 Middle Prong Trail

SLEEPING
8 Abrams Creek Campground
9 Cades Cove Campground
10 Look Rock Campground

INFORMATION
11 Great Smoky Mountains Heritage Center

Hike to Abrams Falls

THE PARK'S MOST VOLUMINOUS WATERFALL

Easily accessible from the Cades Cove Loop (p70), the **Abrams Falls Trail** is one of the Smokies' classic hikes. The total walking time for this out-and-back jaunt is only about 2½ hours, but you should allow at least half a day to make the most of the beautiful setting at the base of the falls, where many linger to picnic or sun themselves on the rocks.

A turnoff just half a mile north of Cades Cove Visitor Center (p71) leads to the trailhead at the far side of a large parking lot. From here, the trail crosses a log bridge and hugs Abrams Creek for the first mile or so, undulating as it goes. Around the 1-mile mark, the creek disappears from sight as it makes a big horseshoe bend around a promontory, which the trail crosses via a low pass. After descending back to the creek, you'll continue another mile or so to reach the falls.

The falls are not high (only 20ft or so), but they carry a greater volume of water than any other cascade in the park, and the surrounding rock shelves are more spacious and welcoming than at many of the park's other waterfall hot spots.

Ambitious hikers can also hike into the falls from Abrams Creek Campground (p72) to the west, but the hike is longer (5 miles) and more sparsely traveled.

LIFE OF A BEAR CUB

In the Smokies, denning female bears give birth one to four cubs around late January. The moms emerge from their torpor, give birth, then go back to 'sleep' but remain attentive to their young.

Newborns resemble black lab puppies – blind, nearly furless and weighing about eight ounces. They begin nursing and, by the time the family emerges in April, the cubs weigh around 5lb. They nurse for up to eight months and then begin foraging in summer. The mom grooms, protects and teaches the cubs until they reach 18 months.

WHERE TO EAT & DRINK NEAR THE WESTERN PARK

Peaceful Side Social
Hipster haven in Townsend with draft beers, taco truck, sandwiches, pizza, a playground and indoor-outdoor seating. **$$**

The Abbey
Chilled-out Townsend spot for beer, cider, sandwiches, salads and daily specials, with an uber-delightful riverside patio. **$$**

Trailhead Steak & Trout House
Friendly service, reasonable prices, seasonal vegetables and later hours make this a useful Townsend option. **$$**

BICYCLE TOUR

Enjoy the Cades Cove Loop

Thanks to its history, wildlife and pastoral scenery, the Cades Cove Loop has become one of the Smokies' most sought-after tourist destinations. Alas, its popularity all too often translates into traffic congestion. To fully appreciate Cades Cove's ravishing beauty without the crowds, set off at dawn or in late afternoon. Better yet, come on Wednesdays, when motor vehicles are prohibited and cyclists and walkers rule the road.

1 Cades Cove Campground
Start at the Cades Cove Campground Store, where you can rent bikes for the journey and park your 'other' vehicle.

The Ride: Exit the campground and turn left onto Cades Cove Loop, which soon becomes one-way. The idyllic, tree-lined route rolls through open meadows to your first stop.

2 John Oliver Place
It's well worth taking the 0.3-mile footpath off the main road to this historic homestead tucked into a clearing at the edge of the forest. Dating to the early 1820s, this is the oldest-surviving log home in Cades Cove, and a tranquil spot to contemplate the valley, even when cars crowd the roadway below.

The Ride: Continue 1.2 miles west on the main road, then take the signposted 0.4-mile detour on your left for the Primitive Baptist Church.

3 Primitive Baptist Church
Few spots in the park are as evocative as this simple Baptist church down a side road, with its serene adjoining graveyard. Deer sometimes come to graze at the cemetery's edge in early morning, and many

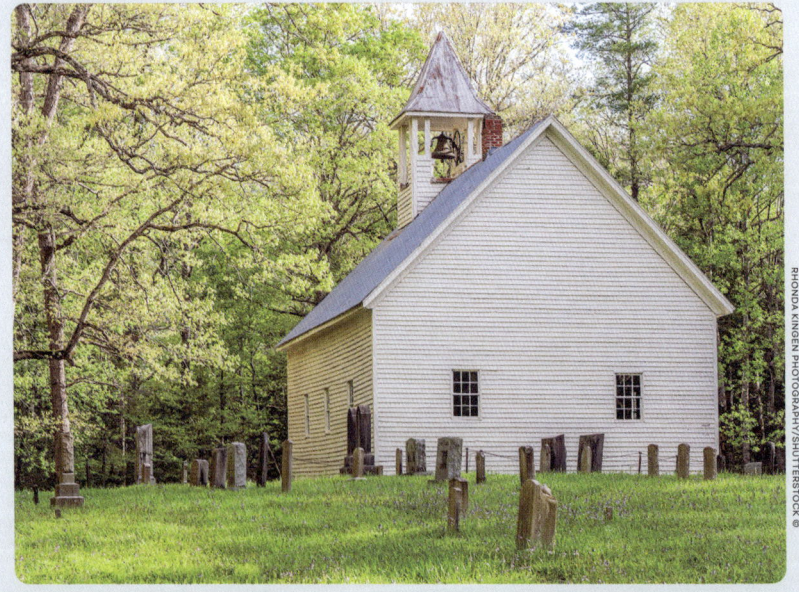

Primitive Baptist Church

familiar Cades Cove names are chiseled on the tombstones here.

The Ride: Return to the main road and bear left, passing two more churches and mountain-backed meadows before a steep descent to the Elijah Oliver parking area (2.3 miles further west).

4 Elijah Oliver Place

Park your bike and walk the lovely half-mile path to this old homestead, complete with smokehouse (for preserving hams), springhouse (for chilling dairy products) and corn crib (for storing corn).

The Ride: It's an easy 1-mile jaunt south to your next stop; en route is an optional turnoff for the Abrams Falls Trail (p69), one of the Smokies' prettiest waterfall hikes.

5 Cable Mill Area & Cades Cove Visitor Center

This attractive streamside assemblage of historical buildings beside the Cades Cove store and visitor center makes the perfect midway picnic stop. The star attraction here is the Cable Mill – a historic grist-mill flanked by a picturesque mill race, a blacksmith shop, a cantilever barn and other 19th-century structures.

The Ride: Your return trip begins here! You'll be following the southern edge of the cove the rest of the way. Continue 2 miles east to your next stop.

6 Tipton Place

The most attractive of several homesteads on your return route, Tipton Place features a shingle-roofed clapboard 1870s home with a collection of outbuildings straddling both sides of the road.

The Ride: Complete the loop, riding 2.9 miles past another historic cabin and the Cades Cove Stables to return to your starting point.

GUIDED HIKES & EXPERIENCES

In addition to ranger-led hikes and programs, several nonprofit partners celebrate the Smokies through hikes, classes and special events.

- **Friends of the Smokies** (friendsofthesmokies.org) leads a Classic Hikes of the Smokies series, showcasing the park's wildflowers, waterfalls and mountain vistas.
- The **Great Smoky Mountain Association** (smokyinformation.org) offers naturalist events around the park, including observing peregrine falcons at Alum Cave, studying salamanders at Sugarlands and tagging monarch butterflies at Cades Cove.
- The University of Tennessee's **Smoky Mountain Field School** (smfs.utk.edu) sponsors one-day courses inside the park, from foraging and fireflies to orienteering and Cherokee plant lore.
- Biologists and specialists lead guided explorations of Smokies plants and animals during April's four-day **Spring Wildflower Pilgrimage**.

Gregory Bald

Camping in the Western Park

CADES COVE AND BEYOND

The park's western section offers three very distinct camping options.

Cades Cove Campground is the park's second-largest and the ideal jumping-off point for exploring the Cades Cove Loop (p70). There's a ranger station and a store selling ice, firewood and limited groceries, and campers get special 24-hour rates at the on-site bike rental shop. RVs find easy parking in Loop A and B – so expect your mornings to be interrupted by the roar of generators, or opt for a quieter site in generator-free Loop C. There are 11 Americans with Disabilities Act–approved sites here, but no waterfront camping. The closest gas stations, restaurants and other services are in Townsend, 20 minutes away.

Near the park's western boundary, the remote **Abrams Creek Campground** is a tranquil paradise for camping, hiking and fishing, with nine of its 16 sites right along Abrams Creek. The approach to the campground involves a steep winding descent on a narrow gravel road with potholes and no guardrails; trailers and RVs are not recommended. Several trails fan out from the campground, including a back-door hiking route to Abrams Falls and Cades Cove.

WHERE TO EAT & DRINK NEAR THE WESTERN PARK

The Artistic Bean
Comfy Townsend venue for terrific coffee, tasty iced Earl Grey with lavender, and fresh pastries. $

Blackberry Farm
Converted warehouse space in Maryville with famed brews and tasty pub fare. $$

Burger Master Drive-in
This popular Townsend eatery has lured locals and tourists with burgers, shakes and ice cream since 1967. $

Look Rock Campground (70 sites) was revamped – for RVs, especially – and reopened in 2022. Ten sites have water and electricity hookups and are the only such sites in the park. Given its location – nearly an hour from Cades Cove on the Foothills Parkway – Look Rock feels isolated from the park proper. Aside from a short trail to nearby Look Rock Tower, hikers must drive elsewhere to find a trailhead.

Climb to Gregory Bald

EXPERIENCE A HIGH MOUNTAIN MEADOW

The Smokies abound in high-altitude clearings known as 'balds.' **Gregory Bald**, high on the ridge line above Cades Cove, is one of the park's most spectacular viewpoints, reached by a 5-mile ascent on the **Gregory Ridge Trail**. From the trailhead, 2.4 miles south of Cades Cove Visitor Center (p71) via unpaved Forge Creek Rd, the trail meanders 2 miles upstream along the rhododendron-clad banks of Forge Creek to backcountry campsite 12, then switchbacks up, up, up for the next 3 miles to a junction with the Gregory Bald Trail. A left-hand turn at this signposted junction would take you to the Appalachian Trail, but bear right here for the short remaining climb to Gregory Bald. Within half a mile, the trees part and you emerge into a vast grassy patch fringed with flame azaleas, which explode with vibrant pink, red and orange blooms in late June. On a clear day, the view extends far to the north and west, well beyond Cades Cove.

Day hikers can head back down the way they came (allow about six hours for the 11-mile round trip). Alternatively, overnight just beyond Gregory Bald at backcountry site 13 (Sheep Pen Gap), a 15-minute walk down the hill along the Gregory Bald Trail.

> **GET ORIENTED TO CADES COVE...IN TOWNSEND!**
>
> If you're entering the park from the west and heading for Cades Cove, your easiest first stop isn't the Cades Cove Visitor Center. Instead, stop in Townsend, TN, at the **visitor center** on Lamar Alexander Parkway. It's one of three official information centers outside the park. You can get your parking tag, maps, hiking, activity guides – you name it! – and be out the door in a flash.
>
> Traffic patterns make Cades Cove Visitor Center functionally inaccessible, unless you're driving the entire 11-mile Cades Cove Loop – a journey that can be maddeningly slow during peak travel times, as bear sightings cause heavy traffic.

Everything Cherokee at the Heritage Center

CHEROKEE CULTURE AND APPALACHIAN LIFE

One of the great surprises of the **Great Smoky Mountains Heritage Center** is its coverage of Native American history and culture. In 1999, federally mandated studies prior to expanding Hwy 321 unearthed a 2000-year-old pottery vessel – and thus began the Townsend Archeology Project. The multi-year excavation found evidence of settlements spanning 5000 years. The thoughtful and engagingly designed exhibits at the center look at the foodways, pottery, basketry, hunting technology and housing of Native Americans

> **CHEROKEE ARTS, CULTURE & HISTORY**
>
> For a deeper dive into Cherokee arts, culture and history, don't miss the **Museum of the Cherokee Indian** (p151) and the **Qualla Arts & Crafts Mutual** (p152) in Cherokee, NC, a scenic drive over the mountains from Townsend.

WHERE TO SLEEP IN TOWNSEND

KOA Kampground & Kabins	**Strawberry Patch Inn**	**Dancing Bear Lodge**
The closest non-National Park Service campground to Cades Cove, offering both camping and cabins. $	Apartments with kitchens and a log cabin aesthetic, plus shared deck and garden spaces. $$	Townsend's cushiest sleeping option, with luxurious cabins and a high-end bistro on a forested hillside. $$$

BEST BOOKS & MAPS FOR GREAT SMOKIES HIKERS

The following resources, available at bookstores and centers throughout the region, are indispensable.

Hiking Trails of the Smokies, by the Great Smoky Mountains Association Colloquially known as the the 'Bible,' this chunky guidebook provides comprehensive route descriptions, details on flora, and local history.

Great Smoky Mountains National Park Map, by National Geographic & Trails Illustrated This 1:70,000 topographic map traces every hiking route in the park.

Great Smoky Mountains Hiking Map, by the National Park Service This map is a good general reference for the park's trails.

---

from roughly 10,000 BCE to 1600 CE. Coverage of the Cherokee language, cosmology, clan structure, music and games is especially fascinating. The Eastern Band of the Cherokee and the McClung Museum of Natural History at the University of Tennessee are partners in this endeavor.

The center's presentation of Appalachian life and culture is equally fascinating. Indeed, its interpretive displays and outdoor historic structures are far better contextualized and signposted than much of what you'll find in the park. Many of the historic structures are furnished – making it easier to later imagine the homes and lives behind the necessarily empty structures in the park. Don't miss the moonshine still and the wonderful video of distiller extraordinaire Charlie Williams, who says that all it takes to make moonshine is 'enough arm muscle and tail muscle to stir the mash,' plus 'enough time and nerve.' The center also has an heirloom garden and orchard, and an ongoing calendar of events that includes live music, storytelling and skills demonstrations.

Get Back to Nature at Tremont
NATURALIST-LED PROGRAMS FOR ALL AGES

Close to 100 years ago, Tremont was synonymous with hell-for-leather logging, but today, it's a great place to learn about and experience nature. The **Great Smoky Mountains Institute at Tremont** is a nonprofit environmental education center, located inside the park, about 10 miles northeast of Cades Cove Campground (p72). Tremont aims to connect people with nature in ways that promote curiosity, awe and wonder. In summer, it offers camps for kids and families, with themes ranging from backpacking to fly fishing to science. Adults can get in on the fun all year-round, with classes including naturalist studies and photography. Tremont announces its camps and classes for the upcoming year in early October – and many sell out quickly. For further info, sign up for their newsletter at gsmit.org.

Walk a Former Logging Railroad
LOGGING GHOSTS AND LOVELY WATERFALLS

Nowadays, the former logging boomtown of **Tremont** is one of the sleepier corners of the national park, tucked down a dead-end dirt road a few miles north of Cades Cove. It's a delightful place to explore, even if the visible remnants of the lumber boom are few and far between. For a great short hike, drive **Tremont Rd** to its terminus south of Townsend and park in the lot at the far end, where Tremont's hotel, post

---

AMENITIES FOR CADES COVE CAMPERS

KOA Townsend Gas & Convenience
The closest gas, ice and groceries stop from Cades Cove Campground; a lifesaver.

Townsend Laundromat
DIY or a wash, dry and fold service; conveniently next door to Artistic Bean and Ace Hardware.

Four Daughters Farm, Walland
Go to the farmstand Sundays 4pm to 6pm or order online and they'll deliver to your campsite Monday.

Little River Railroad and Lumber Company Museum

office and general store once stood, alongside the catch-all school, church and movie theater affectionately known as the 'house of education, salvation and damnation.'

Cross a beautiful wooden bridge over the Middle Prong of the Little River and turn left at a sign for **Middle Prong Trail**. You'll now be following an old logging railway bed gently upstream, with abrupt rock faces to your right testifying to the blasting necessary to create this passage nearly a century ago. Log benches invite a stop at 0.3 miles, where you pass a gorgeous chute of rushing water, and again at the three-tiered **Lynn Camp Prong Falls** (0.7 miles). Simply retrace your steps from here, or continue to yet another waterfall at **Indian Flats**, a few miles further upstream. For more historical details about this area of the park, look for the interpretive booklet *Tremont's Logging History* at park visitor centers, and visit Townsend's **Little River Railroad and Lumber Company Museum**.

LOGGING AT ELKMONT & TREMONT

Prior to 1900, most logging in southern Appalachia was small-scale, aimed at meeting local needs; but with the depletion of forests further north, big lumber set its sights on the Smokies. During the first four decades of the 20th century, the Little River Lumber Company founded and ran the company towns of Elkmont and Tremont, whose crews collectively harvested an estimated one billion board feet from one of North America's last great virgin deciduous forests.

After Elkmont's heyday fizzled in 1926, the action moved to Tremont until 1938, when the company's logging rights finally expired. Wonderful vintage photos of its logging days are on display at Townsend's Little River Railroad and Lumber Company Museum.

GETTING AROUND

Laurel Creek Rd is the only two-way driving route into Cades Cove, running 7.5 miles south from the junction of Lamar Alexander Hwy and Little River Gorge Rd in Townsend, TN, then merging into the Cades Cove Loop Rd near the entrance to Cades Cove Campground. The 11-mile Cades Cove Loop Rd is one-way only, and closed to motor vehicles on Wednesdays. Drivers can leave Cades Cove by returning north on Laurel Creek Rd, or via two unpaved roads: the twisting 12-mile Rich Mountain Rd to Townsend, TN, or the rugged 8-mile Parson Branch Rd toward Fontana Lake, NC. To reach Look Rock and Abrams Creek Campgrounds, drivers must head west through Townsend on the Lamar Alexander Parkway, then turn southwest on the Foothills Parkway to follow the park's western edge.

CATALOOCHEE & THE EASTERN PARK

For travelers seeking a peaceful refuge, the eastern outposts of Cataloochee, Big Creek and Cosby are little slices of heaven. A century ago, Cataloochee was among the most heavily settled places in the Smokies, but with the advent of the national park, the valley has reverted to a more natural state. Roads are still mostly hard-packed dirt or gravel; elk and bears wander peacefully among the ghostly remnants of early settlers' homesteads; and the campsites feel more intimate.

Beyond Cataloochee, near the park's northeastern corner, Big Creek and Cosby offer two less-visited ports of entry, both convenient jumping-off points for rafting on the Pigeon River and hiking the Appalachian Trail. Here, the park's outskirts are more sparsely populated, and visitors come primarily to settle into the slower rhythms of fishing, wildlife watching and hiking – to relax, breathe fresh air and fall asleep to the sounds of the river.

TOP TIP

This part of the park is harder to reach and much slower to navigate by vehicle. Access roads are narrow and winding – often unpaved – with plenty of potholes and precipitous dropoffs. Plan on traveling more slowly, and if camping, make sure you gather all necessary provisions outside the park and arrive before dusk.

Elk, Cataloochee Valley

Watch Wildlife in Cataloochee Valley

WALK AMONG WILD ELK

Thanks to its remote end-of-the-road location, the **Cataloochee Valley** is a prime spot for wildlife watching. Stretching out to the west of Cataloochee Ranger Station is a 2-mile-long series of open meadows frequented by elk, wild turkeys and occasional bears. For the best viewing, set off in the early morning or late afternoon when the animals are most active. Elk can often be seen grazing in the fields as you head west along the main road, but for an even more intimate experience, consider stopping and getting out of your car along the final mile-long stretch between

WHY I LOVE CATALOOCHEE VALLEY

Gregor Clark, writer

For me, Cataloochee Valley is a place of solace and a refuge from our increasingly wired and fast-paced world. The climb over Cataloochee Divide on a bumpy dirt road feels like a rite of passage. One minute you're dodging tractor-trailers on I-40, the next you're descending into the peaceable kingdom.

Mornings here are especially sweet: waking up early to the sounds of birdsong and the rushing creek, and heading off into Cataloochee's open meadows to watch elk grazing in the mist.

To fully experience the valley's tranquil magic, reserve a site at Cataloochee Campground and spend at least a couple of nights here; you won't regret it!

WHERE TO EAT NEAR CATALOOCHEE

Haywood 209 Cafe
Friendly, high-quality truck stop serving breakfast, lunch, dinner and homemade pies at Exit 24 off I-40. **$**

Birchwood Hall Southern Kitchen
Southern-influenced farm-to-table fare in a refined Main St setting in Waynesville, NC. **$$**

The Sweet Onion
A local favorite for onion soup, sandwiches, salads, pasta and steaks in Waynesville. **$$**

WALKING TOUR

The Historic Sites of Cataloochee Valley

The 1910 census showed that Cataloochee and Little Cataloochee had a combined population of 1251, making these twin valleys the largest settlement in the Great Smoky Mountains. Nowadays, Cataloochee is one of the sleepiest and most remote corners of the park. Still, a few traces of the old community remain, preserved for posterity by the National Park Service. On this tour, you'll get to visit several of them.

1 Palmer Chapel & Cemetery

Start your walk 1.5 miles west of Cataloochee Campground at this picturesque white chapel, set at the far side of a large open meadow. Built in 1898, it served as Cataloochee's Methodist church, holding sermons once a month when the circuit riding minister came to town. These days, it remains the site of an annual service for old Cataloochee families who come here to share a meal and maintain family graves.

The Walk: The main road turns to dirt near the chapel, making this a delightful place for slow-paced exploration on foot. Walk the 0.2 miles west to Beech Grove School.

2 Beech Grove School

Slumbering serenely by the roadside, this two-room schoolhouse, with desks and chalkboards still intact, was built in 1901. It's the only surviving school among the three that used to serve Cataloochee Valley. Classes were held here in the winter months only, and were discontinued with the establishment of the national park.

Beech Grove School

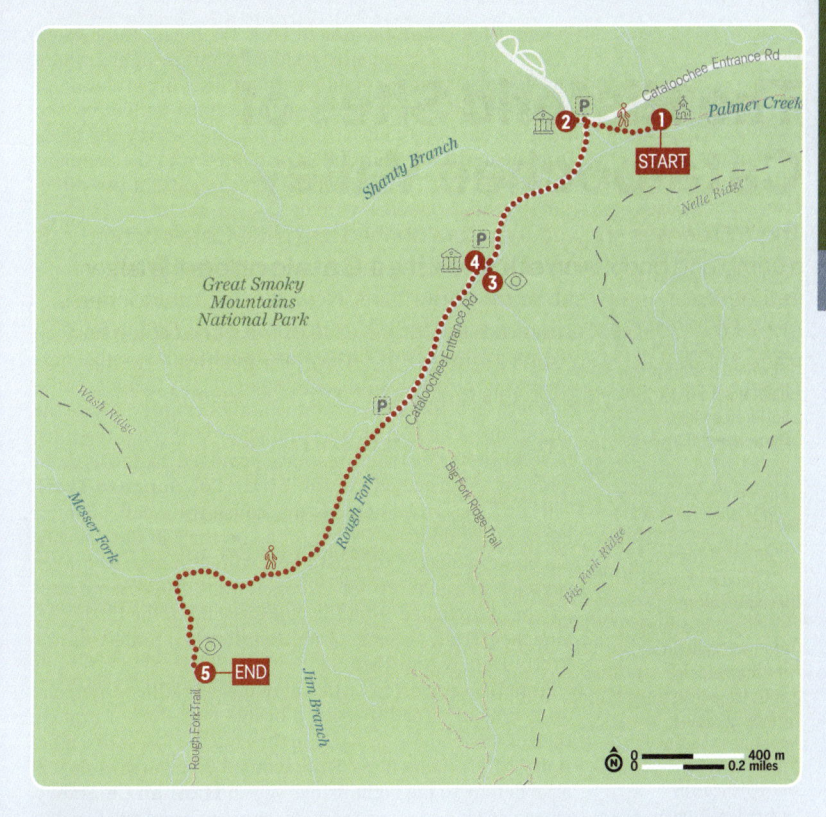

The Walk: Walk half a mile down the road and cross a small bridge over the Rough Fork of Cataloochee Creek on your left to reach Caldwell House.

3 Caldwell House

This striking two-story home with its robin's-egg-blue trim and steeply pitched tin-shingled roof was built around 1903. Compared to the older log homes preserved elsewhere in the park, it feels downright elegant, with nine rooms, a wraparound porch, wide hallways and interior wood paneling throughout. Don't miss the ads for chinchilla coats, lambskin pull-on gloves and other vintage finery, still legible in the old newspapers used to insulate the upstairs bedrooms.

The Walk: Walk back across the bridge and cross the main road to reach the Caldwell Barn.

4 Caldwell Barn

Climb to the hayloft of this massive barn for a lovely view of the meadows on either side. It's a pleasant spot to watch for wildlife, serenaded by the rushing waters of Cataloochee Creek. Downstairs are animal stalls and a large open space for wagons and other farm equipment.

The Walk: Walk 0.4 miles down the road till it dead-ends into a parking lot, then proceed 1 mile further down the signposted Rough Fork Trail to Woody Place.

5 Woody Place

This white clapboard house with its wide front porch began as a one-room log cabin. Owner Steve Woody built several additions between 1901 and 1910, enlarging the place to its current proportions. The Woody family earned extra income by renting rooms to early-20th-century tourists who came to Cataloochee to fish for rainbow trout.

The Walk: Retrace your steps down the Rough Fork Trail and the main road to Palmer Chapel. (The total distance is about 2 miles.)

A MOUNTAIN VOICE

In the 1930s, when Great Smoky Mountains National Park was created, most Cataloochee Valley residents were forced to leave their homes behind, an echo of the more profound displacement suffered by the Cherokee a century earlier, when thousands were exiled from their ancestral lands at gunpoint on the Trail of Tears.

A handwritten letter to future visitors, dated April 2015 and kept on the mantelpiece at Cataloochee's Caldwell House, captures some of the wistful feelings experienced by 79-year-old Irene Caldwell Sutton, who grew up here and was among the last to leave Cataloochee Valley in 1968: 'My family hated to leave this place. And the ones of us left still miss and love it.'

Palmer Chapel and the Rough Fork Trailhead. Here, you'll find a couple of excellently secluded vantage points where you can observe the animals without drawing attention to yourself. Park your vehicle in the small dirt pullout next to the sign for Doc Caldwell Cemetery, and survey the fields from behind a screen of trees, or climb up to the 2nd floor of the old Caldwell Barn, where you can gaze in two directions through big open windows.

Walk the Little Cataloochee Trail

STEP BACK IN TIME

If Cataloochee Valley feels like the back end of beyond, then the parallel valley of **Little Cataloochee**, accessible only by foot or horseback, takes things a notch further. Walking here feels like stepping into another century, where the phantoms of an earlier time and place still roam the hills. Several historic structures have survived in Little Cataloochee, all accessed via the **Little Cataloochee Trail**. The walk described here begins from a trailhead 5.6 miles north of Cataloochee Campground on the Old Cataloochee Turnpike, a rugged dirt road best suited to high clearance vehicles. If you're up for a longer walk, these same sites can be approached from the opposite end of the Little Cataloochee Trail, accessed from Cataloochee Valley via the Pretty Hollow Gap Trail.

From the signposted Little Cataloochee trailhead, descend on a wide dirt road to cross a bridge over Correll Branch, then climb moderately back up through the forest to a junction with the Long Bunk Trail at mile 1.0. A worthwhile 0.2-mile detour to the right brings you to **Hannah Cemetery**, where dozens of grave markers commemorate the families who once lived here. Return to the trail and turn right, reaching another turnoff for the **John Jackson Hannah Cabin** after just 0.1 mile. This rustic dwelling of hand-hewn logs with its brick fireplace dates to 1864. Back on the main trail, descend to cross Little Cataloochee Creek, then climb more steeply to reach the **Little Cataloochee Baptist Church**, serenely sited on a hilltop at the 2-mile mark. You can retrace your steps from here, or continue another 0.7 miles to the **Dan Cook Place**, a nicely restored 19th-century log cabin adjacent to the ruins of an old stone apple house from Little Cataloochee's agricultural heyday.

WHERE TO EAT NEAR COSBY & BIG CREEK

The Bean Sprout
Start your day with good coffee and great bagels near Exit 447 off I-40. $

Doc's 321 Cafe
Lovable hippie diner in a converted school bus, serving homemade BBQ, lemonade and pies. $$

Beantrees Cafe
Perfect place for a bite after rafting the Pigeon River, with a riverside deck and live music. $$

Raft the Pigeon River

RIDE THE SMOKIES' RAPIDS

For most travelers, the teeny town of **Hartford** (population 1000) is just a convenient refueling outpost off I-40, but thanks to its proximity to the **Pigeon River**, it's also the center of a vibrant rafting community. A dozen different rafting companies operate along the riverbank off Exit 447, most offering a choice between an easy Class I and II downstream float on the Lower Pigeon, or a more invigorating rapids-running adventure on the Upper Pigeon. If you opt for the latter, expect to get soaked as you navigate some of the Upper Pigeon's most exhilarating rapids, including the Class III Rollercoaster, Rooster Tail and Microwave, or the most ominous-sounding Class IV Lost Guide and Accelerator. Whatever your style, you can expect a half-hour safety and orientation session, followed by 1½ hours on the river. Well-established companies operating here include Nantahala Outdoor Center (p153), **Smoky Mountain Outdoors** and **Rip Roaring Adventures**. Excursions take place from May through Labor Day, with schedules dependent on water releases from the dam upstream.

Crowd-Free Camping in the Eastern Park

THE SMOKIES' QUIETER SIDE

Travelers seeking tranquility will love the park's three easternmost campgrounds.

Big Creek Campground is a blissful spot, featuring 12 walk-in, tent-only sites and a day-use picnic area clustered within earshot of Big Creek's rushing waters. Sites 10, 11 and 12 enjoy especially privileged positions directly overlooking the creek. Three different trailheads lead to adventure, including a favorite swimming hole and waterfall within 2 miles of the campground.

Idyllically tucked into a deep valley on the banks of Cataloochee Creek, **Cataloochee Campground** is the park's most remote frontcountry campground, accessed by a rugged gravel road with potholes, ruts, exposed rocks and steep drop-offs. Those who make the effort to get here are rewarded with prime wildlife-watching in the meadows just down the road, along with abundant hiking trails and easy access to the historic structures of Cataloochee (p78) and Little Cataloochee valleys. Six of the 27 campsites here (Numbers 3, 5, 7, 8, 9 and 10) directly adjoin Cataloochee Creek.

CHEROKEE NATIONAL FOREST: OUTDOOR ADVENTURES

Hugging the northeastern and southwestern edges of the national park, the 650,000-acre **Cherokee National Forest** offers campgrounds and a multitude of outdoor activities. The forest is split into two non-contiguous sections, both in Tennessee. For white-water rafting, head for the Pigeon (p81), French Broad and Nolichucky Rivers in the north; or the Ocoee and Hiwasee rivers in the south. Note that the Ocoee Whitewater Center was destroyed by fire in April 2022. At time of research, the Forest Service was assessing future plans for the site.

For a walk on the wild side, try backpacking in one of the forest's federally designated wilderness areas, such as Sampson Mountain to the northeast or Citico Creek to the southwest.

CAMPERS' RESOURCES NEAR THE EASTERN PARK

Ingles Supermarket	Exit 20 Service Stations, Waynesville, NC	Exit 447 Service Stations, Hartford, TN
Gather food and supplies for your Cataloochee campout at this huge supermarket in north Waynesville.	Gas, ice and firewood at the BP and Exxon stations off I-40, 30 minutes from Cataloochee.	Gas, ice, firewood and groceries at Citgo and BP, off I-40, 15 minutes from Big Creek.

> **BEARS & ELK – OH MY!**
>
> Beyond Cataloochee, the park boasts several fine wildlife-viewing spots. Elk roam the fields and roadsides around **Oconaluftee Visitor Center** (p63), while bears are frequently sighted in **Cades Cove** (p68); watch for cubs standing on their hind legs as they explore with mom!

Black bear, Cataloochee

REINTRODUCTION OF THE ELK

On February 25, 2001, 13 male and 12 female elk were brought to Cataloochee Valley from Land Between the Lakes in Kentucky. On April 2, they were released: elk had returned to the Smokies.

Before European settlement, an estimated 10 million elk ranged across America, including southern Appalachia. By the mid-1800s, the region's elk were gone – extirpated by habitat loss and overhunting. Reputedly, the last elk in eastern Tennessee was shot in 1849.

Today, the herd's population has risen to 200, and elk now range throughout the park; look for them in the Cataloochee and Oconaluftee valleys.

The largest campground in the eastern park, **Cosby Campground** lacks the wow factor of Big Creek and Cataloochee but still feels off the beaten track. Campsites snake up a north-facing mountainside. Forty of Cosby's 157 sites are generator-free, 45 are walk-in, and three are ADA-accessible. Hikers will appreciate Cosby's wealth of trails that depart directly from the campground, including three that interconnect with the Appalachian Trail.

Campers at all three campgrounds, Cataloochee especially, should plan ahead and bring all necessary food and supplies, as services on this side of the park are limited.

Hike the Big Creek Trail

BIG BOULDERS AND RUSHING WATERS

One of the park's most versatile hikes is this easy out-and-back ramble along the **Big Creek Trail** from Big Creek Campground. For most of its 5.8-mile length, the trail climbs only gradually, hugging the banks of beautiful Big Creek on an old logging road. An appealing option for families with children is to hike the first 1.5 miles and then spend the afternoon at **Midnight Hole**, where Big Creek's waters cascade over massive boulders into a deep green pool. More

---

HIKES FROM YOUR CAMPGROUND

Boogerman Trail from Cataloochee Campground
Old-growth trees, stone walls and several stream crossings are highlights of this 7.5-mile loop.

Big Creek Trail from Big Creek Campground
Creekside classic featuring mossy boulders, cascades and a blue-green swimming hole.

Low Gap Trail from Cosby Campground
After a climb to the Appalachian Trail, head north for views from Mt Cammerer's fire tower.

energetic hikers can forge on past **Mouse Creek Falls** at 2 miles and continue further upstream to reach a pair of backcountry campsites. Site 37, open to hikers only, is tucked a few hundred feet back from the creek at the 5.2-mile mark, while campsite 36 sits directly adjacent to the creek at the 5.7-mile mark, with a nifty set of 20 horse stalls to accommodate equestrians' mounts. With the necessary wilderness permit, you could spend a single night at either campsite and retrace your steps to Big Creek Campground the next day. Alternatively, it's possible to make a much larger backcountry loop back to Big Creek via Mt Cammerer on the Low Gap and Appalachian Trails, or Mt Sterling via the Swallow Fork and Sterling Ridge Trails.

Lunch at Doc's 321 Cafe

COSBY'S QUIRKIEST ROADSIDE EATERY

Every great road-trip deserves a colorful roadside diner, and **Doc's** delivers! At first glance, you might mistake the place for a junkyard, with its parking lot crammed full of mannequins, old cars and cast-off road signs, but sharpen your focus and you'll realize you're in the hands of a creative genius. Take time to admire the purple-and-yellow camper van topped with its adorable pig statue, then run the gauntlet of flamingo lawn ornaments to reach a vintage school bus wedged into the back of the lot and topped with a bright orange 'Doc's 321 Cafe' sign.

Inside this quirkiest of diners, a warm welcome awaits. Sidle up to a Dalmatian-spotted formica table, lean back in your Naugahyde-lined bus-seat booth and peruse a tie-dyed menu whose star attractions include award-winning smoked pork BBQ, homemade lemonade and sandwiches named after '60s celebrities. Bumper stickers plastered on the walls and graffiti from past admirers scrawled on the ceiling give you plenty of reading material while you wait for your order. If you've still got room, dare to try one of Doc's legendary (and weird as they sound) smoked pies for dessert.

To get here, head north 2 miles from Cosby Campground, then left on TN-32 and left again on US-321 toward Gatlinburg.

THE SMOKIES BY LAND & WATER

Andy Gallatin is a Master Guide for the Nantahala Outdoor Center (p153) and an Appalachian Trail thru-hiker.
@river_weasel

Hiking

Appalachian Trail
Anything on this!

Clingmans Dome (p89) Standing on the highest peak of the entire park gives you a top-of-the-world feeling

Mt Cammerer The beauty of this tower that was sourced from the mountain below your feet nearly a century ago takes you back in time.

Max Patch Bald The prettiest bald on the entire trail. The 360-degree views will take your breath away.

Rafting

The Upper Pigeon River. It's friendly for first timers and splashy for experienced thrill-seekers. The first Class III rapid, Powerhouse, will have you hooked.

GETTING AROUND

I-40 offers the most convenient access to the eastern park's three main points of entry: Cataloochee, Cosby and Big Creek. Take Exit 20 for Cataloochee, then drive 11 winding miles (30 minutes) to the campground via Cove Creek Rd and the Cataloochee Entrance Rd. For Big Creek, take Exit 451. For Cosby, take Exit 435 if coming from Knoxville, or Exit 447 if coming from Asheville. It's possible to drive from Cataloochee to Big Creek and Cosby via backroads such as the unpaved NC Hwy 1397, but you'll need a high-clearance vehicle, and I-40 will almost always be faster.

HIGH COUNTRY

Great Smoky Mountains: the name conjures up grand visions of mountain waves ensconced in mist – and that's exactly what you'll find in the national park's spectacular High Country. Unlike many other American national parks, the Smokies' highest elevations are easily accessible by motor vehicle, so even a day-tripper can enjoy the stunning scenery. However, it really pays to linger awhile up top, whether that means spending a night at a backcountry shelter, the mile-high Balsam Mountain Campground or even the legendary LeConte Lodge. If you're able-bodied enough to hit the trail, don't pass up the opportunity to explore beyond the paved pullouts and sidewalks of Newfound Gap and Clingmans Dome. The park's network of High Country trails is breathtaking, and even a relatively short day-hike at these higher elevations is likely to stick with you as one of the fondest memories of your Smoky Mountains visit.

TOP TIP

Newfound Gap Rd and Clingmans Dome Rd are deservedly famous for their high-altitude scenery, but if you're looking for a more off-the-beaten-track experience, try exploring Balsam Mountain Rd, another high country route off the Blue Ridge Parkway that climbs more than a mile above sea level, offering similarly dramatic vistas without the crowds.

Charlies Bunion

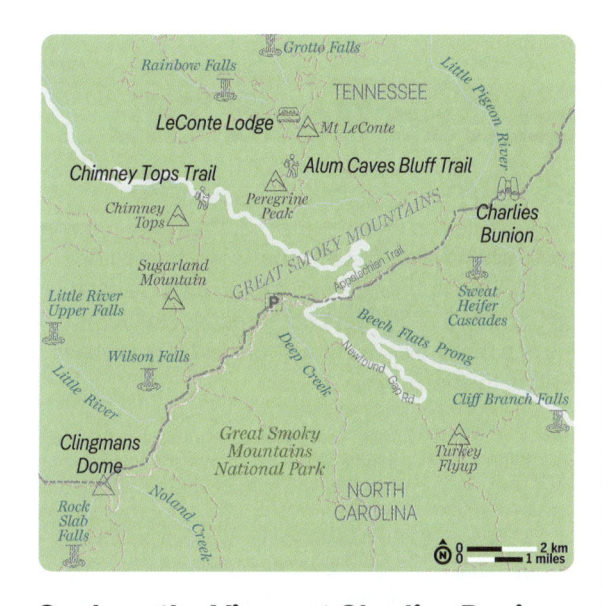

Soak up the Views at Charlies Bunion

A TASTE OF THE APPALACHIAN TRAIL

For a taste of America's oldest long-distance trail, nothing beats the iconic hike to **Charlies Bunion**. From Newfound Gap, this 8-mile out-and-back jaunt follows the Appalachian Trail along the North Carolina–Tennessee border to one of the national park's most jaw-dropping viewpoints,

A sign at the west end of the Newfound Gap parking lot beckons you onto one of the oldest sections of the Appalachian Trail, nonchalantly noting that Mt Katahdin, MA, is only 1972.0 miles away. After an abrupt 1-mile climb through rocky and root-riddled terrain, the trail emerges on a ridge line, yielding occasional glimpses of Mt LeConte through the trees to the west. The terrain rises and falls gently past junctions with the Sweat Heifer Trail and Boulevard Trail (2.7 miles). A long, steady descent ensues, passing the popular **Icewater Spring shelter** (3.0 miles) and continuing through a forest of diseased Fraser firs. Bottoming out near the 3.7-mile mark, the trail pushes briefly upward to a signposted left turn for Charlies Bunion. This bare rock outcrop commands extraordinary views of the ridges and valleys to the northwest, and is one of the Smokies' most photogenic spots. Here you'll surely encounter Appalachian Trail thru-hikers making their way from Georgia to Maine, an opportunity to swap hiking tales while admiring the view.

FALL FOLIAGE IN THE SMOKIES

Fall in Great Smoky Mountains National Park is an exuberantly colorful season, thanks to the biodiversity of its deciduous forests. As temperatures cool, the park's wide-ranging mix of maples, oaks, beeches, birches, hickories and other trees burst into vibrant shades of orange, yellow and red, contrasting pleasantly with the green meadows of Cades Cove and Cataloochee and the darker hues of the evergreens.

The parade of colors lasts from late September to early November, moving gradually down the mountainsides into the valleys. One of the best places to appreciate this annual transition is at the overlooks along Newfound Gap Rd.

BEST SCENIC OVERLOOKS FOR DRIVERS

Newfound Gap
Mountain ridges stretch out forever at this dreamy, easy-to-reach viewpoint on the North Carolina–Tennessee border.

Clingmans Dome
On a clear day, the 360-degree panoramas from the national park's highest viewpoint (6643ft) are unparalleled.

Balsam Mountain Picnic Area
From the parking lot, walk a few hundred paces down Flat Creek Trail for jaw-dropping vistas.

DRIVING TOUR

Newfound Gap Road Trip

There's no better vantage point for appreciating the Smokies' spectacular scenery than Newfound Gap Rd, the main highway running northwest–southeast through the High Country, between the visitor centers of Sugarlands and Oconaluftee. Climbing to an altitude of 5046ft, the road passes through a wide variety of forest ecosystems and boasts a long series of scenic pullouts that afford bird's-eye views of the Smokies stretching to the horizon.

1 Sugarlands Visitor Center
Start at the Sugarlands Visitor Center, the gateway to the northern park.

The Drive: At the T-intersection just east of Sugarlands, turn right on Newfound Gap Rd (Hwy 441) toward Cherokee and drive 3.2 miles to the Huskey Gap trailhead.

2 Huskey Gap Quiet Walkway
Here you'll find one of the park's best maintained Quiet Walkways (short trails designed to get visitors out of their cars and into nature). Follow the broad signposted path into the forest from the right-hand side of the parking area. A few minutes along, look for an unmarked right-hand turnoff to an old cemetery encircled by stone walls. Continue descending to discover a lovely spot by the Little Pigeon River, where you can sit on boulders and enjoy the rushing water.

The Drive: Turn left out of the parking lot and drive 0.8 miles southeast to the Carlos Campbell Overlook.

3 Carlos Campbell Overlook
This overlook on the left side of the highway commands fine views of Mt LeConte, the park's third-highest summit, rising dramatically from Gatlinburg

Carlos Campbell Overlook

The Drive: Continue 10 miles to the Morton Overlook, passing turnoffs for the Chimneys Picnic Area (p55) and the Chimney Tops Trail (p88), then circling through the Loop, a whimsical bit of highway engineering designed to navigate a steep section of the climb.

4 Morton Overlook

You're really in the High Country now! The view here encompasses the entire valley to the west, with Chimney Tops and the road you just drove up visible far below, and the attractive patchwork of evergreen and deciduous vegetation checkerboarding the higher slopes.

The Drive: Climb a further 0.7 miles to the summit of Newfound Gap Rd.

5 Newfound Gap Overlook

Panoramic views unfurl from the highway's highest (5046ft) and most dramatic viewpoint, where waves of mountains stretch clear to the eastern horizon. The giant parking lot here straddles the Tennessee–North Carolina border, with the Appalachian Trail signposted at the far end.

The Drive: Cross into North Carolina and continue 2.2 miles to the next overlook.

6 Deep Creek Valley Overlook

This unmarked overlook on the right-hand side commands spellbinding views south toward Bryson City and the Deep Creek Valley. If you want to ditch your car here and walk down to the Deep Creek Campground (p65), it's only 14.2 miles via the Deep Creek Trail!

The Drive: Continuing 14 miles east, enjoy a long and winding descent into the Oconaluftee River Valley.

7 Oconaluftee Visitor Center

You've made it to the park's southern entrance! Check out the visitor center and the adjacent Mountain Farm Museum (p63).

HIKING THE CHIMNEY TOPS TRAIL

The **Chimney Tops**, two dramatic rock outcrops jutting above Newfound Gap Rd, have long been a hikers' magnet. Nowadays, their fiery name seems even more fitting, after the 2016 Gatlinburg fire reduced the surrounding landscape to a wasteland of burnt-out tree trunks.

From the trailhead 10 miles south of Gatlinburg, descend to cross Walker Camp Prong, then begin an unrelenting 1.75-mile climb. Halfway up, after crossing your fourth bridge, turn right at a junction with the Road Prong Trail and climb a steep series of log and stone staircases. Near the summit, the trail veers right, climbing more moderately to a viewpoint with in-your-face views of the fire-scarred Chimney Tops. A gate here blocks access to the unstable, dangerous terrain beyond.

Alum Cave

Hike the Alum Cave Trail

EVERYONE'S FAVORITE GREAT SMOKIES HIKE

The **Alum Cave Trail** is one of the Smokies' most popular, thanks to its scenic beauty and variety. Because it's an out-and-back trail, you can choose to turn around wherever you like. A few steps off the busy main road, you'll find yourself immersed in a gorgeous green forest where canopies of rhododendrons overhang the rushing waters of Walker Camp Prong. The trail's wide and flat first mile offers a delightful stroll with minimal exertion. At 1.4 miles, the trail crosses a log bridge and spirals up through **Arch Rock**, a photogenic cleft navigated by graceful stone steps. From here, a more pronounced climb, punctuated by breathtaking views of the valley below, leads to **Alum Cave** (2.3 miles), a dramatic overhang of sandy-hued stone that contrasts fetchingly with the surrounding forest and serves as a convenient umbrella during rainstorms.

Most people retrace their steps from here, but you can continue 2.7 miles further on the steep trail toward the summit. The views just keep getting better, while strategically placed cables serve as handholds for navigating slippery stretches of rock underfoot. At trail's end (5.0 miles), turn right on Rainbow Falls Trail to reach LeConte Lodge, **Mt LeConte** summit and a pair of classic viewpoints: Cliff Tops and Myrtle Point. Arrive early (before 8am) for the best shot at a parking spot, or reserve a shuttle (p59) in Gatlinburg.

BEST VIEWPOINTS FOR HIKERS

Charlies Bunion
The quintessential Great Smokies photo op, this rocky promontory on the Appalachian Trail offers astounding views.

Myrtle Point
At 6500ft, this is the classic vantage point for sunrise after an overnight on Mt LeConte.

Gregory Bald
Feast your eyes on flame azaleas and expansive panoramas at this iconic high-mountain meadow.

Overnight at LeConte Lodge

SLEEP AT THE SUMMIT

Spending the night in the legendary **LeConte Lodge** is one of the Smokies' most memorable experiences. The 10 rustic cabins clustered at 6400ft above sea level offer the national park's only indoor accommodations. While amenities are simple – bunk beds, kerosene lamps, front porch rockers, a wash basin and a shared outhouse – the effort required to snag a spot here makes the memory even sweeter for those who succeed. Reservations are accepted, beginning October 1 each year, and rooms fill up almost instantly. The lodge is accessible only by foot, via the Alum Cave, Rainbow Falls (p56), Trillium Gap or Boulevard Trail. Rates include breakfast and dinner, served in the lodge's dining room overlooking the Smokies, with supplies brought in thrice weekly by llamas.

Short trails from the lodge lead to two of the park's most stunning viewpoints: **Cliff Tops** (0.3 miles) and **Myrtle Point** (0.7 miles). If you come up short-handed during the brief October booking window, it's worth trying again in early November, as reservations not paid for within the first 30 days are automatically cancelled and made available again to the general public. Last-minute cancellations are also occasionally announced on the lodge's Twitter feed.

Greet the Dawn at Clingmans Dome

ENJOY SENSATIONAL MOUNTAINTOP VISTAS

At 6643ft, **Clingmans Dome** is the highest point in Great Smoky Mountains National Park. In 1959, the National Park Service added a space-age **viewing platform** near the summit, which elevates visitors another 45ft, affording 360-degree views of the Smokies' grandeur. For an unforgettable experience, come here early in the morning on a clear day to see the sun cresting the Smokies' eastern slopes, with mists hanging in the valleys below. Plaques placed at the four corners of the viewing platform identify distant peaks, from Mt Mitchell (6684ft) in the east to Thunderhead Mountain (5527ft) in the west. Clingmans Dome is reached from Newfound Gap (p86) via a 7-mile spur road. Upon arrival at the Clingmans Dome parking lot, look for the paved trail at the far end; it's a stiff half-mile climb from here to the viewing platform.

BACKCOUNTRY SHELTERS

Hikers in the Great Smoky Mountains can stay overnight in dozens of backcountry campgrounds and 15 backcountry shelters, including 12 on the Appalachian Trail. Accommodations at the shelters are very basic, with wooden bunks and an occasional privy – but they're sturdily built, offering protection from the elements and a chance to commune with other hikers.

All shelters and backcountry campsites need to be reserved ahead at smokiespermits.nps.gov. Simply choose your shelter or campsite on the map, pay your fee online and obtain a backcountry permit instantly. If you're already in the park and prefer to reserve in person, you can visit the national park's backcountry office at Sugarlands Visitor Center (p58).

GETTING AROUND

The easiest driving access to Great Smoky Mountains National Park's High Country is via two heavily traveled paved roads: Newfound Gap Rd (US Highway 441), which runs 33 miles from Gatlinburg, TN, to Cherokee, NC; and Clingmans Dome Rd, which climbs 7 miles from Newfound Gap to Clingmans Dome. Both highways get crowded during peak travel times, and parking can be difficult at popular trailheads unless you arrive very early; taking a shuttle (p59) is a worthwhile alternative.

EAST TENNESSEE GATEWAYS

SPRINGBOARDS TO SMOKY ADVENTURES

Embrace the small-city pleasures of artsy, outdoorsy Knoxville, or dive into theme-and-adventure-park fun in Gatlinburg and Pigeon Forge.

Eastern Tennessee is defined by its mountains. Its music, food, culture and history are all deeply shaped by the southern Appalachians and the demands of hill-farm living. Its very history sets it apart from the rest of the state. Indeed, in the 1780s it broke off to form the short-lived state of Franklin. For the traveler coming to Great Smoky Mountains National Park, the most important aspect of the Tennessee towns near its borders is the flavor of experience each might add to the trip.

Most convenient for those arriving by plane is Knoxville, which combines the friendliness of a small town with the cultural sophistication of a larger city. From here, you can reach the Cades Cove, Sugarlands, Cosby or Big Creek entrances to the park in about an hour.

Gatlinburg and Pigeon Forge offer a completely different take on the Smokies. Gatlinburg literally borders the park, yet many visitors dip in for a quick peek only, devoting most of their time to Gatlinburg's adventure parks, Ripley's attractions and moonshine distilleries. Pigeon Forge is synonymous with Dollywood, one of the world's most captivating theme parks. It makes a convenient base if Dollywood is the main focus of your trip.

THE MAIN AREAS

KNOXVILLE
A small, artsy and outdoorsy city. **p94**

GATLINBURG & PIGEON FORGE
A true theme-park destination. **p101**

Above: Tennessee Theatre (p97), Knoxville. Left: Ole Smoky Moonshine (p108), Gatlinburg

Find Your Way

Home to eastern Tennessee's largest airport and only 35 miles from the national park, engaging, easygoing Knoxville makes the ideal Great Smokies gateway. An hour east, tourist-driven Gatlinburg and Pigeon Forge sit even closer to the park.

CAR
US 441 connects Knoxville with Pigeon Forge and Gatlinburg. US 129 heads south from Knoxville to McGhee Tyson Airport in Alcoa, the region's car rental hub; from here, US 321 heads east toward Townsend and Cades Cove Visitor Centers.

BUS
Gatlinburg and Pigeon Forge have free or low cost trolley services serving popular destinations such as Dollywood. Knoxville Area Transit (KAT) buses reach some Knoxville attractions, but there's no public transit between the airport and downtown.

Knoxville, p94
Friendly, cosmopolitan, artsy and outdoorsy, eastern Tennessee's largest city makes an appealing and convenient jumping-off point for exploring the Great Smokies.

Gatlinburg & Pigeon Forge, p101
Anchored by delightful Dollywood, these tourist meccas on the national park's edge are all about theme-park thrills and decadent family fun.

Market Square (p95), Knoxville

Plan Your Time

Day and night, there's always something going on in tourist-friendly Knoxville, Gatlinburg and Pigeon Forge. In summer, theme parks such as Dollywood and Anakeesta keep longer hours.

If You Only Do One Thing

If your time is limited, make the most of it with a day trip to **Dollywood** (p102), where you'll find everything from traditional Appalachian music, food and crafts to raptor shows, kiddie rides and adrenaline-pumping roller coasters. Alternatively, if theme parks aren't your thing, explore Knoxville's delightful downtown on foot, starting at **Market Square** (p95), or stroll the **Tennessee River Boardwalk** (p99) south of town.

More Time to Explore

Extend your time in Knoxville, visiting some of its excellent **museums** (p96), taking in a **show** (p97), exploring the **Urban Wilderness** (p98) and sipping drinks at the city's **breweries** (p96) and **rooftop bars** (p100). When it's time to move on, embrace the holiday mood on the **Gatlinburg Strip** (p106), escape into the national park via the **Gatlinburg Trail** (p109) or spend a day (or three) at fabulous **Dollywood** (p102).

Seasonal Highlights

SPRING
Performers from around the globe bring their talents to Knoxville during the annual **Big Ears Festival** (p95).

SUMMER
Hit Knoxville's Urban Wilderness for mountain biking, kayaking and swimming at Mead's Quarry.

FALL
Admire fiery fall foliage. Artists and craftspeople from across Appalachia display their wares at the **Gatlinburg Craftsmen's Fair**.

WINTER
Dollywood shimmers with colorful lights and festive family fun during the ever-popular **Smoky Mountain Christmas** (p103).

KNOXVILLE

Knoxville bills itself as a 'nature-loving adventure-seeking artsy kinda town' – and the description fits! Its 1300-acre-plus Urban Wilderness provides plenty of room to hike, run, mountain bike, climb, watch birds, swim and paddle. And that doesn't begin to count the roughly 86 regular city parks and the mighty Tennessee River that cuts through town on its looping journey toward the Mississippi.

Knoxville's vibrant arts scene boasts a symphony orchestra, two operas, numerous professional theaters, dance companies, choral societies, an art museum, lots of galleries and nonstop festivals throughout the year. Anchored around the beloved Market Square – a gathering place for the whole town – Knoxville's lively downtown is fun, varied and walkable. The third-largest city in the state and the largest in eastern Tennessee, Knoxville is home to the flagship University of Tennessee, with its 30,000-plus students and championship athletics. Visitors will notice that Knoxville is a friendly place – and locals love to share their love of it.

TOP TIP

Base yourself as close to Market Square as possible. Here in the walkable heart of the city, Knoxville's sights, shops, performances, galleries, street art, restaurants, cafes and bars are all right at your doorstep. Downtown parking garages are conveniently located and reasonably priced, making it easy to grab your vehicle when needed.

Dogwood Arts Festival

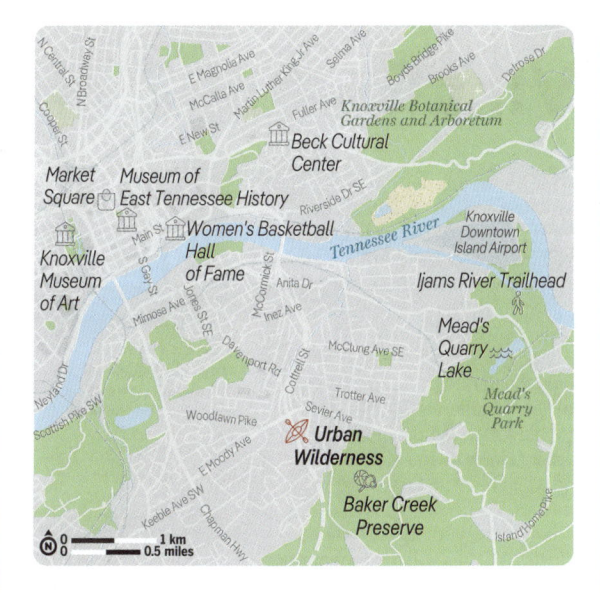

Explore Market Square

KNOXVILLE'S CONVIVIAL LIVING ROOM

The beating heart of downtown Knoxville is **Market Square**, a pedestrianized plaza lined with shops, bars and restaurants and shaded at one end by six magnificent sawtooth oaks. Stroll the square day or night and you'll find something going on. The **Market Square Farmer's Market** takes place from May to December and features only products grown or made within a few hours' radius of Knoxville; dozens of vendors sell their produce, including honey, jelly, crafts, cut flowers and more. Many of the square's restaurants have outside seating, and there's a pleasant bustle at all hours. In summertime, kids gravitate to the small-but-effective grouping of splash fountains, and folks bring picnic baskets and folding chairs for free evening concerts on the big open stage. Under the towering oaks, don't miss the **Tennessee Woman Suffrage Memorial**, which honors the three women who lead the suffrage movement. Tennessee was the 36th state to ratify the 19th amendment, making it the final vote needed to give women the right to vote.

Market Square began as a public produce market in 1854, and other businesses soon sprang up around it. Over the

BEST ARTS & CULTURAL FESTIVALS IN KNOXVILLE

Big Ears Festival
Acclaimed as 'one of the world's greatest music bashes,' this March festival draws locals and international visitors alike.

Chalk Walk
Locals love this April event where chalk artists create their works on the spot.

Dogwood Arts Festival
The World's Fair Park explodes with art, crafts, music and food in late April.

HoLa Festival
The dynamic HoLa Hora Latina puts on Tennessee's largest celebration of Hispanic/Latinx culture in September.

Knoxville Pride Festival
The South's largest free Pride festival celebrates equality, community and activism in October.

WHERE TO EAT IN KNOXVILLE

Oli Bea
An iconic breakfast spot beloved for its fluffy biscuits, farm-fresh ingredients and ample vegan offerings. **$**

Chivo Taquería
Tasty tacos, guac and margaritas are served under the chandeliers at this buzzy, high-ceilinged eatery. **$**

Jackie's Dream
Fried chicken, fried green tomatoes and friendly service stand out at Knoxville's favorite soul-food joint. **$**

FOR MORE ART...

For hands-on immersion in the arts, check out the multiday workshops offered by the **Arrowmont School of Arts and Crafts** (p108) in Gatlinburg. Also worth a visit is their Gatlinburg gallery, where shows by resident artists alternate with exhibitions of traditional crafts from Arrowmont's permanent collection.

Market house bell

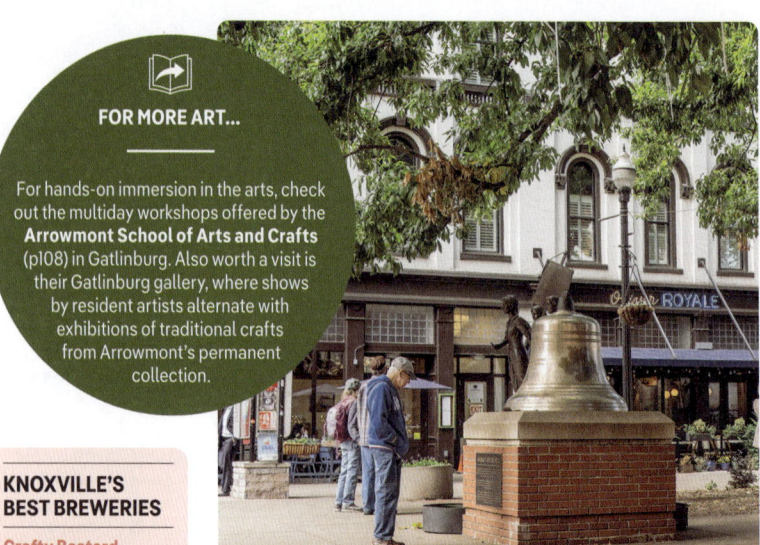

KNOXVILLE'S BEST BREWERIES

Crafty Bastard
A perennial North Knoxville favorite, thanks to its rotating beer selection, atmospheric warehouse interior, ample outdoor seating, live music and food trucks.

Pretentious Beer Co.
In Knoxville's Old City, this creative mix of brews is served in hand-blown glassware from the sister business next door.

Gypsy Circus Barrelhouse
Forty taps feature Gypsy Circus's exceptional barrel-aged, wild yeast ciders, alongside artisanal meads and craft beers from other local breweries.

years, the square has been home to newspaper offices, saddleries, a candy factory, sausage-makers, a sculptor's studio and more. The original Market House was replaced with a grander two-story structure in 1897. Then, as times changed in 1960, the whole thing was razed, and the square pedestrianized. Not until 2000 did the city restore something of the square's Victorian charm and bring back the farmers market. The original **market house bell** is displayed in the square.

Discover Eastern Tennessee History

VOICES OF THE LAND

The **Museum of East Tennessee History** is one of Knoxville's greatest treasures. Its outstanding 'Voices of the Land' exhibit traces the broad sweep of human history in the region, from First Nations to European settlement, and from the Civil War to the establishment of Great Smoky Mountains National Park. Beautifully designed displays and compelling objects greet you at every turn: a Cherokee ball stick (the forerunner of modern-day lacrosse), a map of Hernando de Soto's circuitous course through the Smokies from 1539 to 1540 and a panel documenting the State of Franklin, formed

WHERE TO DRINK IN KNOXVILLE

Balter Beerworks
Enjoy a flight and a bite on the spacious back patio at this downtown gas-station-turned-brewery.

Bernadette's Crystal Gardens
Choose from three different levels at this atmospheric bar with rooftop terrace and sparkling gemstone decor.

Peter Kern Library
Creative cocktails and intimate, low-lit atmosphere are the twin draws at this speakeasy near Market Square.

by eight self-governing East Tennessee counties that separated from North Carolina and petitioned for statehood in the 1780s. The museum is centrally located on Gay St, just steps from Market Square (p95).

On Show at the Beck Cultural Center

SHOWCASING KNOXVILLE'S BLACK COMMUNITY

East of downtown, the **Beck Cultural Center** celebrates the city's African American history and culture. Photos and documents showcase everything from the razing of Knoxville's Black neighborhoods in the name of urban renewal (aka 'urban removal') to the Civil Rights-era sit-ins, pickets and other peaceful civil disobedience that finally brought desegregation to Knoxville's downtown businesses in the 1960s. Photos and biographies of prominent Black Knoxvillians line the staircase to the 2nd floor, spanning over a century of local history. Upstairs, visitors can thumb through vintage copies of the *Green Book,* a travel guide used by Black motorists to safely navigate racism on road trips throughout the United States.

History & Heroes at the Women's Basketball Hall of Fame

CELEBRATE WOMEN ATHLETES

Knoxville is crazy for its sports teams, and you can't take two steps here without encountering the garish orange team colors of the University of Tennessee. Even non-sports fans will be moved by this museum's portrayal of the powerful, tough and confident individuals who have brought women's basketball to prominence over the past century.

Don't miss the 25-minute video in the first room, which traces a century of basketball history – from the early days when women took the court in full-length skirts and tight-fitting blouses, to the most recent national college tournaments. Footage and memorabilia spanning six decades convey the grace, exuberance, determination and joyful camaraderie of some of the most successful women's teams in history. Among the athletes featured here are the **All-American Red Heads**, who barnstormed across America, busy knocking off men's teams in the '30s, '40s and '50s (check out their limo-length station wagon!), and beloved University of Tennessee coach Pat Summitt, who led Knoxville's **Lady Volunteers** to a record-breaking eight national championships. If you're feeling inspired to shoot some hoops of your own, head for the basketball courts downstairs.

PERFORMING ARTS IN KNOXVILLE

Knoxville has a thriving performing-arts scene. The renovated **Tennessee Theatre** offers Broadway shows, national music acts, tours and movies – in a grand, historic setting. The **Knoxville Jazz Orchestra** and **Knoxville Symphony Orchestra** perform at the landmark **Bijou Theatre**, which brings in regional and national acts.

Several professional companies offer live theater. The **Tennessee Stage Company** specializes in Shakespeare and new work. At the University of Tennessee's **Clarence Brown Theatre**, professionals and students work side by side. The **River and Rail Theatre Company** stages contemporary plays, while **Carpetbag Theatre** creates new works and gives voice to historically silenced communities. For opera and choral music, seek out the **Knoxville Opera**, the **Marble City Opera**, the **Appalachian Equality Chorus** and the **Knoxville Choral Society**.

WHERE TO SLEEP IN KNOXVILLE

The Oliver Hotel
A stone's throw from Market Square, this boutique hotel has comfy, high-ceilinged rooms and impeccable service. **$$**

Hyatt Place Knoxville
A renovated historic hotel with rooftop bar and prime downtown location near the Tennessee Theatre. **$$**

The Tennesseean
This high-rise four-star is conveniently located between downtown and the University of Tennessee. **$$**

THE ARTS SCENE IN KNOXVILLE

Enrique Cruz is Executive Director of the nonprofit HoLa Hora Latina. *@HoLaHoraLatina*

Knoxville is a hidden gem for the arts. Everywhere you go, every coffee shop, every bar and museum is filled with local art and a celebration of what it means to be an artist.

On **First Fridays**, all of Knoxville becomes an art gallery. You get to walk around and interact with the artists. Every month you discover something new.

There's a great curiosity here about Hispanic culture. Something like Día de los Muertos sparks conversations about culture and passion. Our **HoLa Festival** (p95) is a celebration of Latinx artistry, with lots of dancing, music and food. Most recently, we had poets come on stage and recite their poems.

A Celebration of East Tennessee Artists

LOCAL ROOTS, INTERNATIONAL TIES

From the pink Tennessee marble on its facade to the stunning display of one of the world's largest installations of figural glass (Richard Jolley's *Cycle of Life*), the **Knoxville Museum of Art** is all about East Tennessee artists and the region's connections to national and international art movements. The permanent exhibit, 'Higher Ground,' focuses on regional art of the 19th and 20th centuries. The museum holds the world's largest collection of works by the brilliant but neglected African American painter Beauford Delaney, as well as works by his brother, Joseph, both Knoxvillians. Each year, the museum holds a juried exhibition of works by East Tennessee students from grades 6–12, while an ever-changing series of temporary exhibits shines a line on emerging and established regional artists. Also of interest are the museum's international collection of contemporary glass and the 'Thorne rooms,' a collection of miniature dioramas made in the 1930s.

Explore Knoxville's Urban Wilderness

GO WILD AT THE CITY'S EDGE

Knoxville's **Urban Wilderness** is a sprawling urban green space offering recreation, education and spiritual renewal to residents and visitors alike. Its 1381 acres comprise 10 distinct natural areas clustered near the Tennessee River's southern banks, all within Knoxville's city limits. The Urban Wilderness was launched in 2008 by the Knoxville-based Legacy Parks Foundation, which helps East Tennesseans access green space. Thanks to their efforts, the Wilderness just keeps growing: each area has its own identity and offerings, and many are interconnected by trails. The largest patch is the state wildlife agency's **Forks of the River Management Area**; then there's the **Ijams Nature Center** – a private, nonprofit environmental education center. The **River Bluff Wildlife Area** is a city park and former Civil War battle site, and more Civil War history is found around the well-preserved earthen fort at **Fort Dickerson Park**.

Mountain bikers can head for the pyrotechnic trails of Baker Creek Preserve (p100), while parts of the **Dogwood Community Trail** are designed for wheelchair accessibility.

There are quarries to paddle and swim in, trails for running and hiking, green spaces to play in, cliffs to climb, and plenty of places to just enjoy nature, bird-watch and take in the river views. With so many acres and so many options, the

WHERE TO GEAR UP FOR THE NATIONAL PARK

Outdoor Gear Revival
Excellent selection of name-brand, secondhand outdoor gear, from clothing to stoves, coolers, backpacks and tents.

Mast General Store
Find hiking guides, maps and outdoor apparel downstairs at this popular shop near Market Square.

Three Rivers Market
Hikers and campers can stock up on healthy provisions at Knoxville's venerable community food co-op.

Ijams River Trail

hardest part is deciding what to do! You can grab an Urban Wilderness map at the **Knoxville Visitor Center** on Gay Street, or check out the Urban Wilderness website – but the easiest place to start is at the Ijams Nature Center, where helpful staff can help match your interests with the Urban Wilderness's offerings.

Walk the Tennessee River Boardwalk

WHERE THE TENNESSEE BEGINS

Among the standout experiences in Knoxville's Urban Wilderness is the **Ijams River Trail**, starting just outside the Ijams Visitor Center. This easy 1-mile loop descends to the forested bottomlands along the Tennessee River. Near its midpoint, the trail ambles along a lovely wooden boardwalk bolted into the sandstone cliffs, bringing you face to face with the wide, languid river, whose placid waters exquisitely reflect the trees on the far bank.

Standing here, less than a mile downstream from the spot where the French Broad and Holston Rivers converge to create the Tennessee, it's hard to believe that downtown Knoxville is so close: all you see is river,

KNOXVILLE FOR KIDS

There's a world of activities for kids to explore in Knoxville. For outdoor fun, don't miss the sky-high splash fountains in **World's Fair Park** and the evening zip-line tours at **Navitat Knoxville**. If you're feeling artsy, catch a show at the **Knoxville Children's Theatre**, check out the miniature Thorne rooms at the **Knoxville Museum of Art**, explore outdoor sculptures in **Krutch Park** or scout out downtown Knoxville's many murals (hint: start at the Visitor Center).

When it's time for a treat, choose from 500 types of penny candy at **Mast General Store**, sidle up to the old-fashioned soda fountain at **Phoenix Pharmacy**, or cool off with ice cream at local dairy **Cruze Farm**.

MORE FUN FOR KIDS

Don't miss the amazing lineup of animal- and plant-themed rides at Dollywood's **Wildwood Grove** (p104). In Great Smoky Mountains National Park, kids will also love meeting horses and taking a wagon ride at **Smokemont Riding Stables** (p65).

WHERE TO TAKE THE KIDS IN KNOXVILLE

Muse
Kids will love the interactive science exhibits and planetarium at Knoxville's favorite children's museum.

Zoo Knoxville
Mingle with cute red pandas and African elephants, and hop aboard the Zoo Choo train.

Navitat Knoxville
Get the wiggles out with daytime and evening treetop zip-line adventures in Knoxville's Urban Wilderness.

trees and sky. Thus begins the river's loopy journey south to Chattanooga and Alabama, where it will eventually double back north through Tennessee and Kentucky.to finally feed into the Ohio, and thence the Mississippi.

Mountain Biking at Baker Creek Preserve

RIDES FOR EVERY STYLE

With 50-plus miles of trails just minutes from downtown, Knoxville is a paradise for mountain bikers. The center of the action is **Baker Creek Preserve**, 3 miles south of the city center. Here, you'll find experiences for all ages and abilities. Two state-of-the-art **bike parks**, complete with pump tracks and jump line, give young riders a place to hone their skills and show off their aerial wizardry. Directly adjacent are five multi-use trails, including the 1.2-mile **Sycamore Loop**, a mostly level circuit suitable for families with small kids. Hard-core riders will love Baker Creek's three dedicated downhill runs, epitomized by the notorious double black diamond **Devil's Racetrack**. If you're hungry for more, the Baker Creek trails connect to a vast network extending east through other sections of the Urban Wilderness to the Tennessee River.

Swim at Mead's Quarry Lake

ESCAPE KNOXVILLE'S SUMMER HEAT

On a sultry summer day, there's no better place to beat the heat than **Mead's Quarry Lake**. Ten minutes southeast of town, this lovely lake, backed by rosy stone cliffs, is the perfect place to swim or sunbathe on the long wooden dock. In the 19th century, Mead's Quarry supplied the prized pinkish-gray limestone known as 'Tennessee marble' to clients up and down the East Coast, including the National Gallery of Art in Washington, DC, and New York City's Grand Central Station. These days, the abandoned quarry is part of Knoxville's Ijams Nature Center (p98).

Other popular activities here include kayaking and paddleboarding (rentals available on site), or perambulating the quarry on the **Tharp Trace Loop Trail**. Big Fun Tuesdays and Bluegrass Sundays add an extra dose of magic with food trucks, beer and live music.

SUNSET DRINKS ON THE ROOFTOP

At day's end, Knoxvillians head for the rooftop bars above Market Square (p95) to watch evening settle over the city. Joining this nightly pilgrimage is one of Knoxville's quintessential pleasures.

Amid the cluster of popular bars at the square's northeast corner, **Bernadette's Crystal Gardens** stands out for its crystal-themed decor and fanciful roof terrace adorned with sculpted ceramic trees, paper flowers, tinsel garland flamingos and colorful lights. Downstairs, a labyrinth of staircases leads to Bernadette's two other venues, the **Knox County Quartz House** and the **Amethyst Lounge**. At the latter, you can sip gemstone-themed drinks in a crystal-walled booth while admiring the purple glow from a bar encrusted in amethysts.

GETTING AROUND

Walking is the best way to experience Knoxville's compact downtown, centered on Market Square and fanning out north along Gay and Central streets into the Old City neighborhood, with its cafes, restaurants, bars and galleries. Parking at places such as the State St and Market Square garages is free on nights and weekends, and surprisingly affordable on weekdays. For trips further afield, having your own wheels makes life easier, as KAT's limited routes don't serve key destinations such as the Ijams Nature Center, Mead's Quarry Lake, or the McGhee Tyson (TYS) Airport, 14 miles south in Alcoa.

GATLINBURG & PIGEON FORGE

Perched 2 miles north of Sugarlands Visitor Center, Gatlinburg is Great Smoky Mountains National Park's busiest gateway. This town of about 3600 residents hosts a good portion of the park's roughly 13 million annual visitors. Backed by the Smokies and hemmed in by hills and creeks, Gatlinburg's crowded main drag brims with so many shops, snacks, chairlifts and other distractions that you might never set actually foot in the park. It's a pedestrian and vehicular mob scene, but it's fun – in large part because of its walkability and the easy glimpses of nearby nature.

A few miles northwest, along a scenic parkway, is Pigeon Forge and its 5-mile, six-lane strip of chain motels, restaurants and arcade attractions. Pigeon Forge shines brightest as the home of the award-winning Dollywood theme park, while also offering less expensive accommodations and easier parking. Further north is Dolly Parton's hometown, the sedate county seat of Sevierville.

TOP TIP

Save money and avoid parking headaches by using the excellent trolley bus systems of Gatlinburg and Pigeon Forge. Park for free at the trolley stops near Gatlinburg Welcome Center and Patriot Park. From the latter, buy a low-cost day pass for the eight-minute ride to Dollywood.

HIGHLIGHTS
1 Dollywood

SIGHTS
2 Gatlinburg Strip
3 The Old Mill

ACTIVITIES, COURSES & TOURS
4 Anakeesta
5 Arrowmont School of Arts & Crafts
6 Gatlinburg SkyPark
7 Ober Gatlinburg

EATING
8 Crockett's
9 The Appalachian

DRINKING & NIGHTLIFE
10 Ole Smoky Moonshine
11 Sugarlands Distilling Co

Scan this QR code for prices and opening hours.

TOP SIGHT

Dollywood

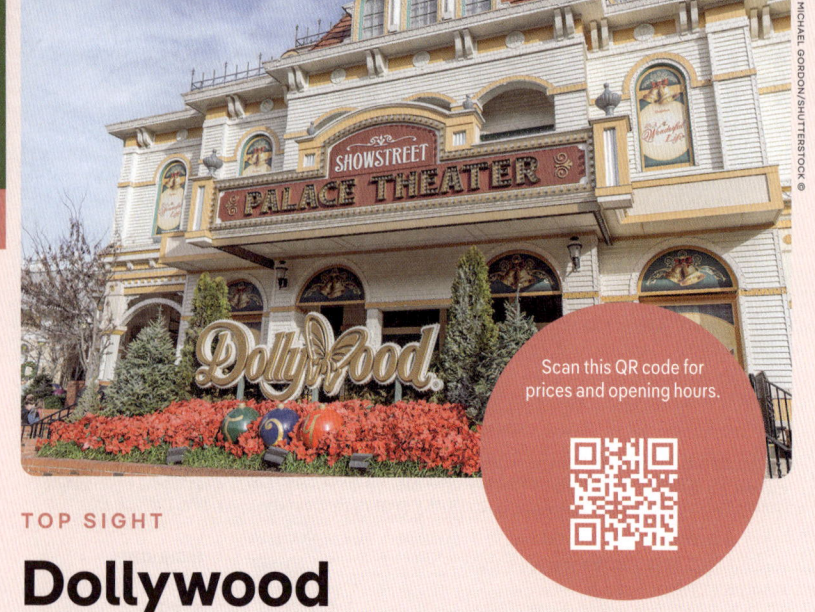

Aficionados now rate award-winning Dollywood among the world's top 10 amusement parks. With its colorful Appalachian-themed rides, fanciful neighborhoods and beautifully landscaped grounds, Dollywood is unlike any other theme park on Earth. Rides range from heart-stopping to toddler-friendly, while the live music, down-home food and a scattering of traditionally constructed buildings offer a taste of mountain culture.

DON'T MISS

Lightning Rod roller coaster

Eagle Sanctuary and raptor show

Live bluegrass

Dolly's Tennessee Mountain Home

Amazing Flying Elephants ride

Dolly's Home-on-Wheels tour bus

The Dollywood Express

Lands of Dollywood

You can have a fine (if footsore) day just setting out from the front gate and wandering around Dollywood. But a better day awaits – especially with kids in tow – if you understand Dollywood's 11 themed areas, each of which has its own personality and offerings.

Showstreet

Showstreet, at the park's entrance, offers lots of music – two indoor theaters and two outdoor stages – plus treats, snacks, shopping and a sit-down cafe, along a pastel-colored Victorian main street. Musical offerings include bluegrass and gospel. National acts perform at the **Celebrity Theater**, and visitors services, like rentals, Ride Accessibility and Ride Measuring centers are just to the left as you enter.

Adventures in Imagination

Adventures in Imagination – across the landscaped creek from Showstreet – offers all things Dolly. Here, you can see **Dolly's tour bus**, buy Dolly clothes and hear Dolly's songs at the **Dreamsong Theater**. The **Chasing Rainbows Museum** (formerly Rags to Riches: The Dolly Parton Story), dedicated to Parton's life story, is set to reopen in a reimagined format in 2024.

Jukebox Junction

Just beyond Adventures in Imagination, **Jukebox Junction** is a paean to Parton's childhood in 1950s Sevierville. Here, you'll find Dollywood's most popular roller coaster, Lightning Rod, and **Rockin' Roadway**, where you can 'drive' a miniaturized Thunderbird, Cadillac or Corvette around a track. The sock-hop vibe continues with **Red's Drive-In** – a 1950s-themed burger joint – and live music at the **Pines Theater**.

Rivertown Junction

Rivertown Junction features the replica of the **one-room cabin** on Locust Ridge, near Sevierville, where Parton grew up. There's lots of food and drink here, including the family-style **Aunt Granny's** restaurant. You can also listen to live music or ride the rapids at Smoky Mountain River Rampage.

Country Fair & The Village

Tucked just behind Rivertown Junction, these two neighborhoods are nestled side by side. **Country Fair** recreates a nostalgic county fair with classic carnival rides and games. There are more little kids' rides here (no height restrictions) than anywhere else in the park – don't miss the Amazing Flying Elephants (p105); nearby are more adventurous rides for older kids, as well as plenty of treats and snacks.

The Village is the only place in the park where you can board the **Dollywood Express**, a 110-ton coal-fired steam engine that makes a scenic circuit of the park. This is one of Dollywood's longest-standing attractions, dating back to 1961, when the park's predecessor, Rebel Railroad, was founded. The Village has Dollywood's only **carousel**, plus live music at the **Depot Stage** and ongoing showings of the film, **Heartsongs**, a Dolly's-eye view of the Smokies.

Craftsman's Valley & Owens Farm

Craftsman's Valley draws on the architecture and features of mountain towns from the late 19th century. Chief among these is the working **Grist Mill**, built in 1982 using traditional techniques and material, and famous for its cinnamon bread. Nearby, you can observe blacksmithing, candle-making, leather-working and glass-blowing, though much of the merchandise on sale is imported. This area also houses the huge **aviary** for non-releasable eagles and an entertaining and info-packed **raptor show** featuring owls, hawks, falcons, vultures and eagles. Craftsman's Valley is also home

---

SMOKY MOUNTAIN CHRISTMAS

November through early January, Dollywood decks itself out with dozens of Christmas trees, six million lights and countless festive shows and exhibits. Other seasons also get their own festivals. Look for huge sculptures made from live flowers during the **Spring Food and Flower Festival**, and more than 12,000 glowing pumpkins during the **Harvest Festival**.

TOP TIPS

- If you buy the one-day ticket, Dollywood will let you upgrade to a multiday ticket later the same day.
- Grab the 'This Week at Dollywood' guide at the entrance.
- Ride wait times are posted throughout the park.
- Live music and raptor showtimes are in 'This Week at Dollywood' and posted live throughout the park.
- Height requirements and thrill levels are posted at all rides, alongside the height-measuring stand.
- Weekdays, especially Wednesdays and Thursdays, tend to be less crowded.
- Opening hours and dates of operation vary, so double check the park website for details.
- Download the Dollywood app!

> **TIPS FOR FAMILIES**
> - Make the Ride Height Measuring Center (left of the entry) your first stop! Color-coded wristbands show ride eligibility, save time and prevent heartbreak.
> - Parent Swap lets one parent ride with eligible kids while the other waits nearby with littler ones, then the parents swap places.
> - Small playgrounds are tucked around the park: Firehouse Fun Yard and Wildwood Creek feature water play. Hidden Hollow offers indoor play for toddlers.
> - Eating areas differ: Market Square has live bluegrass; Wilderness Pass Plaza has a lovely fountain; and there are covered eating areas at Country Fair and Eagle Mountain.
> - Gonna get splashed? Bring an extra set of dry clothes.

to a one-room schoolhouse, country chapel, the Tennessee Tornado and the Daredevil Falls. Food here includes **Granny Ogle's**, with its signature mountain menu of ham, pinto beans, greens and cornbread.

Owens Farm sits in a cul-de-sac alongside Craftsman's Valley. Aside from two somewhat tired-looking playgrounds for little kids, the main attraction here is the **Barnstormer** swing ride, themed around the stunt pilots of the 1920s.

Wilderness Pass & Timber Canyon

Thrill-seekers will head immediately for these two areas, which feature many of the park's most daring rides. Climbing uphill from Craftsman Valley, you'll find **Wilderness Pass**, with its roller coasters – the **FireChaser Express** and Wild Eagle. Younger kids will love spraying each other with firehoses at **Fire House Fun Yard**. Nearby **Wilderness Pass Plaza** is pleasantly landscaped around a fountain and a great place to chill.

The lumber-camp-themed **Timber Canyon** offers the high-thrill rated roller coasters of Mystery Mine and Thunderhead, and the junior-level Whistle Punk Chaser. Test your muscle strength at the **Lumberjack Lifts**, or plunge a thrilling 230ft at **Drop Line**.

Wildwood Grove

Dollywood's newest area (opened May 2019) is geared to families and built around a nature theme, with colorful rides featuring mockingbirds, frogs, bears, leaves and acorns. Rides here accommodate all ages, from the easygoing Black Bear Trail to the more daring Dragonflier and Big Bear Mountain roller coasters. **Wildwood Grove** offers two play areas: **Hidden Hollow**, with its special toddler zone, and **Wildwood Creek**, an engaging outdoor space where kids can experiment with music and splash in the water to their hearts' content.

Dollywood Rides You Gotta Try

Rides are a Dollywood highlight, from hair-raising roller coasters to gentle animal-themed jaunts that will put a smile on any toddler's face.

Roller Coasters for Thrill-Seekers

The legendary hot-rod themed **Lightning Rod** is Dollywood's fastest roller coaster, clickety-clacking up to speeds of 73mph. Vintage wood-coaster fans will also love **Thunderhead**, whose track zigzags over and under itself 32 times. The steel-wing **Wild Eagle** climbs up, up, up to 210ft, then plunges into midair, with no track below to break the sensation of soaring. Older but still beloved are the **Tennessee Tornado** (Dollywood's fastest steel coaster) and the rickety-looking **Mystery Mine**, with spooky animatronic ravens, lightning, simulated explosions and mine collapses.

Roller Coasters for Younger Kids

The 'high adrenaline' rides above require minimum heights of 48in to 50in – but Dollywood has fantastic alternatives for younger kids 39in or taller. **Dragonflier**'s suspended cars mimic the pattern of a dragonfly in flight, while firefighter-themed **FireChaser** features bells, sirens, fireworks and thrilling reverse acceleration. **Big Bear Mountain**, 3990ft long and new in 2023, is the park's longest coaster.

Fun for Toddlers

Really, who can resist a parade of ebullient elephants with legs outstretched in graceful flight? The **Amazing Flying Elephants** will delight kids of any age. Other 'no height limit' rides embracing the happy-animal theme include **Frogs & Fireflies**, **Lucky Ducky** and **Piggy Parade**. Kids over 36in will love bouncing down the track on smiling bears' backs at **Black Bear Trail**.

Fun in the Water

Beat the heat at **Smoky Mountain River Rampage**, a rollicking simulation of white-water rafting, and **Daredevil Falls**, where your log boat plunges over a 60ft waterfall, sending up watery plumes from the pool below.

ACCESSIBILITY

The Ride Accessibility Center (RAC) is just to the left of the entrance. At the RAC, you can rent strollers, wheelchairs and motorized convenience vehicles, ask about the Calming Room for guests with sensory overload issues, and ask about accessibility. You can get help customizing your Dollywood visit, including availing yourself of a Boarding Pass tailored to your needs and choices.

See the park's website for more details about accessibility.

BEST GEARING-UP STOPS FOR THE SMOKIES

This pair of excellent outfitters makes it easy to gear up for the Smokies.

Nantahala Outdoor Center, Gatlinburg
Located just paces from the park, this well-stocked store is a dream come true for hikers and campers. A dizzying array of high-quality gear is spread across three levels, from tents and trail maps to stove fuel and sleeping bags, while the sale rack upstairs offers deals on name-brand merchandise.

REI Co-op, Pigeon Forge
This national chain offers a good selection in a shopping center with easy parking.

OUTDOOR GEAR ON THE CHEAP

Looking to save money on a last-minute hiking or camping gear purchase? Head to **Outdoor Gear Revival** (p98) in Knoxville, where high-quality, name-brand and secondhand gear sells for less.

Believe It or Not Museum

Stroll the Gatlinburg Strip

THE SMOKIES' MINI-LAS VEGAS

Folks flock to Gatlinburg for a special kind of family fun that's heavy on arcade games, theme parks and mini-golf, and fueled by corn dogs, funnel cakes and fried Oreos. There's no better way to experience Gatlinburg's unique breed of hedonism than by walking the **Gatlinburg Strip**, a mile-long stretch of US 441 that begins just north of the national park boundary. As you make your way through town, a bevy of pancake houses and moonshine merchants crowds both sides of the street, while a barrage of signs advertises everything from axe throwing to Gatlinburg's Best Frickin' Chicken. Halfway up, a smoke-breathing T-rex gazes down from the rooftop of **Ripley's Moving Theater**, the first in a series of Ripley's attractions that also includes **Ripley's Aquarium of the Smokies**, the **Marvelous Mirror Maze**, the **Haunted Adventure** and the **Believe It or Not Museum**. Pause at the latter to admire its mad-genius facade, where canoeing bears and a banjo-plucking raccoon cavort among the giant trees. Near the end of the strip, don't miss the diminutive **log cabin** of one of Gatlinburg's earliest settlers, languishing in the shadow of a multi-story parking garage.

WHERE TO EAT IN GATLINBURG & PIGEON FORGE

The Peddler, Gatlinburg
Hickory-grilled meats, a well-stocked salad bar and river views make this Gatlinburg's favorite steakhouse. **$$$**

The Local Goat, Pigeon Forge
An easygoing eatery famous for its burgers, craft beers, mixed drinks and decadent desserts. **$$**

Pottery Cafe at the Old Mill, Pigeon Forge
Salads, sandwiches and more, on a welcoming outdoor patio or beside the fire in winter. **$$**

Visit a Sky-High Adventure Park

FAMILY FUN ON THE HILLTOPS

Gatlinburg specializes in high-altitude family fun at a trio of theme parks in the hills above town. All three offer impressive views of the Gatlinburg area, with restaurants and outdoor decks to relax and soak it all in.

Reached by a chairlift from downtown, the **Gatlinburg Sky Park**'s star attraction is its 680ft **SkyBridge**, the longest pedestrian suspension bridge in North America. For a cheap thrill, pause mid-span and gaze through the glass floor into the deep valley below.

At alpine-themed **Ober Gatlinburg**, ride a Swiss-built aerial tramway up the mountain for a seasonally changing mix of adrenaline sports, from skiing and snow tubing in winter to mountain biking in summer. Other popular attractions include the alpine slide, mountain coaster, rock-climbing wall, ice bumper cars and high-flying chair swings.

Anakeesta, the newest of the three and still expanding, whisks visitors by chairlift, gondola or **Ridge Rambler** monster truck to a whimsically landscaped hilltop village. Up top, you can wander the forest canopy on the **Treetop Skywalk**, zoom down the mountainside on the **Rail Runner** mountain coaster, climb the **Anavista** tower for 360-degree mountain views, or ride parallel zip lines with family and friends. Themed play areas like **Treehouse Village** and **Bearventure** keep younger kids happy. At day's end, it's worth sticking around for sunset views and the **Astra Lumina** night walk, which winds through an enchanted forest of colorful lights.

Breakfast at Crockett's

BREAKFAST WITH A SIDE OF HISTORY

The crowds don't lie. **Crockett's** is Gatinburg's best breakfast spot. This vast log-cabin eatery serves up regional favorites like biscuits and gravy, grits, corn pone and fried bologna, as well as citified breakfast classics like eggs Benedict. Most famous of all is Crockett's monster cinnamon roll – big as a plate and drenched in sugary white icing or fried up in egg batter to satisfy even a lumberjack's appetite. (If your sweet tooth isn't quite that sweet, you can ask them to hold the icing.) Adding to the ambience are poster-size historic photos of Smokies logging, railroading, hard-working mules and mountain people, a menagerie of taxidermied beasts hanging above the big stone fireplace and a soundtrack of Appalachian roots music – the real deal.

DOLLY PARTON: AN AMERICAN TREASURE

Singer, songwriter, savvy businesswoman, saint – the superstar status of **Dolly Parton** is multifaceted. There's how she rose from humble beginnings in a one-room shack to captivate the entire world; there's her voice; there's how she's channeled the 'high lonesome sound' and gutsy bellowing of Appalachian music into pop glory; and there's her uncanny self-assurance. Just watch her 1967 debut on the *Porter Wagoner Show*, singing 'Dumb Blonde,' and you know she's a force of nature.

Over and over, Parton has used her success for good. Perhaps most emblematic is her **Imagination Library**, which sends free, high-quality books to children from birth to age five, regardless of income. To date, over 200 million books have been put in kids' hands.

WHERE TO SLEEP IN GATLINBURG & PIGEON FORGE

KOA, Pigeon Forge
Near the Dollywood trolley, this well-kept KOA has camping, cabins, RV sites, pool and playground. **$**

Margaritaville Resort, Gatlinburg
Frozen drinks, outdoor pool with mountain views, and a full-service spa. **$$$**

DreamMore Resort, Pigeon Forge
Perks include theme-park packages and the option to stay in Dolly's former tour bus. **$$$**

Get Crafty at Arrowmont

ARTS AND CRAFTS WORKSHOPS FOR ALL

Providing an unexpected counterpoint to Gatlinburg's touristy frivolity, the **Arrowmont School of Arts and Crafts** is a renowned community arts center with deep mountain roots. Originally established as a school and Appalachian crafts shop, Arrowmont began offering summer workshops in 1945. Instructors teach everything from banjo building to pine-needle basketry to glass jewelry-making. Workshops last from six days to two weeks.

Dinner at the Appalachian

FARM-TO-TABLE, APPALACHIAN STYLE

For a memorable dinner near Pigeon Forge, head for the red brick calm of Dolly Parton's hometown, **Sevierville**, where you'll find the exceptional **The Appalachian**, which opened here in 2021. Chef David Rule elevates traditional Appalachian food to cuisine level, using locally sourced ingredients. The decor is understatedly elegant and the atmosphere easygoing, with an open kitchen where you can watch the chefs at work by the wood-burning hearth. While this farm-to-table restaurant calls itself the best in Sevierville, it's really the best in the Smokies. The menu includes traditionally hunted and foraged ingredients, like elk, wild mushrooms, ramps (wild alliums) and elderflowers. Classics like fried okra, greens, ham hocks and lima beans sit alongside steelhead trout with garlic scapes and claytonia pesto. You can try a flight of Appalachian whiskeys or sample craft cocktails with Smokies-suggestive names like 'Mountain Laurel.'

Prices are incredibly reasonable, given the care behind each dish. Each day's menu lists the local/regional farms and suppliers behind the meals. Before or after dinner, a one-block pilgrimage leads to the lawn of the nearby **Sevier County Courthouse**, where you can pay homage to the famous **Dolly Parton statue**.

Explore the Old Mill

DISCOVER PIGEON FORGE'S FORGOTTEN ROOTS

Tucked down an unassuming side street off Pigeon Forge's six-lane highway, the **Old Mill** is a remnant of an earlier time, when passenger pigeons still filled Tennessee's skies and water power ruled the day.

Today's Old Mill is the heart of a tourist complex where visitors come to shop and eat. It's also one of the oldest continually

---

DIVIDED LOYALTIES OF THE CIVIL WAR

During the Civil War, some 31,000 Tennesseans broke ranks with their Southern compatriots and joined the Union Army. Loyalty to the US was strongest in the eastern part of the state, and while a statewide referendum in June 1861 made Tennessee the last state to join the Confederacy, eastern Tennessee voted no. Indeed, Sevier County voted 96% *against* secession.

Undaunted, eastern Tennessee counties petitioned the state government to let them go their own way. In response, the now Confederate state branded the petitioners as traitors and sent in Confederate troops. Unionist refugees from eastern Tennessee were among those who formed the 9th Tennessee Cavalry at the Union's Camp Nelson in central Kentucky.

WHERE TO DRINK IN GATLINBURG

Sugarlands Distilling Company
Sample a dozen sips of moonshine for five bucks at this downtown Gatlinburg distillery.

Ole Smoky Moonshine
Salty watermelon, mango habanero...in short, enough moonshine flavors to keep you all night!

Smoky Mountain Brewery
Near the Gatlinburg Strip, this long-established brewery serves up six flagship brews, plus seasonal offerings.

Old Mill

operating gristmills in America, enshrined on the **National Register of Historic Places** and the **Tennessee Civil War Trail**. William Love built this mill on the banks of the West Prong of the Little Pigeon in 1830; his family also operated an iron forge nearby. The original 2300lb millstones came from France and were dragged here, over the Smokies, by sled.

Excellent historic signposting at the mill and restaurant next door tells you how Pigeon Forge was founded and got its name, how watermills work, the central role of mills in the local community, and more. During the Civil War, a secret garment factory on the mill's 2nd floor made cloth for Union Army uniforms and boots, using leather from a nearby tannery. Mill owner John Trotter was pro-Union, as were many East Tennessans, and his son captained Company H of the Union's 9th Tennessee Cavalry.

THE TRAIL TO THE SMOKIES

When Gatlinburg's non-stop barrage of manufactured entertainment gets to be a bit much, it's easy to escape into the national park. Just beyond Gatlinburg's southernmost stop light, a peaceful oasis of forest and creek opens up along the **Gatlinburg Trail**. This easy, 45-minute walk to the Sugarlands Visitor Center (p58) climbs gently upstream along the Little Pigeon River, dipping in and out of earshot of the main road, which runs parallel the entire way. Benches and side trails offer plenty of opportunities to contemplate the scenery or dip your toes in the water. Walk the full 2-mile trail, or turn around whenever you like.

GETTING AROUND

Pedestrian-friendly Gatlinburg sits at the national park's doorstep, just 2 miles north of Sugarlands Visitor Center via US 441. From here, it's an 8-mile drive north to Pigeon Forge. Gatlinburg's popularity and compact geography makes parking expensive; most lots charge $10 to $20 per day, so see if you can snag one of the free spots on River Rd. Pigeon Forge is brimming with mega parking-lots, most free of charge; those at Patriot Park and the Island are among the most popular.

Both towns also operate excellent public trolley services. Gatlinburg's is free, while Pigeon Forge's offers a good-value day pass. Both trolleys converge at the Gatlinburg Welcome Center, 2 miles north of Gatlinburg. Note that driving down Gatlinburg's main strip can be excruciatingly slow due to heavy traffic and frequent pedestrian crossings. Commercial shuttles (p59) offer convenient transport from Gatlinburg into the national park.

Above: Devil's Marbleyard (p125). Right: Fiddler, Floyd (p135)

NORTH CAROLINA GATEWAYS & BLUE RIDGE PARKWAY

WATERFALLS, SCENIC VISTAS & APPALACHIAN CULTURE

Mountains bring the backdrop. Fiddles and banjos bring the soundtrack. And small towns? They bring the biscuits and the welcome.

The Blue Ridge Parkway unfurls for 469 sumptuous miles across the Blue Ridge Mountains, stretching south from Virginia's Shenandoah National Park to Great Smoky Mountains National Park in North Carolina. A national parkway designed as a contiguous unit, the road rolls above a mountain-and-valley landscape home to historic farms, scenic rivers, grazing wildlife, epic trails and a lifetime's supply of waterfalls. Old-time mountain music is regularly heard – these hills are where country music was born – and nearby wineries and craft breweries offer tastings on mountain slopes with sweeping views. What you won't find? Billboards or a single stoplight.

In Virginia, vibrant college towns like Charlottesville and Lexington lure drivers down from the parkway with farm-to-table fare and boutique inns. Hikers hit nearby trails for look-at-me rock formations like Natural Bridge, Devil's Marbleyard and McAfee Knob – all catnip for social media feeds. The Appalachian Trail runs roughly parallel to the parkway north of the Roanoke Valley, then swings westward north of Roanoke. Mountain music concerts happen nightly in southwest Virginia and the High Country of North Carolina, which is dotted with adventure-minded gateway towns not far from Great Smoky Mountains National Park. Craggy peaks, mossy trails and hidden waterfalls bring whispers of the fantastic. Continuing south, Asheville is the last urban anchor, an epicenter of culture, cuisine and craft beer on the westward road to the national park.

THE MAIN AREAS

CHARLOTTESVILLE
Thriving college town. **p116**

STAUNTON & LEXINGTON
History, hiking and paddling. **p122**

ROANOKE
Urban amenities and mountain biking. **p129**

NORTH CAROLINA HIGH COUNTRY
Blue Ridge Parkway adventures. **p139**

ASHEVILLE
Art, microbreweries and fantastic restaurants. **p144**

Find Your Way

The Blue Ridge Parkway begins at the southern end of Shenandoah National Park in Virginia, linking it to Great Smoky Mountains National Park in western North Carolina. In North Carolina, you'll find numerous gateway towns along the parkway.

NORTH CAROLINA GATEWAYS & BLUE RIDGE PARKWAY

Asheville (p144)

Immerse yourself in art, stroll the Biltmore, hike beside the parkway and get primal at the drum circle. Sample more beer than you ever imagined.

North Carolina High Country (p139)

With magnificent waterfalls, craggy viewpoints, fun trails and abundant wildlife, the Blue Ridge Parkway is living its best life in this northwest corner of North Carolina.

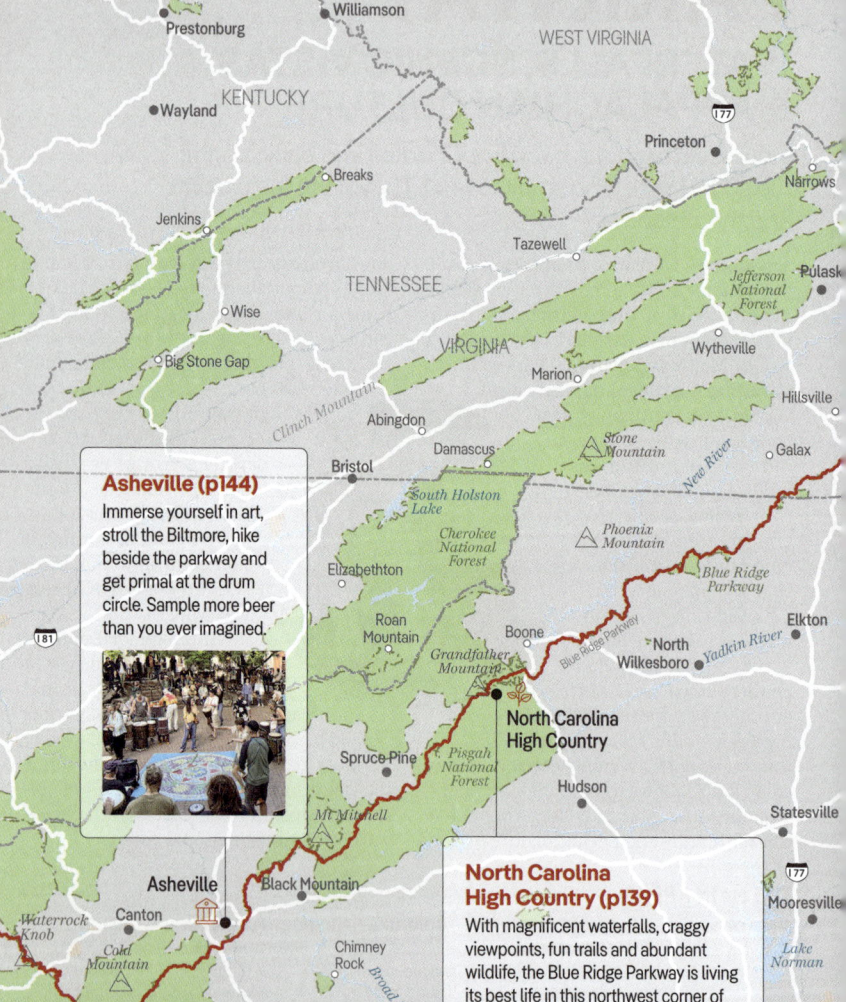

Staunton & Lexington (p122)

These historic small cities are culture-minded base camps with good regional hiking, biking and paddling. Also expect festive breweries and an abundance of Southern hospitality.

Charlottesville (p116)

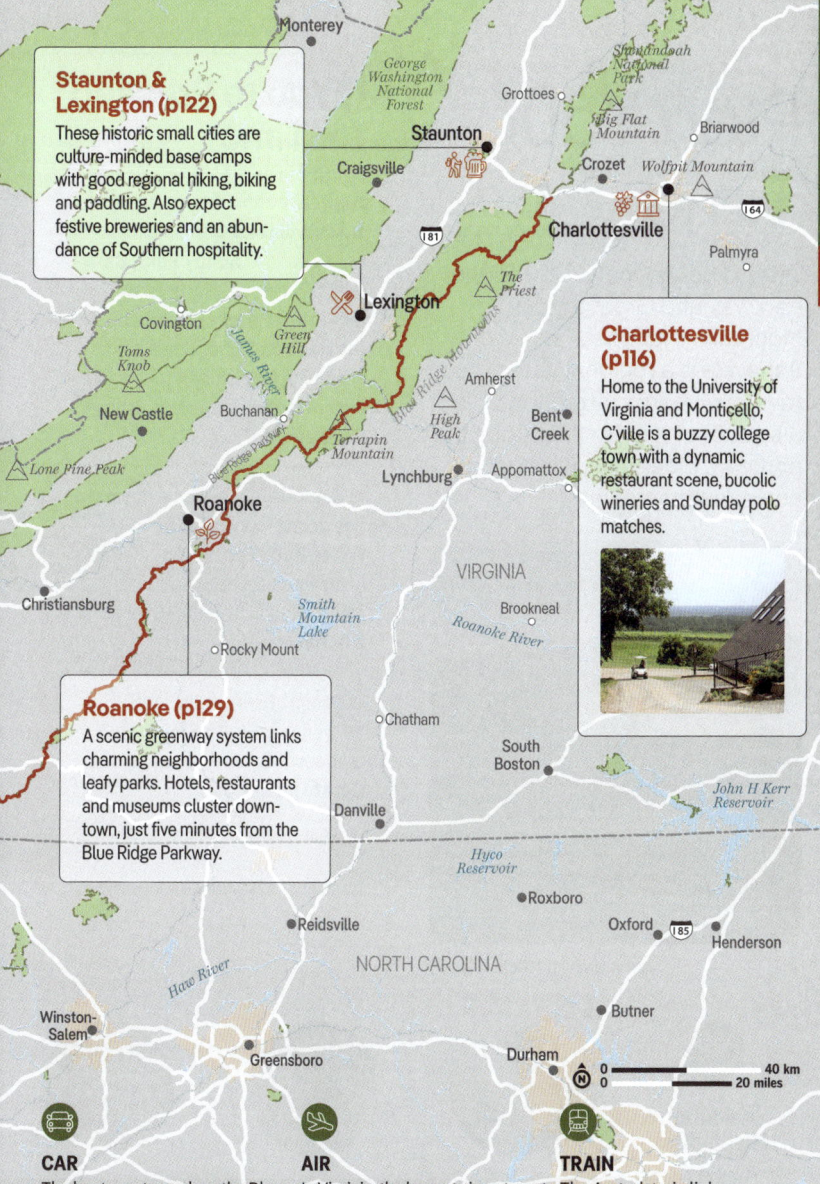

Home to the University of Virginia and Monticello, C'ville is a buzzy college town with a dynamic restaurant scene, bucolic wineries and Sunday polo matches.

Roanoke (p129)

A scenic greenway system links charming neighborhoods and leafy parks. Hotels, restaurants and museums cluster downtown, just five minutes from the Blue Ridge Parkway.

CAR

The best way to explore the Blue Ridge Parkway and the gateway towns is by car. In Virginia, I-81 and I-64 are the primary interstates near the parkway. You'll also want your own wheels to get around mountain towns in the High Country and western North Carolina.

AIR

In Virginia, the largest airport west of the Blue Ridge Mountains is Roanoke–Blacksburg Regional Airport. Asheville Regional Airport is the gateway to the North Carolina mountains. Charlotte Douglas International Airport, 120 miles east of Asheville, is an American Airlines hub.

TRAIN

The Amtrak train links Washington, DC, with Charlottesville and Roanoke along the daily Northeast Regional route. Amtrak also stops in Spartanburg and Greenville, SC; both are about one hour south of Asheville on the Crescent Route.

THE GUIDE

NORTH CAROLINA GATEWAYS & BLUE RIDGE PARKWAY

113

JOE FLOOD/FLICKR/ CC BY-NC-ND 2.0 ©, EMANUEL TANJALA/ALAMY STOCK PHOTO ©

Plan Your Time

Tucked between the Blue Ridge Parkway and Great Smoky Mountains National Park, Asheville is a regional launchpad for many nearby attractions. It's also a lot of fun. Further along the parkway, bluegrass, waterfalls and adventure await.

View from Mt Mitchell (p147)

If You're Pressed for Time

● If you're short on time, wake up in Asheville and grab breakfast on the patio at **Sunny Point Cafe** (p149). Then drive north on the Blue Ridge Parkway to soak up the views atop East Coast height champion **Mt Mitchell** (p147) and admire the wildflowers at **Craggy Gardens** (p147).

● Return to Asheviile for lunch beside the French Broad River at **White Duck Taco** (p148), then take in the murals, shops and studios along Foundy St in the **River Arts District** (p146).

● Sample beers at the craft breweries in **South Slope** (p147), then savor Spanish tapas at **Cúrate** (p148).

Seasonal Highlights

Wildflowers bloom and festival season begins in spring, while seasonal attractions open in summer. In fall, leaf peepers admire colorful foliage. In winter, after snow, sections of the parkway may close.

MARCH
Meet authors and attend literary panels in Charlottesville during the **Festival of the Book** (p120).

APRIL
Wildflowers bloom along creek beds in the mountain foothills while azaleas show off at the Biltmore Estate.

MAY
Hikers and backpackers converge on Damascus to celebrate the AT during the **Trail Days** (p138) weekend.

Three Days to Explore

● After a day in **Asheville** (p144), hop onto the Blue Ridge Parkway. Shop at the **Folk Art Center** (p146), then stop by the **Blue Ridge Parkway Visitor Center** for info. Continue south on the parkway, veering west onto US 276 to drive the **Forest Heritage Scenic Byway** (p152). Return to the parkway and drive south to waterfalls at **Graveyard Fields**.

● In Cherokee, learn about the Trail of Tears at the **Museum of the Cherokee Indian** (p151), then enjoy dinner and an overnight at the **Everett Hotel** (p151) in Bryson City.

● Next morning, explore **Nantahala Gorge** (p153), grab lunch in **Sylva** (p154) and then tour the **Biltmore Estate** (p145).

If You Have More Time

● For Appalachian culture, drive north to Virginia, where the **Crooked Road** (p137), a music-themed driving route, swoops past old-time jams and historic mountain-music sites. Book a room in Bristol, home of the **Birthplace of Country Music Museum** (p135).

● Next up is a scenic pedal on the **Virginia Creeper National Recreation Trail** (p138) near Abingdon. Spend the night in **Floyd** (p135), a one-stoplight town vibrant with the sounds of live old-time music, especially during the **Friday Night Jamboree** (p135).

● Near Roanoke, hike the Appalachian Trail to **McAfee Knob** (p131) and its iconic Catawba Valley view. End in Lexington with a **carriage ride** (p126) through the historic downtown.

JUNE
Rhododendrons bloom exuberantly along the Blue Ridge Parkway while **Shindig on the Green** (p149) concerts kick off in Asheville.

SEPTEMBER
Celebrate all things Harry Potter during the **Queen City Mischief & Magic Festival** in Staunton.

OCTOBER
Fall foliage begins its colorful transformation in the mountains while Roanoke hosts its outdoorsy **GO-Fest**.

DECEMBER
The Biltmore Estate celebrates the holiday season with extensive decorations, plus luminaries at night.

CHARLOTTESVILLE

A hub of culture, cuisine and history bumping against the foothills of the Blue Ridge Mountains, Charlottesville is regularly ranked as one of the country's best places to live. This convivial town is home to the architecturally resplendent University of Virginia (UVA), which attracts Southern aristocracy and artsy lefties in equal proportions. The UVA grounds, Main St and the pedestrian Downtown Mall area overflow with students, professors and visiting tourists, endowing 'C'ville' with a lively, well-educated and diverse atmosphere. More than 100 wineries are located just beyond the city, alongside rural villages, grand colonial estates, breweries, cideries and distilleries.

In 2017, clashes over the removal of Confederate statues and the subsequent horror of a white nationalist rally cast a pall over the city, as did the fatal shootings of three football players by a fellow student in 2022. The Charlottesville community today is reflective but also resilient. It remains a compelling and stimulating base for regional exploring.

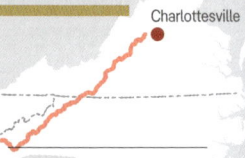

TOP TIP

If you're planning to hike Old Rag Mountain (p166) from March through November, secure a day-use ticket online (recreation.gov) before you arrive at the parking lot, which is one hour north of Charlottesville. This ticket requirement is currently a pilot program aimed at easing congestion, but may be implemented permanently.

Pippin Hill Farm & Vineyards (p121)

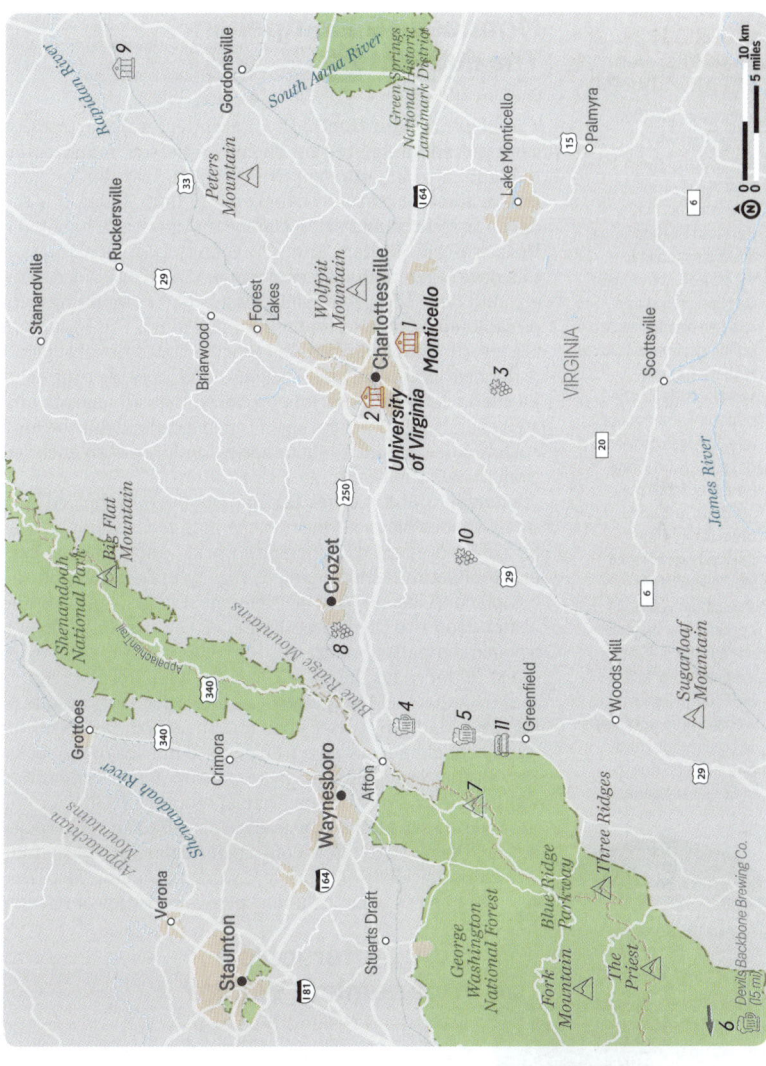

HIGHLIGHTS
1 Monticello
2 University of Virginia

SIGHTS
3 Blenheim Vineyards
4 Blue Mountain Brewery
5 Brewing Tree Beer Co.
6 Devils Backbone Brewing Co.
7 Humpback Rocks
8 King Family Vineyards
9 Montpelier
10 Pippin Hill Farm & Vineyards

SLEEPING
11 Indigo House

Downtown Mall (p120)

NORTH CAROLINA GATEWAYS & BLUE RIDGE PARKWAY CHARLOTTESVILLE

THE GUIDE

Monticello & Montpelier: The Full Picture

FASCINATING HOMES, COMPLICATED HISTORIES

The house at **Monticello** is an architectural masterpiece designed and inhabited by Thomas Jefferson, founding father, and third US president, who spent 40 years building his dream home – eventually completed in 1809. Today, it is the only presidential and private home in America designated a Unesco World Heritage Site. The centerpiece of a plantation that once covered 5000 acres, it can be visited on guided tours (ground floor only), while its grounds and outbuildings can be explored on themed and self-guided tours. The 45-minute 'Slavery at Monticello' walking tour (included in ticket price) is the highlight of any trip. Guides don't gloss over the complicated past of the man who declared that 'all men are created equal' in the Declaration of Independence, while owning enslaved people and likely fathering children with enslaved woman Sally Hemings.

Jefferson and his other family members are buried in a small wooded plot near the home. A high-tech exhibition center delves deeper into Jefferson's world – including exhibits on architecture, enlightenment through education and the complicated idea of liberty. Frequent shuttles run from the visitor center to the hilltop house, or you can walk along a wooded footpath to reach it.

Just 25 miles northeast of Charlottesville (off Hwy 20), is James Madison's **Montpelier** – another spectacular estate in the area. Madison, a statesman and the fourth US president, was a brilliant but shy man who devoted himself to his books. He was almost single-handedly responsible for developing and writing the US Constitution. Guided tours shed a light on the life and times of Madison, as well as his gifted and charismatic wife, Dolley. Carefully reconstructed cabins show what life was like for Madison's enslaved workers, and the 'Mere Distinction of Colour' exhibit explores the legacy of slavery.

UVA: Jefferson's 'Academical Village'

WANDERING THE GROUNDS OF UVA

Old and new collide with compelling – and sometimes jarring – effect while strolling around the University of Virginia (UVA). Thomas Jefferson founded the school and designed what he called an 'Academical Village' to embody the spirit of communal living and learning. The hub of this 'village' is **The Lawn**, a sloped grassy

---

BLUE RIDGE PARKWAY: GETTING STARTED

In Virginia, the Blue Ridge Parkway begins just south of the southern entrance to Shenandoah National Park and Skyline Drive. It is accessed at Exit 99, off I-64 at Rockfish Gap, which is home to a few abandoned buildings, a food truck for kettle-corn (a sweet, old-fashioned popcorn) and parking lots. There is no fee to drive the Blue Ridge Parkway. From the northern entrance, drive 6 miles south to Humpback Rocks, where you'll find a seasonal visitor center. The maximum speed limit is 45mph. In winter, check the Blue Ridge Parkway website (nps.gov/biri) to confirm the road is not closed due to inclement weather.

FOR MORE BLUE RIDGE

The spooky **Blue Ridge Tunnel Trail** (p167), near the beginning of the Blue Ridge Parkway just south, is a 2.25-mile path on an abandoned railway line. A favorite of kids, it stretches through a dark mountain tunnel for nearly a mile. Headlamps are a must!

WHERE TO EAT IN CHARLOTTESVILLE

Bodo's Bagels
Students are regulars at this Charlottesville institution, lured by its wonderful bagels and UVA location. **$**

Oakhart Social
The patio here is a prime spot for enjoying the seasonally inspired small plates and wood-fired pizzas. **$$**

Public Fish & Oyster
If you're a raw-oyster virgin, this is the place to change that story. Also try the twice-cooked Belgian fries. **$$$**

Rotunda, University of Virginia

field that is fringed by columned pavilions, student rooms, the Standford White-designed **Old Cabell Hall** (1898) and Jefferson's famous **Rotunda**, modeled on Rome's Pantheon and the centerpiece of the entire school. The Rotunda was constructed between 1822 and 1832 and has always functioned as a library. By edict of Jefferson himself, the UVA campus is referred to as 'the Grounds.' Rooms on The Lawn, though small and lacking bathrooms, are a prestigious residence open to only 50 or so seniors who apply for the honor of living there. The rooms, which have fireplaces, date to the early 1800s, but the political commentary on some doors is pure 21st century – and sometimes quite controversial.

Together, the original neoclassical and Palladian-style university buildings and Jefferson's Monticello comprise a Unesco World Heritage Site. Free **guided tours** (uvaguides.org) of the original university and lawn area are offered daily from the Rotunda at 11am, plus a 3pm tour on Saturdays, during the school year.

Brews with Mountain Views
TRAVELING THE BREW RIDGE TRAIL

The vast patio at **Blue Mountain Brewery** is the place to be on a sunny afternoon, especially after a hike. Blue Mountain joins a string of craft breweries and cideries stretching west

OLD RAG & CHARLOTTESVILLE

It's a little-known fact that before tackling the adventurous ascent up the 3238ft Old Rag Mountain (p166) in the lovely Shenandoah National Park, hikers in the know spend the night in Charlottesville, which is a far more convenient base than Skyline Drive for accessing the main trailhead. The trailhead is near Nethers, VA, just one hour north of Charlottesville.

🛏 **WHERE TO SLEEP IN CHARLOTTESVILLE**

South Street Inn
This elegant 1856 building houses a heritage-style B&B with 11 well-sized and beautifully presented rooms. **$$**

The Draftsman
This hotel is named for the three presidents from Virginia who penned the country's founding documents. **$$$**

Clifton
Elegant boutique inn with manor house and cottages in the hilly countryside near UVA. **$$$**

LOCAL EVENTS: BOOKS, MOVIES & HORSES

Charlottesville hosts a wide variety of festivals and events throughout the year. You'll find UVA students and alums – affectionately known as Wahoos or Hoos – tailgating beside **Scott Stadium** during home football games in the fall. In March, authors and bibliophiles gather for the **Virginia Festival of the Book**.

In April and October, steeplechase races bring the horsey set (and inebriated college students) to the track during the **Foxfield Races**.

Catch upcoming indie films and panel discussions during the **Virginia Film Festival** in November.

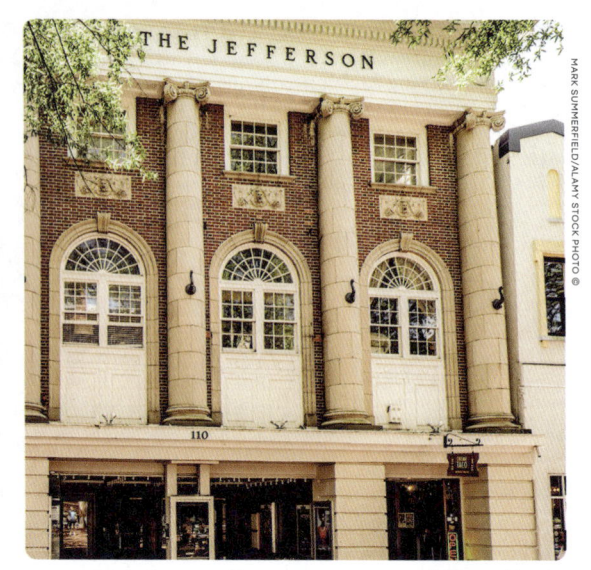

Jefferson Theater

from Charlottesville along Hwy 151, which ribbons along the base of the mountains below the Blue Ridge Parkway. Part of the **Brew Ridge Trail**, these breweries produce fine craft beer; many also offer mountain views, great food and convivial patios. **Hop On Virginia** (virginiahopontours.com) shuttles between many of them. Other good picks for beer and food include the stream-side **Brewing Tree Beer Co.** and the regional Goliath of **Devils Backbone Brewing Co**.

Hwy 151 is also lined with homes offering short-term rentals for weekend adventurers and group getaways. For a low-key but welcoming B&B, check out the breezy rooms at new-on-the-scene **Indigo House**. Each room is inspired by a national park.

Strolling the Historic Downtown Mall

BOUTIQUES, PATIOS AND PERFORMANCE HALLS

A go-to destination for alfresco dining and romantic strolls, the **Downtown Mall** is a paved pedestrian area about a mile and a half east of UVA. This multi-block collection of boutiques, bookstores, restaurants, coffee shops, movie theaters and live music venues is a community hub and festival hot spot. For casual eats, try the gourmet burgers at **Citizen Burger Bar** or the sandwiches, salads and daily soups at **Revolutionary**

WHERE TO EAT PIZZA IN CHARLOTTESVILLE

Lampo Neapolitan Pizza
True Italian-style pizza in cozy digs in the trendy Belmont neighborhood. **$$**

Crozet Pizza
Kicky sauces draw pizza-philes to this perennial favorite near the Brew Ridge Trail. Open since 1977. **$$**

Dr Ho's Humble Pie
Everything's made by hand and ingredients are locally sourced; located 15 miles south of the city. **$$**

Soup. Cocktails are skillfully crafted at **The Alley Light** and the nearby **Whiskey Bar**. For live music, check the schedule for the outdoor **Ting Pavilion** or the more intimate **Jefferson Theater**. Small memorials mark the spot where 32-year-old Heather Heyer was deliberately hit by a car and killed while protesting a white nationalist rally in 2017. The road, formerly 4th St SE, has been renamed Heather Heyer Way.

Sip Wine like Royalty
WINE TASTING AND POLO MATCHES

At halftime, spectators remove their shoes to stomp on dirt clods, called divots, kicked up by the ponies during the Sunday polo match at **King Family Vineyards**. It's fun to gussy up for this free summer social event, marked by field-side picnics and roaming golf carts that sell bottles of wine. This vineyard consistently ranks as one of Virginia's best wineries; try its flagship Meritage, a merlot, cab franc, petit verdot and malbec varietal. Flights of King Family's various wines are available in the tasting room daily (10am to 5pm; $15 to $20).

The Piedmont area, with its rolling hills, wineries and vineyards, has also drawn wine-loving visitors for decades. Charlottesville-area favorites include **Pippin Hill Farm & Vineyards**, where wonderful views over the Piedmont complement the well-regarded viognier and cabernet sauvignon, and **Blenheim Vineyards**, which is owned by musician Dave Matthews. His chardonnay is eminently quaffable, and the setting is sheer bucolic joy. For a full list of local wineries, follow the **Monticello Wine Trail** (monitcellowinetrail.com).

Hiking & History at Humpback Rocks
ROCKY SUMMIT WITH BIG VIEWS

You will likely be huffing and puffing while climbing the 1-mile trail that slings hikers from the Blue Ridge Parkway to **Humpback Rocks** (Mile 6), a sloped rock ledge jutting from the summit of Humpback Mountain. From the rocks, you can see the Shenandoah Valley to the west and the flat Piedmont to the east. The Blue Ridge Mountains roll north and south between them. Pop into the visitor center at the base of Humpback Mountain, then stroll the adjacent interpretive trail, which passes rustic cabins and farm buildings that showcase 1890s mountain life.

BLACK HISTORY IN THE BLUE RIDGE

To learn more about Black history in Charlottesville, download the **Discover Black Cville Passport** (visit charlottesville.org), which stops at notable sites and Black-owned businesses in Charlottesville and Albemarle County.

Get started at the **Jefferson School African American Heritage Center**, which showcases Black history and culture. Black-owned businesses include **MarieBette**, a popular stop for lunch, pastries and coffee, and **The Ridley**, located inside the Draftsman Hotel. Serving seafood and southern fare, the upscale restaurant is named for Dr Walter N Ridley, the first Black graduate of UVA.

In the Roanoke area, about two hours southwest of Charlottesville, you can delve into Black history at the **Harrison Museum of African American Culture** and the **Booker T Washington National Monument**.

GETTING AROUND

Parking can be tight in Charlottesville, especially near UVA and the university hospital. Good options are the Water Street Parking Garage (200 E Water St) and the Omni Hotel parking lot, both near the Downtown Mall. For exploring UVA, try the 14th St NW lot. Charlottesville is walkable in spots, but you will need a car to explore beyond the city. The walk between the Rotunda and the Mall is just under 1.5 miles.

A free trolley (look for a T sign) connects UVA and the Mall via W Main St. It runs every 15 minutes between 6:40am and 11:37pm Monday to Saturday and from 8am to 5:47pm on Sunday. The Amtrak station (810 W Main St) is also on the trolley line.

STAUNTON & LEXINGTON

Beverley St is the fun-loving heart of Staunton, a small city near the northern entrance of the Blue Ridge Parkway. Historic and walkable, Beverley St has a fantastic food scene. The city closes the street on occasion in summer for socializing and for the wildly popular Queen City Mischief & Magic weekend, a three-day ode to Harry Potter in September. The city's wonderful American Shakespeare Center is a repertory theater inside a recreation of Blackfriars Theater.

Lexington, the southern gateway to the Shenandoah Valley, is 35 miles south of Staunton. Home to Washington & Lee University and the Virginia Military Institute, the city and its historic downtown exude a vibrant, youthful energy supported by a slew of new hotels, bars and restaurants. Civil War generals Robert E Lee and Stonewall Jackson lived and are buried here, and Lexington has long been a favorite stop for Civil War enthusiasts. Today, you'll see many adventurers using Lexington as a launchpad for mountain fun.

TOP TIP

Traffic jams are common on I-81, particularly on weekends. If traffic starts to look congested, exit onto Route 11, which runs parallel to the interstate highway through much of the state. Route 11 is bordered by picturesque farmland between Staunton and Lexington and is frequently four-lane.

Beverley St, Staunton

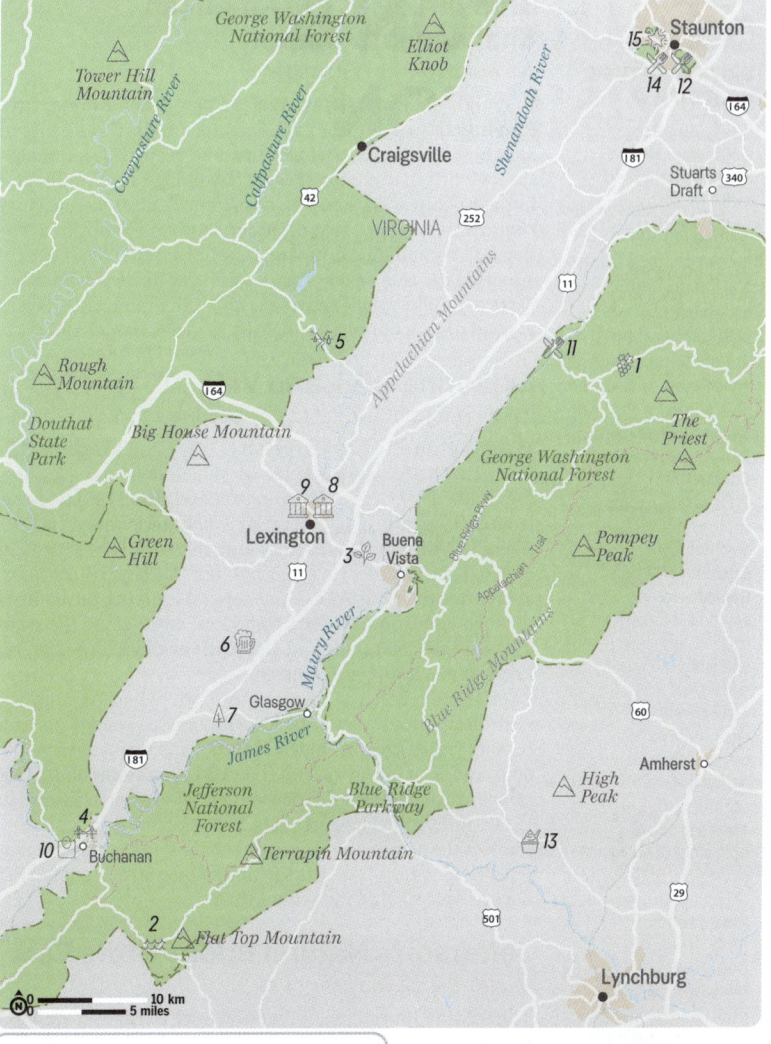

SIGHTS
1 12 Ridges Vineyard
2 Abbott Lake
3 Ben Salem Wayside
4 Buchanan Swinging Bridge
5 Goshen Pass
6 Great Valley Farm Brewery & Winery
7 Natural Bridge State Park
8 Virginia Military Institute
9 Washington & Lee University

ACTIVITIES, COURSES & TOURS
10 Twin River Outfitters

EATING
11 Gertie's Country Store
12 Kathy's
13 Woodruff's Cafe and Pie Shop
14 Wright's Dairy-Rite

ENTERTAINMENT
15 Blackfriars Playhouse

University Chapel (p124)

Break a Leg at the American Shakespeare Center

THE WORKS OF THE FAMOUS BARD

You might find yourself part of the play at the **Blackfriars Playhouse** in Staunton, where actors from the American Shakespeare Center perform inside a recreation of Shakespeare's original indoor theater. Two plays are usually performed per season, and the small but dedicated repertory troupe often acts in two different shows on Saturdays. The theater is small and intimate, and brave guests can choose a seat on the side of the stage. With beer and wine on sale – we're sure Will would approve – it's a fun evening out. Several good dining options are nearby.

Exploring W&L and VMI

CAMPUS HISTORY AND ECLECTIC MUSEUMS

Washington and Lee University (W&L) and **Virginia Military Institute** (VMI) sit side-by-side in downtown Lexington. Named for George Washington and Robert E Lee, W&L is a pretty and preppy liberal arts college founded in 1749. George Washington saved the young school in 1796 with a gift of $20,000. Confederate general Robert E Lee served as president after the Civil War in the hope of unifying the country through education. Visitors today can stroll along the striking redbrick Colonnade and visit **University Chapel**, where Lee and his family are interred.

You'll be greeted with friendly nods when passing the well-disciplined cadets at VMI, the only university to have sent its entire graduating class into combat (plaques to student war dead are touching). The **VMI Museum** houses the taxidermied carcass of Stonewall Jackson's horse among its 15,000 military-related artifacts. Free 45-minute cadet-guided tours of the campus depart from the museum at noon during term time. A full-dress parade takes place on designated Fridays at 4pm during the school year.

Jefferson's Natural Bridge State Park

MAJESTIC ARCH AND DARK SKIES

The soaring limestone arch at **Natural Bridge State Park** has impressed travelers for centuries. The 215ft-high span was once touted to be one of the seven natural wonders of the world. Thomas Jefferson purchased the arch in 1773 for just over £10 and hired a free Black man to pay the annual property taxes and serve as caretaker. There are 6 miles of

---

DRIVING HISTORIC ROUTE 11

Rte 11 follows the Great Wagon Road, a historic path used by Scots-Irish and German settlers traveling south from Pennsylvania in the 1700s. Today it parallels I-81 through Virginia and is dotted with quirky attractions.

Closer to Shenandoah National Park, the **Route 11 Potato Chips** factory in Mt Jackson offers short tours and free samples. In Staunton, **Edelweiss German Restaurant** has served schnitzel, house-made beer and accordion tunes since 1981.

Just north of Lexington, pull in on weekends for a double-feature at **Hull's Drive-in Theatre**, one of only eight drive-ins in Virginia. South of Lexington, the **Pink Cadillac** is a 1950s-loving diner. Down the road, feed exotic animals from your car at the **Virginia Safari Park**.

WHERE TO EAT IN STAUNTON

Chicano Boy
This former food truck whips up fresh tacos, burritos and bowls near downtown. $

Yelping Dog
Breezy wine shop with innovative cheese boards and deliciously gourmet grilled-cheese sandwiches. $

The Shack
A James Beard Award semi-finalist, Ian Boden creates dinners inspired by his mountain roots and Jewish heritage. $$$

Natural Bridge State Park

trails in the park, including a moderate trail that drops to **Cedar Creek**, then passes under the arch to a reconstructed **Monacan Indian village** and a **waterfall**. Disc golfers can play through hills and forests on the new 18-hole **disc golf course**. The park was named an International Dark Sky Park in 2021, and stargazing events are held here monthly.

A Lazy Day on the James

FLOAT DOWN A SCENIC RIVER

All you need is sunscreen, a bathing suit and river shoes for a half-day float on the **James River**. This mighty waterway flows from the foothills of the Blue Ridge all the way to Richmond and eventually the coast. Flanked by forested hills and fed by trout-filled streams, the James is a Virginia Scenic River and part of the 74-mile **Upper James River Water Trail**. Owned by twin brothers, **Twin River Outfitters** in Buchanan rents kayaks and inner tubes for half-day floats, and a shuttle ride is included. The fun **Buchanan Swinging Bridge** crosses the James north of downtown, beside Rte 11. After tubing, drive a few miles north to **Great Valley Farm Brewery & Winery** for a craft beer and sweeping mountain views.

BEST HIKES NEAR LEXINGTON

Crabtree Falls
This 5 miles round-trip trail ascends beside a 1200ft waterfall with five scenic sections.

Mountain Pleasant Scenic Area
Hike the Appalachian Trail across a magnificent bald atop Cole Mountain or ascend to rocky overlooks on Mt Pleasant.

Devil's Marbleyard
A 1-mile trail leads to a fun scramble up a vast quartzite boulder field blanketing a mountain slope.

Apple Orchard Falls
Start from the Sunset Fields Overlook on the Blue Ridge Parkway or from Arcadia in the foothills for views of a 200ft-high waterfall.

WHERE TO EAT IN LEXINGTON

Heliotrope Brewing
Small-batch brewpub serving wood-fired sourdough pizzas, salads and some really addictive hummus. **$$**

Taps
This lounge doubles as Lexington's living room – stop for elevated pub fare, cocktails and gossip. **$$**

Red Hen
Intimate restaurant with limited menu featuring creative, French-focused fare and local produce. Great cocktails. **$$$**

DOWNTOWN LEXINGTON ON FOOT

This half-mile walk passes numerous historic buildings and churches. From the **1 Visitor Center of Lexington**, walk west on Washington St to the **2 Jackson House Museum**, once owned by Confederate general Stonewall Jackson. The **3 Milinery de Rousselot Mural** on the corner of Washington and Main Sts is not an 1800s holdover. It was painted for the movie *Sommersby*, a Civil War-era drama filmed here in 1992.

Turn right on Main St, where you'll spot exposed foundations and a few oddly placed doors – in 1851, the street levels were lowered to improve the steep grades that had been a hazard for 75 years. Reminders of this project include the **4 Jacob Ruff House** at 21 N Main St. Cross Main at **5 First Baptist Church**, a Black church built in the 1890s, and pass the **6 Willson-Walker House**, c 1830. Harry Lee Walker, one of the city's most prominent Black citizens, bought the building in 1910 and ran a butcher shop here, one of the anchors of the Black business district during the Jim Crow era. The **7 Alexander-Withrow House** on the corner of Main and Washington St dates to the late 1700s. Note the diamond pattern of glazed bricks on its upper-level exterior walls.

Continue west on Washington St to **8 Grace Episcopal Church**, where former Confederate general Robert E Lee served as warden while president of Washington College. Next door is the **9 Lee House**, his former residence. The doors to the garage, formerly a stable, always remain open in case the ghost of Lee's horse, Traveller, returns from his wanderings. From here, return to the Lexington Visitor Center. Horse-drawn carriage rides and the Haunting Tales ghost tour begin here.

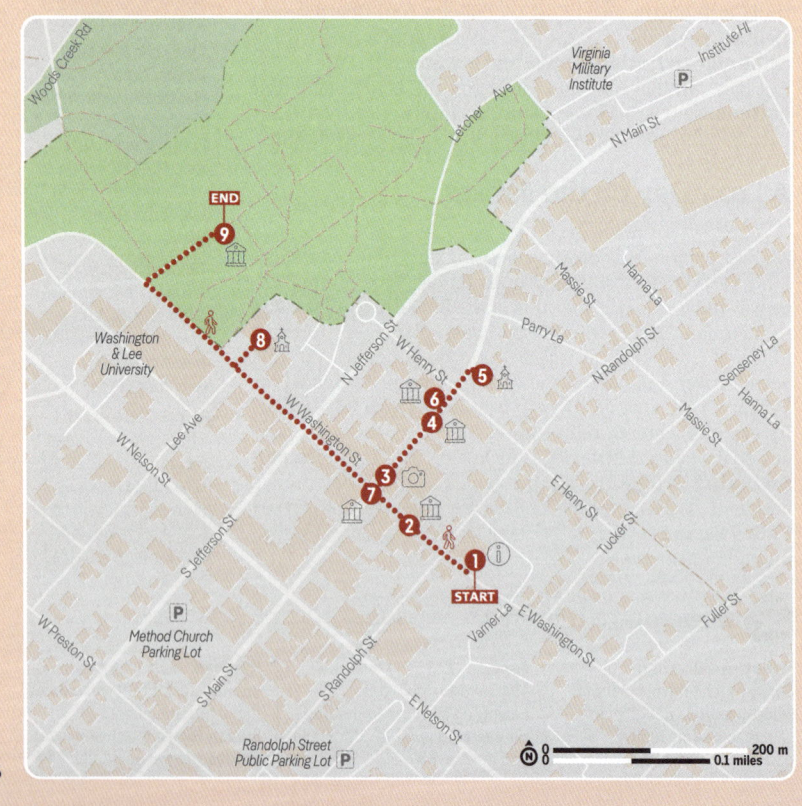

Appalachian Lore at the Peaks of Otter
ROCKY SUMMIT AND APPALACHIAN HISTORY

Three pretty peaks – Sharp Top, Flat Top and Harkening Hill – surround tiny **Abbott Lake** on the Blue Ridge Parkway (Mile 85). From the summit of **Sharp Top**, you'll enjoy views that sweep in the lake, the Shenandoah Valley and the eastern Piedmont. It's 3 miles round-trip to the top, but a shuttle loops to the summit in summer. The **Johnson Farm Trail** leads to an 1850s **farmhouse**, and trails also climb the other two peaks and pass rocky cascades, where deer sightings are likely. The farmhouse is typically staffed by a ranger in summer, who can share stories about the family who lived here and grew apples that were sold to a long-gone local hotel. Stop by the **Peaks of Otter Lodge** for a meal beside the lake. There's a **campground** here, too.

Sip Wine atop the Blue Ridge
WINE TASTING BESIDE THE PARKWAY

The terrace appears to float beside the clouds at **12 Ridges Vineyard** – the highest altitude vineyard in Virginia. And it has all of the breathtaking mountain views you'd expect. Open since 2019, 12 Ridges is a young, small-batch winery offering tastings of internationally acclaimed high-elevation and cool climate wines, plus a few of its own inaugural wines, as it builds its offerings. The winery borders the Blue Ridge Parkway at Mile 25. Since commercial signage is not permitted on the parkway, plug the address at 24981 Blue Ridge Parkway into your GPS and look for the gravel drive. Leashed pets are permitted, and it's open Friday through Sunday, noon to 5pm.

Swimming Holes & Swinging Bridges
SUMMER FUN BY THE WATER

'Swimming holes and swinging bridges' may sound like a country song, but both are also fun and photogenic destinations in summer. For ease of access, it's hard to beat the **Ben Salem Wayside**, which borders Route 60 just off I-81 between Lexington and Buena Vista. Beside the Maury River, the park is also home to a historic 1800s lock. For a swimming hole with boulders perfect for jumping, continue east on Route 60 and pass beneath the Blue Ridge Parkway. Turn right on Panther Falls Rd and continue to the trailhead for **Panther Falls**. Camping is popular here, and it can get busy on weekends.

Another attractive spot for splashing around is **Goshen Pass** on Route 39. On the drive, pull over for the creaky **swinging bridge** beside the Rockbridge Baths Post Office. Once you get

---

STONEWALL JACKSON LORE

Confederate general Thomas Jonathan 'Stonewall' Jackson was a physics professor at the Virginia Military Institute (VMI) in Lexington before the Civil War. The VMI Museum (p124) displays the stuffed carcass of his horse, Little Sorrel, as well as the raincoat Jackson was wearing when he was mortally wounded by friendly fire during the war.

According to local mythology, he walked around town sucking on lemons for his health. To this day, visitors leave lemons on his grave at the **Oak Grove Cemetery** downtown. Not all of the general is buried here, however. His arm was amputated in a field hospital outside Fredericksburg before his death and was buried nearby.

WHERE TO STAY IN LEXINGTON

Hampton Inn Col Alto
A lobby and several rooms occupy an historic 1827 home a few blocks from Main St. **$$**

Stonegate
Elegant B&B in a columned, redbrick house frequented by Robert E Lee. Ask about the secret door. **$$$**

The Georges
Set in several historic buildings downtown, the classy rooms feature high-end furnishings and luxury linens. **$$$**

WHY I LOVE LEXINGTON

Amy C Balfour, writer

I live in Lexington and attended Washington & Lee University, and my mom grew up here, so Lexington has been a big part of my life for years. I love the merging of old and new in the historic downtown and the energy and sophistication of it being a college town. On weekends, you'll catch me sipping cocktails and enjoying fish tacos at **Taps at the Georges**, eating Sunday breakfast at **Niko's** and popping into **Pumpkinseeds** and **Purveyors on Main** for gifts.

A short drive drops me at a wonderful loop hike across the **Cole Mountain** balds. A favorite gathering spot is Great Valley Farm Brewery & Winery (p125) near Natural Bridge, where sunset views of the Blue Ridge are downright magnificent.

Wright's Dairy-Rite

to Goshen Pass, park at the designated wayside or find a pull-off and walk down to the Maury, where enormous rocks are a bit more isolated and perfect for relaxing. There's another **swinging bridge** 1.7 miles west of the wayside. Turn right at the gravel road, which leads to a parking lot and kiosk. The parking lot is also the trailhead for the pleasant **Chamber Ridge's Trail**.

Old-School Eats

HOMEMADE FARE AND SOUTHERN HOSPITALITY

There's something about a welcoming smile and good comfort food that can set a day right. The diners and country stores in the foothills of Virginia do both exceedingly well. Your breakfast is served up fast if you're sitting at the counter at **Kathy's** in Staunton, where everybody on staff is ready to keep you happy. Down the highway, you can pull in for carhop service with burgers, fries and shakes at **Wright's Dairy-Rite**. Be sure to sign the wall at **Gertie's** in Vesuvius, a tried-and-true lunch spot frequented after hiking the Crabtree Falls Trail. And pie? A few miles off the parkway, and located in an old gas station, **Woodruff's Cafe and Pie Shop** has served delicious chocolate and fruit-filled pies for decades.

GETTING AROUND

Staunton and Lexington can be reached by car from I-61 and I-81. Both cities have historic downtowns that are compact and pedestrian-friendly, and street parking is free and plentiful in both cities. You'll need a car to reach trailheads and attractions outside of the downtown areas.

ROANOKE

Illuminated by the neon lights of the Mill Mountain Star, which overlooks downtown, Roanoke is the largest city in the Roanoke Valley, and is a convenient launchpad for exploring the Blue Ridge – downtown is just five minutes from the parkway and a short drive from the Appalachian Trail. The community, originally known as 'Big Lick' thanks to its game-attracting salt licks, took off as a railroad town in the early 1880s. At about the same time, the town changed its name to 'Roanoke,' a derivation of the Algonquian word 'rawrenock,' a shell bead that was traded and worn by regional tribes. A century or so later, the railroad companies were gone, and Roanoke grew a bit sleepy. But today? An expanding greenway system, a burgeoning arts scene, mountain biking bone fides and a growing portfolio of farm-to-table restaurants have energized the city, flipping Roanoke from sleepy to almost hip.

TOP TIP

Before stepping into Roanoke's famous Texas Tavern (p133) for a meal, lock down the lingo. A 'cheesy western' is a burger topped with a fried egg, cheese, relish, pickles and onion. For chile topped with onions, order a 'chile with.'

Downtown Roanoke

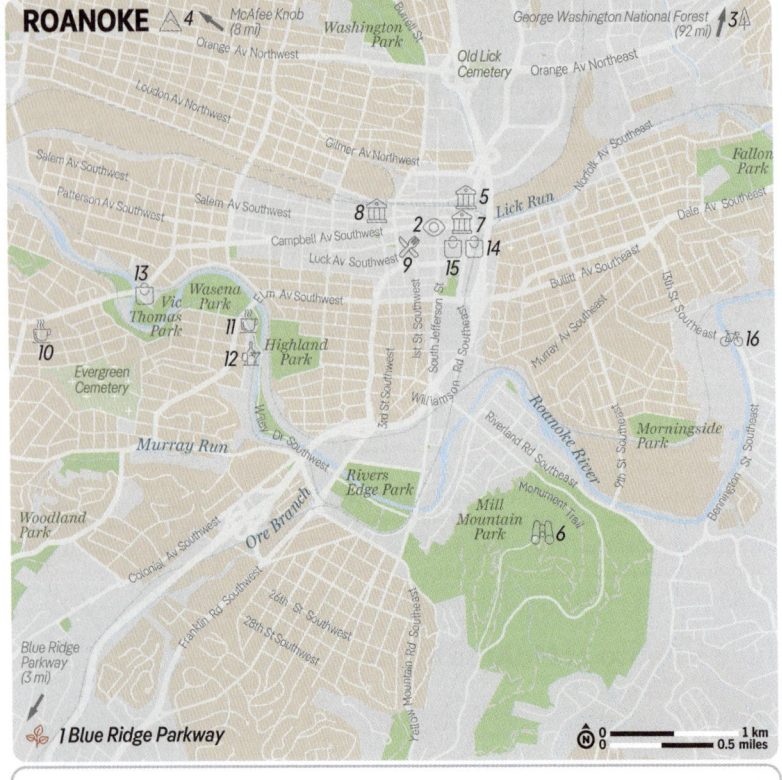

ROANOKE

HIGHLIGHTS
1 Blue Ridge Parkway

SIGHTS
2 Center in the Square
3 George Washington National Forest
4 McAfee Knob
5 O Winston Link Museum
6 Roanoke Star & Mill Mountain Park
7 Taubman Museum of Art
8 Virginia Museum of Transportation

EATING
9 Texas Tavern

DRINKING & NIGHTLIFE
10 Cardinal Bicycle & Cafe
11 Green Goat
12 Wasena City Tap Room

SHOPPING
13 Black Dog Salvage
14 Chocolate Paper
15 Walkabout Outfitter

TRANSPORT
16 Roanoke River Greenway

Up Close with the Roanoke Star

ADMIRE A NEON LANDMARK

First illuminated in 1949, the towering **Roanoke Star** glows nightly over downtown Roanoke from its perch atop Mill Mountain. Weighing 10,000 pounds and rising 88.5ft, it is the largest freestanding illuminated star in the world. A short drive up the Mill Mountain Spur Rd ends at the base of the star, near a platform with broad views of downtown and the Roanoke Valley. The 3.3-mile round-trip hike on the **Star Trail**, from the base of Mill Mountain, is a good workout that ends with a rewarding

Roanoke Star

view. A small **zoo** and a discovery center are located in the adjacent **Mill Mountain Park**.

Railways & Photography at O Winston Link

STEAM TRAINS IN BLACK AND WHITE

The name of this **museum** doesn't stir excitement, but trust us: train-spotters aren't the only ones who will find this place fascinating. Housed in the former passenger station of the Norfolk and Western Railway, the museum is home to photographs, sound recordings and film by O Winston Link (1914–2001), a New Yorker who spent nine months recording the last years of steam power on the Norfolk and Western (N&W) Railway in the 1950s. The N&W Railway was the last major American railroad to operate exclusively with steam power – it carried locally mined coal, so stayed profitable when other such railway lines closed.

The gelatin silver prints of Link's B&W photographs are hugely atmospheric and dramatic – many were shot at night, a rarity at the time. As well as photographs including Link's well-known *Hotshot Eastbound at the Drive-in Movie* (1956), the collection includes some of his photographic equipment and a recreation of his darkroom.

Take a Photo at McAfee Knob

DRAMATIC ROCK LEDGE

A rocky ledge jutting over Catawba Valley, **McAfee Knob** is one of the most recognizable spots on the Appalachian Trail (AT). Planting yourself on the ledge for a photo is de rigeur for day hikers and thru-hikers alike. From the ledge, the 270-degree panorama sweeps in North Mountain, Tinker Cliffs and the city of Roanoke. Flat rocks on adjacent cliffs make scenic perches for a picnic. Highlights along the 4.4-mile climb to the 3197ft-high knob include wooden walkways, trailside shelters and imposing boulders. For scenic variety, return on the fire road that parallels the trail.

Along with **Dragon's Tooth** and **Tinker Cliffs**, the knob is one of three visually striking rock formations west of Roanoke collectively known as the **Virginia Triple Crown**. All border the AT, and reaching them is a fun all-day hiking challenge. The trailhead is 16 miles northwest of downtown Roanoke on Rt 311. The main lot fills quickly.

SHUTTLE TO MCAFEE KNOB

The hike to the wildly photogenic **McAfee Knob** has become increasingly popular in recent years, and the trailhead parking lot on Rt 311 regularly fills to capacity. Parking on the highway is not permitted, and you risk a ticket or getting towed if you try. If the lot is full, you can park at other locations in Catawba, but this will extend the hike. Visit the Roanoke Appalachian Trail Club's website (ratc.org) for parking lot locations.

Another option is the seasonal shuttle that runs between the Park-and-Ride off I-81 at exit 181 and the trailhead, Friday through Sunday between March and November (wmcafeeshuttle.com). Also check visitroanoke.com, which dedicates a full page to exploring McAfee Knob.

WHERE TO STAY IN ROANOKE

Hotel Roanoke
First opened in 1882 and now part of the Hilton Group, this Tudor-style grand dame presides over downtown. **$$**

Fire Station One
Boutique hotel in a historic downtown firehouse filled with custom furnishings from the on-site furniture store. **$$**

Liberty Trust
This new 54-room hotel is in a former bank headquarters with smartly elegant rooms. **$$$**

BEST RESTAURANTS IN ROANOKE

Mama Jean's Barbecue
The fantastic BBQ from pitmaster Madison Ruckel is a gateway for a swoony collection of smoked fare. **$**

Tucos Taqueria Garaje
Choose gringo-style or traditional tacos at this convivial taco joint with 90 tequilas on the menu. **$**

Local Roots
Much of the menu rotates seasonally at this farm-to-table restaurant in Grandin Village. **$$**

Lucky
Perennial favorite serving seasonally inspired prix-fixe menu. Wonderful craft cocktails. **$$$**

River and Rail
This modern bistro uses wild-caught and organic local produce to scrumptious ends. **$$$**

Texas Tavern

Cycle along Mountains, Greenways & Gravel

BERMS, ROCK ROLLERS AND GREENWAYS

The only East Coast city designated a Silver-Level Ride Center by the International Mountain Bicycling Association, Roanoke is packed with challenging mountain biking trails, and it's a mountain biking hub for Southwest Virginia. With hundreds of miles of forest roads in **George Washington National Forest**, gravel riding is exploding here, too. Greenways also crisscross the city and surrounding towns, with a mix of short commuter trails and longer scenic paths.

The city's marquee route is the 14-mile **Roanoke River Greenway**, which tracks its namesake river past city

WHERE TO DRINK IN ROANOKE

Big Lick Brewing Co.
Lively downtown brewery serving innovative brews in a beer garden beneath a stop-you-in-your-tracks mural.

Lucky
Hunter Johnson crafts cocktails surely infused with magic at this intimate spot that's also beloved for its food.

Bar 1882
This circular bar in the Hotel Roanoke evokes a Victorian-era train station with a whisper of steampunk whimsy.

parks, the **Wasena City Tap Room**, an ice cream shop, a skatepark, antique-and-treasure-filled **Black Dog Salvage** and the **Green Goat** cafe. The greenways also link to more challenging trails on Mill Mountain. Rent bikes, stop for repairs, take a guided ride and get the biking lowdown at wonderful **Cardinal Bicycle & Cafe** in Grandin Village. Housed in a former grocery store, its has an in-house cafe, coffee shop, bar and post-ride showers. For greenway maps visit greenways.org.

Explore Downtown
MUSEUMS AND THE CITY MARKET

With its peaked central atrium and gently rolling rooftop, the eye-catching **Taubman Museum of Art** gives an appreciative nod to its mountain-and-valley setting. The jewel in Roanoke's cultural crown, the Taubman curates a small permanent collection that's strong in 19th- and 20th-century American works, including pieces by Norman Rockwell and Sally Mann. Four galleries host temporary exhibitions that really shine, including a recent retrospective of movie costumes designed by Ruth Carter, Oscar winner for Best Costume Design for *Black Panther: Wakanda Forever*. Train buffs can also walk a half-mile west to the **Virginia Museum of Transportation**, which is passionate about locomotives.

From the Taubman, stroll to **Center in the Square**, where you'll find four museums covering African American culture, pinball, science and imaginative play for children. The atrium aquariums and rooftop – with great views of the mountains – are free of charge; admission fees apply for other attractions. Outside, vendors with the **Historic City Market** – which opened in 1882 – sell produce, flowers and arts and crafts. Step into **Walkabout Outfitter** for outdoor gear and apparel, and **Chocolate Paper** for chocolate, greeting cards and gifts. Conclude at at the legendary **Texas Tavern**, a 1930s boxcar-sized diner where you can get 24/7 hamburgers or hot dogs for just $1.50. Trust us on ordering the infamous cheesy western. It's a must.

WHERE TO MOUNTAIN BIKE IN ROANOKE

Dan Lucas, rider experience manager at Cardinal Bicycle. @cardinal_bicycle

Why Roanoke?
You can ride to a fantastic trail system that's about 12 miles worth of trails from downtown. If you drive one hour from the center point of Roanoke you will probably hit 100 to 150 miles of trails.

A Recommendation for Families
Carvins Cove. It's a 12,000-acre park that is owned by the city. The second largest municipal park in the nation – which is pretty cool – it has over 60 miles of fantastic single track. It has everything from beginner to advanced level stuff.

A More Challenging Favorite
The Dody Ridge and Spec Mines loop. It's a 16-mile figure eight.

GETTING AROUND

Amtrak operates daily services between Roanoke and New York City (9½ hours) on the Northeast Regional line. These leave from the downtown train station and travel via Washington, DC (five hours). The airport is 5 miles north of downtown and serves the Roanoke and Shenandoah Valley regions.

Downtown Roanoke is fairly compact and walkable, and you can explore much of the city on a bike via its paved greenways, which also climb Mill Mountain. To access the Blue Ridge Parkway and trailheads along the Appalachian Trail, you will need your own vehicle.

Beyond Roanoke

Farm-dotted valleys and the gentle Blue Ridge Mountains roll south toward North Carolina. This is a picturesque region that showcases a rich Appalachian heritage.

Southwest Virginia, also known as the Blue Ridge Highlands, is one of the most attractive regions in the state. The Blue Ridge Parkway and the Appalachian Trail roll across the mountains here, home to scenic rivers, streams and lakes, and an abundance of trails. Mountain music is a given, and wineries and craft breweries offer tastings in small towns and on mountain slopes. The most rugged part of the region – and the state – is the southwestern tip of Virginia, where mountain music was born. Turn onto any side road, and you'll plunge into dark strands of dogwood and fir, and see fast streams and white waterfalls. Fiddle-and-banjo jams are your likely reward after a scenic day of hiking.

TOP TIP

For Crooked Road planning, the Friday Night Jamboree is in Floyd, and it's a 150-mile drive to the Carter Family Fold's Saturday night show.

Birthplace of Country Music Museum, Bristol

Friday Night Jamboree, Floyd Country Store

Friday Night in Floyd

OLD-TIME MUSIC AND COMMUNITY FUN

Tucked in the foothills of the Blue Ridge Mountains, 40 miles southwest of Roanoke (roughly an hour's driving), tiny, cute-as-a-postcard **Floyd** isn't much more than an intersection between Hwy 8 and Hwy 221. In fact, the whole county only has one stoplight. But downtown explodes during the weekly **Friday Night Jamboree** at the **Floyd Country Store**, and the surrounding sidewalks are packed when folks from far and wide converge for live old-time music and communal good cheer.

The Jamboree starts at 6:30pm, and for $10 you get three old-time bands playing gospel, then dance tunes and the chance to watch happy crowds dancing to regional heritage music. No smokin' and no drinkin', but there's plenty of dancin' (of the flat footing style). On warm nights, step outside to see musicians jamming on the sidewalks. There's also music on Saturdays during **Americana Afternoons**. You can check the website (floydcountrystore.com) for music the rest of the week. You might also see a farmer walk in with produce for the toppings at **Dogtown Roadhouse**, a lively pizzeria serving woodfired pies, including the Appalachian (apple butter

THE CRADLE OF COUNTRY MUSIC

The Victor Talking Machine Co recorded regional musicians in Bristol in 1927 and 1928, drawing the likes of the Carter Family, Jimmie Rodgers and a slew of undiscovered Appalachian musical talents. These recording sessions, now known as the **Bristol Sessions**, produced records that transformed the music industry by introducing mountain music – the forebear of country music – to the world.

These days, Bristol joyfully dubs itself the 'Birthplace of Country Music.' The **Birthplace of Country Music Museum** tells the whole story, while the vast **Bristol Rhythm & Roots Festival** in September celebrates regional sounds.

Fun fact? Bristol straddles the Virginia–North Carolina state line, which runs right down State St, the main drag. Look for the markers on the road.

WHERE TO SLEEP BEYOND ROANOKE

Hotel Floyd
Rooms are large, impeccably clean and very comfortable. Main St is a short walk away. **$$**

Bristol Hotel
In a former office building dating to 1925, this snazzy boutique hotel exudes finger-snapping cool. **$$**

Martha Washington Inn & Spa
Handsome Victorian-era hotel set amid formal gardens in Abingdon, with rocking chairs on the front porch. **$$$**

Mabry Mill

> **DON'T MISS: ABINGDON**
>
> One of the most photogenic towns in all of Virginia, **Abingdon** retains fine Federal and Victorian architecture in its historic district. With its many restaurants, hotels and cultural attractions, from art galleries and museums to the Barter Theatre (p138), Abingdon is an entertaining regional base for cultural pursuits. The magnificent Virginia Creeper National Recreation Trail (p138) also runs through town.

base, sausage, caramelized onion, cheddar and goat cheeses). This is another great spot for live music – think Americana and rock.

Exploring Rocky Knob & Mabry Mill
HIKING, WINE AND HISTORY

At some point during your 10.8-mile hike on the **Rock Castle Gorge Loop Trail**, you will curse your decision to hike here. A remarkably diverse trail in the **Rocky Knob Recreation Area** (Mile 169), it's worth the exertion, but it's still a hike into a steep gorge – meaning you're also going to have to climb out. But the awesome parts of the hike include an atmospheric cove of hardwood forest, seasonal blooms of mountain laurel and Catawba rhododendron, an enchanting stint along Rock Castle Creek and a pretty mountain-top pasture. Near the trailhead, you'll find a **visitor center** and a **campground**. By car, Rocky Knob is just over one hour south of Roanoke.

Just south, pull over at **Chateau Morrisette** (Mile 171.5). The swish tasting room here serves the signature Black Dog dry red and the Our Dog Blue, a blend of riesling, vidal blanc and traminette. There's also a restaurant. Continue south

WHERE TO EAT BEYOND ROANOKE

Girl & The Raven
Innovative and delicious Southern breakfasts and lunches with great vibe and nice owners. **$**

Blackbird Bakery
Folks flock here late night in Bristol for decadent sweets including cheesecake, cupcakes and pies. **$**

Mickey G's Bistro
Savor post-hike pizzas, pastas and sandwiches at this welcoming Italian bistro in Floyd. **$$**

to admire **Mabry Mill** (Mile 176): one of the most photographed buildings in the state, the mill nests in a gloriously green vale. Edwin Mabry's original sawmill and blacksmith shop still stand and often host demonstrations of Appalachian and Blue Ridge crafts.

Mountain Music along the Crooked Road

CELEBRATE THE SOUNDS OF APPALACHIA

Virginia's Heritage Music Trail, the 330-mile-long **Crooked Road** (myswva.org/tcr), passes nine major sites associated with mountain music and its history, along with eye-stretching mountain scenery. It's well worth taking a detour and joining the music-loving fans of all ages who kick up their heels (many arrive with tap shoes) at these festive jamborees. During a live show, you'll witness elders connecting to deep cultural roots and a new generation of musicians keeping that heritage alive and evolving.

Major venues include the festive Floyd Country Store on Friday nights (p135), the joyous Carter Family Fold in Hiltons on Saturday nights and the mountain-topping Blue Ridge Music Center near Galax, close to the North Caroline state line. They say you can find live music along the Crooked Road and its 60 or so affiliate venues every night of the year. Wayside kiosks along the route share historic tidbits and music. For a map and a live music calendar, visit thecrookedoadva.com.

Mountain Music's Blue Ridge Home

If you pull in at the right time, you'll encounter one of the best welcomes around: live mountain music played with heart. Programming at the **Blue Ridge Music Center** (Mile 213), an arts and music hub for the region, focuses on local musicians carrying on the traditions of Appalachian music. Headline performances are mostly on weekends in an outdoor amphitheater with fine mountain views, but local musicians give free concerts on the breezeway of the visitor center most days from noon to 4pm. There's a free 'Roots of American Music' exhibit on-site, too. The music center is a two-hour drive south of Roanoke.

The Birthplace of Mountain Music

In the tiny hamlet of Hiltons in southwest Virginia, you'll find one of the hallowed birthplaces of mountain music. The **Carter Family Fold** continues the musical legacy begun

ORIGINS OF MOUNTAIN MUSIC

A uniquely American genre, mountain music traces its roots to the earliest days of the country. European settlers brought their violins, also called fiddles, to the Virginia coast in the 1600s. Soon after, enslaved Africans were creating music with their own banjo-like instruments. The fiddle and banjo eventually joined forces and their combined sound migrated west.

In the Southern Appalachians, this fiddle-and-banjo music marinated with the songs and stories carried south from Pennsylvania by Scots-Irish and German immigrants, who established farms along the Great Wagon Road in the mid-1700s.

Today, mountain music is a universal term covering old-time music, which is often played for dancing, and the more modern sounds of bluegrass, known for its instrumental solos.

WHERE TO DRINK CRAFT BEER BEYOND ROANOKE

Chaos Mountain Brewing Co.
Eighteen beers on tap, with lots of easy-drinking ales. In Callaway, between Roanoke and Floyd.

Wolf Hills Brewing Co.
For satisfying microbrews and the occasional live music session, head to Wolf Hills in Abingdon.

Damascus Brewery
Sixty beers rotate across eight taps in Trail Town, steps from the Virginia Creeper Trail in Damascus.

> **THE BARTER THEATRE**
>
> Founded during the Depression, the **Barter Theatre** in Abingdon earned its name from audiences trading food for performances. Actors Gregory Peck and Ernest Borgnine cut their teeth on Barter's stage.
>
> A repertory theater, the Barter has two separate stages, and there's a play every night of the week except Mondays and Wednesdays. Recent productions include *Footloose, Sense & Sensibility* and *To Kill a Mockingbird*. Helpfully, the theater is within walking distance of several great restaurants.

by the talented Carter family way back in 1927. The founding members of the trio – discovered during the 1927 Bristol recording sessions (p135) – were AP Carter, his wife Sara and her sister-in-law Maybelle Carter. Their classic tunes include 'Keep on the Sunny Side' and 'Can the Circle Be Unbroken (By and By).'

Every Saturday night, the 800-person arena hosts first-rate bluegrass and gospel bands; there's also a **museum** with family memorabilia and the original mid-1800s log cabin where AP Carter was born. Johnny Cash, husband of June Carter (who was the daughter of Maybelle), played his last live show at the fold. You can learn more about the relationship between Johnny and June in the award-winning movie, *Walk the Line*.

Shows at the fold start at 7:30pm. With no nearby lodging, your best bet is to stay in Abingdon (30 miles east), Kingsport, TN (12 miles southwest) or Bristol, TN (25 miles southeast). The fold is about three hours southwest of Roanoke.

Outdoors at Appalachian Trail Days & Damascus

SLIP INTO YOUR CLEANEST CHACOS

Backpackers, thru-hikers and those who love them celebrate the Appalachian Trail during the three-day **Appalachian Trail Days** festival in **Damascus**, where the white-blazed footpath rolls right through the center of town. An epicenter of outdoor adventure 135 miles south of Roanoke, the town welcomes 20,000 annually for the event, which includes live music, guided nature walks, speakers and the lovingly ragtag Hikers Parade. Trail Days, which kicked off in 1987, is held the weekend after Mother's Day in May. Damascus is also a springboard for pedaling the famed **Virginia Creeper National Recreation Trail**, a 33.4-mile cycling and hiking trail on an old railroad corridor that rolls through the **Mount Rogers Recreation Area**, connecting lofty Whitetop with Damascus and eventually Abingdon.

For bike rentals and shuttles, try **Sundog Outfitters** and grab coffee at **Mojo's Trailside Cafe & Coffee House** next door. The eight-tap **Damascus Brewery** is just steps from the Virginia Creeper Trail. For stylish overnight digs, reserve a room at **Brinkwater's**.

> **GETTING AROUND**
>
> To explore the byways and country roads, you will need a car. The primary interstate here is I-81, running north-south through the western edge of the state. The Blue Ridge Parkway runs parallel to I-81, but it is much slower going. Roanoke is served by Amtrak train, with daily services linking it to New York (9½ hours) and Washington, DC (five hours). The major airport in the region is the Roanoke-Blacksburg Regional Airport.

NORTH CAROLINA HIGH COUNTRY

The High Country of North Carolina welcomes the Blue Ridge Parkway as it rolls in from Virginia with lively mountain music, craggy peaks and a slew of impressive trails and overlooks.

Several inviting communities here are convenient urban hubs for exploring the region and, in winter, enjoying the ski areas. Boone is a vibrant mountain town where the predominantly youthful inhabitants – many of them students at Appalachian State University – share a hankering for the outdoors. Renowned for its bluegrass musicians and Appalachian storytellers, the town is named after pioneer and explorer Daniel Boone, who often camped in the area. Downtown Boone features a fine assortment of low-rise, brick-broad, colonial revival, art deco and streamline moderne buildings.

A stately and idyllic mountain village, tiny Blowing Rock beckons from its perch at 4000ft above sea level, the only full-service town directly on the Blue Ridge Parkway. Shops, taverns and restaurants line its picture-perfect Main St.

TOP TIP

The High Country Host Regional Visitor Center at the corner of Hwy 321 and Edmisten Rd – look for the alpine-style A-frame – is a great resource and worth a stop. Their hiking recommendations are particularly good. An access road to the Blue Ridge Parkway is just south of here.

Boone

NORTH CAROLINA HIGH COUNTRY

BEST KID-FRIENDLY ATTRACTIONS

Tweetsie Railroad
This Wild West–themed amusement park features a 1917 coal-fired steam train that chugs past sheriff and bandits re-enactors.

Foggy Mountain Gem Mine
When your kids go through their treasure-hunting phase, Foggy Mountain is there for you. Enjoy panning for semi-precious stones with the kids.

Mystery Hill
Gravity gets kooky at Mystery Hill, where good-natured guides discuss the science of the anomalies with a side of hokiness.

River and Earth Adventures
These eco-conscious operators offer caving, tubing and rafting trips. Rentals, too.

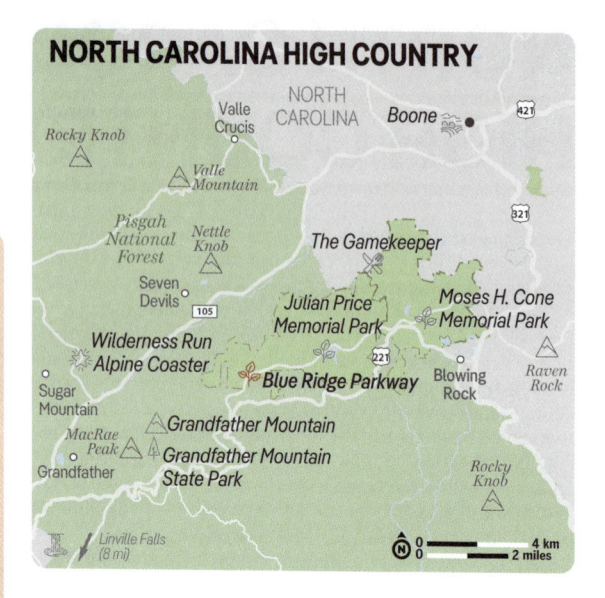

Scenic Walks along the Parkway

CARRIAGE TRAILS, WATERFALLS AND VIEWPOINTS

Three pleasant, easy-to-moderate trails and trail systems begin on the Blue Ridge Parkway near the town of Blowing Rock. Hikers and equestrians share more than 25 miles of carriage trails at **Moses H. Cone Memorial Park** (Mile 294) – site of the former estate of philanthropist and conservationist Moses H Cone, who made his fortune in denim. His 1901 manor, Flat Top, holds a museum and the **Parkway Craft Center**, where the Southern Highland Craft Guild sells superb Appalachian crafts.

Just south of Moses H. Cone Memorial Park, at **Julian Price Memorial Park** (Mile 296), the **Boone Fork Trail** rolls beside Boone Fork Creek as it flows toward the 25ft-high **Hebron Falls**. The trail crosses a fertile and ancient lakebed, meandering through a lush meadow and thick forest on its 1.5-mile journey to the falls. Along the way, you'll pass a footbridge at the junction of the Boone Fork Trail and the state-crossing **Mountain-to-Sea Trail**. Stay left at this junction to reach the falls. For a longer, more strenuous hike, continue past the falls on the Boone Fork Trail for a 5½-mile loop. You'll

WHERE TO EAT IN THE HIGH COUNTRY

Stick Boy Kitchen
Spare digs in Boone serving breakfast bagels, egg dishes and gourmet sandwiches. Coffee and cookies, too. $

Cardinal
Locals hunker down in this barnlike space in Boone for excellent burgers and regional brews. $

Bistro Roca
Lodge-like bistro with atmospheric bar in Blowing Rock, serving upscale New American cuisine. $$$

likely see lots of friendly dog-walkers on the way to Hebron Falls. The Boone Fork Trail begins in the picnic area beside the parking lot, near the restrooms.

A section of the **Tanawha Trail**, accessed from the **Rough Ridge parking area** (Mile 303), shoots to one of the finest overlooks in the High Country. Here, you'll climb to boardwalks with interpretive signage and views of the **Lynn Cove Viaduct** just south. Continue to the rock ledge for even loftier mountain-and-valley views.

Dining Wild at the Gamekeeper

A TOP PICK FOR CARNIVORES

Dinner at the **Gamekeeper** feels like a wild adventure. A twisty mountain drive from Boone ends at the base of a steep hill, with the restaurant perched overhead. One tip? Hand your keys to the valet and let them handle the parking. From here, climb the steps to the patio and the big-windowed dining rooms, which overlook poplars, maples and wild mountain scenery. Eclectic decor inside the stone-walled building keeps the vibe refreshingly offbeat, and the staff are friendly and accommodating. The menu showcases game mains – think emu, bison, elk, venison and wild trout – prepared with an innovative sense of fun, seen in dishes like the 'emo adobo' and the 'anteloaf'; there are vegetarian options available, too. While many say the restaurant is romantic, solos won't feel like total doofuses in the bar area. Make sure you reserve ahead of time, as this place gets busy.

Exploring Grandfather Mountain

LADDERS, CABLES AND BRIDGES

The highest of the Blue Ridge Mountains, **Grandfather Mountain** looms just north of the Blue Ridge Parkway, about 20 miles southwest of Blowing Rock. As a visitor destination, it's famous for the **Mile High Swinging Bridge**, the centerpiece of a private attraction that also includes hiking trails plus a small museum and wildlife reserve. Don't let a fear of heights scare you away; though the bridge is a mile above sea level, it spans a less fearsome chasm that's just 80ft deep. It's a bit pricey, and younger kids may be more enthralled than teens, but it's a classic destination, and crossing the swinging bridge is a notable regional adventure. Much of Grandfather Mountain – including its highest summit, **Calloway Peak** (5946ft) – belongs to **Grandfather Mountain State Park** (ncparks.gov). The park's 13 miles

THE ORIGINAL MAST GENERAL STORE

With its creaky wooden floors, 5¢ cups of coffee and barrels of candy, the **Original Mast General Store** in Valle Crucis (about 8 miles west of Boone) is a portal to the past. The first of the many Mast General Stores that now dot the High Country, this rambling clapboard building still sells many of the same products that it did back in 1883. As well as the traditional bacon, jams, axes and hard candy, you'll now find hiking shoes, gourmet local popcorn and French country hand-towels.

The nearby **Mast General Store Annex** is stocked with outdoor apparel, hiking gear and even more candy. It's worth visiting the Annex, too, especially if you love hard-to-find sweets.

WHERE TO STAY IN THE HIGH COUNTRY

Blue Ridge Tourist Court
Seven rooms in a revamped 1950s motor court are bright and snazzy, with modern amenities. **$$**

Green Park Inn
On the parkway, this clapboard hotel opened in 1891. The Eastern Continental Divide runs through the bar. **$$**

Horton Hotel
This 15-room boutique hotel in a former Studebaker showroom exudes contemporary cool, with a rooftop bar. **$$$**

> ### TRAVERSE THE LINN COVE VIADUCT
>
> The sinuous **Linn Cove Viaduct**, an elevated bridge hugging the slopes of Grandfather Mountain along Mile 304, was the last section of the Blue Ridge Parkway to be completed, opening in 1987. You'll hardly be aware you're on a bridge while driving this beautiful span, which was painstakingly built by landscape architects to protect the fragile flora and fauna and to blend in with the setting.
>
> For a view of the viaduct, climb the **Tanawa Trail** from the **Rough Ridge parking area** (Mile 303) and walk south to the boardwalks (p140).

of wilderness hiking-trails can be accessed for free at Mile 300 on the parkway.

If you want to tackle the epic **Grandfather Mountain Trail**, avoid strapping too many things to your daypack. This multi-challenge adventure squeezes between rocks, climbs steep ladders and shoots up boulders, with steel cables to help you maintain your balance. With all these obstacles, it's easy for water bottles and unsecured hiking poles to get knocked from your pack and fall great distances – not that we'd know anything about that. This 0.9-mile one-way hike ends with a final ladder climb to the summit of **MacCrae Peak**. Bring a picnic to enjoy while taking in the 360-degree views from 5845ft. For some variety, you can loop back on the **Underwood Trail**. Or, for a full-day adventure that includes serious rock scrambling, continue on the Grandfather Trail along the crest of Grandfather Mountain– where you'll see plenty of high-elevation spruce and fir trees. You'll end at the lofty summit of **Calloway Peak**. The full hike is 4.8 miles round-trip. Although much of the trail is within Grandfather Mountain State Park, the main trailhead is beside the Top Shop parking lot within the privately owned Grandfather Mountain. Fill out a hiking permit at the trailhead and return by 5pm. Note that if you have a fear of heights, this hike definitely won't be fun.

Careening Down a Mountain
SLOW CLIMB, WILD PLUNGE

As your alpine coaster slowly glides to the top of the track at **Wilderness Run Alpine Coaster**, it becomes clear that this steep approach was designed for maximum suspense, with plunging corkscrews and steep drops pressing in from every side. At the summit, one simple act – pressing down on the hand-operated brakes – slings your coaster forward. From here, you'll hurtle through heart-lurching drops and impossible turns, potentially at a maximum speed of 27mph. You can slow down by pulling up the brake levers – and it's likely you will. But just know, according to staff, that even at maximum speed you won't fly off the track. One bummer? The wait for a ride can be an hour in summer.

Relaxing in Downtown Boone
URBAN EXPLORATIONS AND A CLIMBING TOWER

There's a bronze **statue** of bluegrass legend Doc Watson in downtown Boone, and his guitar-strumming likeness is a focal point for local creativity. Someone might have draped a

---

WHERE TO DRINK IN THE HIGH COUNTRY

Booneshine Brewing Co.
Sip a Boonerang Trail Ale in the restaurant or beer garden. No moonshine, just Booneshine.

Blowing Rock Ale House
Serving 15 taps of craft suds, including pilsner and chocolate porter, in a 1940s lodge house.

Horton Hotel Rooftop Lounge
Enjoy cocktails and views of the mountains from a rooftop bar in downtown Boone.

Linville Falls

scarf around his neck first time you see him, but later in the day a guy with an accordion may be sitting on the bench beside him playing a tune.

The nearby multi-block King St is energized by a perpetual flow of students from nearby Appalachian State University. The **Rock Dimensions** outdoor climbing tower, which soars 40ft, epitomizes the city's outdoor spirit. Pop into the adjacent **Footsloggers** for outdoor gear and information about lessons and guided climbs with Rock Dimensions. For caffeine, order a small-batch coffee at **Expresso News**. For eating, good restaurants cluster along King and N Depot Sts. There's a Latin flavor to the menu at **Wild Craft Eatery**, with tacos and tamales aplenty, but it also offers Thai noodles, shepherd's pie and good vegetarian dishes. A gastropub, **Lost Province Brewing Co.**, serves pizza with its beers. One lunch standout is **FARM Cafe**, a nonprofit, pay-what-you-can community cafe, meaning everybody eats regardless of their means. Suggested prices are provided by the staff, most of whom are volunteers. Meals are delicious, hearty and locally sourced when possible.

ADMIRING LINVILLE FALLS

For a wonderful, short hike, head up the hour-long Erwin's View Trail to a spectacular view of **Linville Falls**. This moderate 1.6-mile round-trip hike offers great close-up views of the Linville River as it sweeps over two separate falls. Climb the wooded hillside beyond for two more magnificent long-range panoramas over the falls and, if you look downstream, see where the river crashes a further 2000ft to enter the **Linville Gorge Wilderness Area**. Swimming is forbidden at the falls.

GETTING AROUND

The High Country is an easy drive from Asheville or Charlotte, with Charlotte Douglas International Airport the closest air gateway, about 90 miles southeast. Downtown Boone and downtown Blowing Rock are compact and easily explored by foot, but you will want a car to explore the Blue Ridge Parkway and most of its attractions. Blowing Rock is 8 miles south of Boone via Hwy 321. Parking is $1 per hour in metered spaces in downtown Boone (Monday to Saturday, 8am to 5pm). Meters take coins and credit and debit cards.

ASHEVILLE

When you fall for Asheville, it will likely happen when you're wandering downtown. With its historic art deco buildings, whimsical public art, buzzing patios and soulful sidewalk buskers, it's an invigorating spot. Long famous as the home of the Biltmore Estate, today Asheville is the undisputed 'capital' of the North Carolina mountains and one of the coolest small cities in the South. Cradled in a sweeping curve of the Blue Ridge Parkway, it offers easy access to outdoor adventures. An abundance of homegrown microbreweries and a dynamic culinary scene have also become Asheville hallmarks.

Despite rapid gentrification, Asheville recognizably remains an overgrown mountain town that holds tight to its traditional roots. It's also a rare liberal enclave in the conservative countryside, home to a sizable population of artists and hard-core hippies. Alternative Asheville life is largely lived in neighborhoods such as the waterfront River Arts District and, across the French Broad River, West Asheville.

TOP TIP

Download the handy Passport app (passportparking.com), which facilitates paying downtown Asheville's parking meters and paid lots. Although there's very little free parking downtown, public garages are free for the first hour and cost just $2 per hour thereafter.

Biltmore Mansion

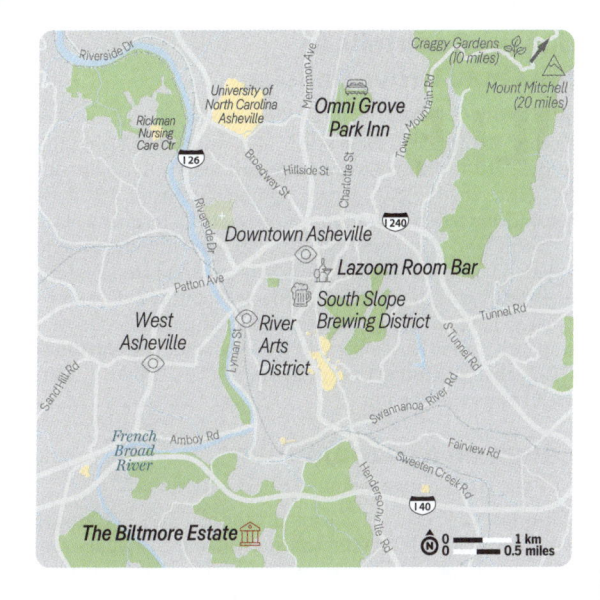

The Biltmore: Inside and Out

TOUR THE MANSION, WANDER THE GROUNDS

Blooms of pink and purple azalea celebrate spring with exuberance across the vast **Azalea Garden** – a dazzling sight you won't soon forget. And yes, you must tour the **Biltmore Mansion**, but if time allows, make sure you wander the gardens, which were designed by Frederick Law Olmstead. The gardens are particularly photogenic in April and May, and again in July and September, when 140,000 sunflowers bloom.

Modeled after three châteaux in France's Loire Valley and completed in 1895, the Biltmore Mansion is the largest privately owned home in the country. The estate and its grounds are Asheville's premier tourist attraction, visited by more than 1.7 million guests every year. Plan to spend a minimum of three hours exploring the house, the gardens and the winery at **Antler Hill Village**, a short drive from the house. House tours include an audio guide. Book ahead for guided specialty tours. To dig into the outdoor offerings – falconry, hiking, horseback and carriage rides – across its 8000 acres, stop by the Biltmore's **Outdoor Adventure Center**.

THE BILTMORE: HELPFUL HINTS

A word of warning: you may experience sticker shock when purchasing your Biltmore **admission ticket** – prices begin at $89 per person. To maximize your visit, plot out your day ahead of time, making sure you include the gardens, the winery and outdoor recreation.

With its crowds and size, the Biltmore is not conducive to a last-minute drop-in. There are no shuttles, so you will have to drive 5 miles from the mansion to **Antler Hill Village** and the winery.

Also be sure to visit the interesting 'Vanderbilts at Home and Abroad' exhibit, also at Antler Hill. The exhibit showcases the family's worldwide travels and includes a vast family tree, where you can trace newsman Anderson Cooper's family lineage.

WHERE TO SLEEP IN ASHEVILLE

Sweet Peas Hostel
A spick-and-span, well-run, contemporary hostel downtown with a loft-like open-plan space. **$**

Glo Best Western
Hip and minimalist accommodations from the Best Western chain with midrange prices near downtown. **$$**

Aloft
Trendy hotel with colorful rooms and knowledgeable staff in the thick of the downtown action. **$$$**

Sunset Cocktails at the Omni Grove Park Inn

COMMANDING VIEWS AND CRAFT COCKTAILS

Mother Nature does some of her best work just beyond the terrace at the **Omni Grove Park Inn**, particularly at sunset. With clouds aglow, forests and mountains on the horizon and crafted stone framing the view, it's an inspiring place to recap your day over cocktails. An arts-and-crafts-style lodge that opened in 1913, the hotel – with its stone exterior, soaring entrance hall and a couple of antique elevators – evokes a long-lost era of glamor and adventure. Make sure you stop by between November and January, when the **National Gingerbread House Competition** displays ornate gingerbread houses at the inn.

Laugh on a Lazoom Tour

RIDE THE WACKY PURPLE BUS

Corny jokes and exuberant actors are the hallmark of **Lazoom Tours**, which leads 90-minute historical tours through Asheville on an open-air purple bus. Introverts may panic for a hot second with all of the jokes and audience interaction, but it's all in good fun, and the local history is quite interesting! Buy beer and wine for the ride at the **Lazoom Room Bar** or at the brewery stop along the way. Specialty tours include the Fender Bender Band and Brewery Tour, as well as a ghost tour and a kids tour.

Embrace Creativity in the River Arts Distict

GALLERIES, MURALS AND CRAFT BEER

A dazzling sky-blue mural draws eyes toward **Wedge Brewing**, which rises temple-like from scrappy Foundy St in the **River Arts District**. It's the perfect centerpiece for this burgeoning neighborhood, a collection of aging warehouses along the river now filling with artists' studios and galleries. Indie restaurants, coffee shops and watering holes have also arrived, ready to provide the requisite support. Technicolor murals just about everywhere keep things real.

A good starting point for exploration is **Riverview Station**, a 1902 building now home to more that 60 artists who open up their work spaces and welcome questions and conversation. Along the adjacent Foundy St, also lined with galleries, you can

FOLK ART CENTER

Handcrafted chairs hang dramatically above the entranceway of the **Folk Art Center** (Mile 382), a gallery and shop showcasing the region's rich Appalachian heritage. The **Allanstand Craft Shop** here is the oldest craft shop in the country, and it sells artisan-made pieces – jewelry, pottery, glassworks, apparel and more – by members of the Southern Highland Craft Guild. Exhibits spotlight the history and craft behind various high-quality works from the Guild's permanent collection.

Stop by for the daily craft demonstrations, from March through December. The Folk Art Center is on the Blue Ridge Parkway, just 6 miles north of Asheville.

WHERE TO SLEEP IN ASHEVILLE

Bunn House
Six rooms and suites in a meticulously restored 1905 home, half a mile north of downtown. $$$

Omni Grove Park Inn
This arts-and-crafts-style stone lodge harks back to a bygone era of mountain glamor. $$$

The Foundry
The vibe is elevated steampunk at this posh newcomer in a former steel factory downtown. $$$

order a latte at **Summit Coffee**, devour a pulled pork sandwich at **12 Bones Smokehouse**, sip a pilsner at Wedge Brewing, catch a movie at **Grail Moviehouse** and practice your ollies at **RAD Skatepark**. Next door is **Marquee**, a design-driven arts market with curated vendors selling antiques, crafts, art, jewelry and home decor. It even has its own bar. The **Hop On Trolley** stops on Foundy St.

Nature Escapes on the Parkway

BALSAMS, WILD FLOWERS AND SUMMITS

The Blue Ridge Parkway curves around Asheville on its push toward Great Smoky Mountains National Park. An easy 30-mile drive from downtown will take you to the parking lot beside the summit of 6684ft-high **Mt Mitchell**, the highest point east of the Mississippi River and the namesake peak at North Carolina's original state park. A short but steep walk ascends to the observation deck and 360-degree views of the Black Mountains, a sub-range of Blue Ridge Mountains. Bring a jacket – the climate and ecosystems of the Black Mountains are similar to those of Canada. Return on the **Balsam Nature Trail**, a 1-mile walk through a lush, high-elevation forest; this trail resembles a portal to a Tolkein-esque magical kingdom.

A few miles south at **Craggy Gardens** (Mile 364), the **Craggy Gardens Pinnacle Trail** climbs to an impressive view of the surrounding mountains. The trail bursts with pink and purple Catawba rhododendron blossoms in mid-to-late July.

Sampling Craft Beer in South Slope

THE HEART OF BEER CITY USA

A walk through **South Slope Brewing District** is an easy introduction to 'Beer City USA' – an apt nickname for a metropolitan area with 50 brewery locations catering to a population of just 94,000. Were it not for the 11 million tourists who join them each year, that would be a lot of beer per person! Formerly a warehouse and industrial district, the pedestrian friendly South Slope – technically an extension of downtown – is the city's craft beer epicenter. With beer gardens, open-air taprooms and live music, the compact neighborhood feels like one big street party, especially on weekends.

Wicked Weed's all-sour taproom at the **Funkatorium** is a temple of tart and funk. The massive **Wicked Weed** mothership – with 58 taps – is just two blocks away. **HI-Wire** is also known for its sour beers and is a pleasant spot on a

BEST PLACES FOR SWEET TREATS

The Hop
Multi-location ice-cream shop with rotating casts of unusual flavors – like lavender vanilla – and vegan options.

Sugar and Snow Gelato
In the River Arts District, this sustainability-minded shop uses ingredients from North Carolina's farms, with seasonal fruit and non-dairy options.

Hole Donuts
Served piping hot in West Asheville, these tasty beauties include vanilla glaze and toasted almond sesame sugar.

Moo Cookie
Chocolate chip cookie connoisseurs, don't miss these hefty handcrafted versions sold in West Asheville.

WHERE TO SHOP IN ASHEVILLE

Marquee
This design-driven warehouse is just as eye-catching as its vast array of curated artistic creations.

New Morning Gallery
It's hard to leave empty-handed after exploring this two-story collection of high-end crafts in Biltmore Village.

Southern Highland Craft Guild
Jury-selected original pieces from artists in nine Appalachian states, with three Asheville stores.

CULINARY ADVENTURES DOWNTOWN

In a city dubbed 'Foodtopia,' showcasing the culinary treasures of just one neighborhood may seem unwise. But with its many top-tier restaurants, downtown Asheville is a worthy gateway for city-wide dining adventures.

Opened in 2011 by Chef Katie Button and her Catalan husband Félix Meana, **Cúrate** was at the forefront of Asheville's transformation into a nationally acclaimed dining destination. This convivial hangout celebrates the simple charms and sensual flavors of Spanish tapas, while adding an occasional Southern twist.

Irresistible Indian street food shines at no-reservations **Chai Pani**, named the Best Restaurant in America by the James Beard Foundation in 2022. Ever-popular **White Duck Taco** serves hefty soft tacos with globally inspired toppings.

Chai Pani

sunny afternoon. Never mind the menacing logo at **Burial**: this friendly joint whips up some of Asheville's finest and most experimental Belgian-leaning styles. Step inside the multi-story Green Mansion at long-running **Green Man** for English-style ales. Its original Dirty Jack's taproom has a scruffy, everybody's-welcome appeal – it's also a favorite of soccer fans.

Exploring Downtown Asheville

ACHITECTURE, ART AND A DRUM CIRCLE

Downtown Asheville promotes two self-guided walking tours: the 30-stop **Urban Trail** and the **Architecture Trail**. The latter passes 14 churches, skyscrapers and government buildings, many built in the 1920s with art deco, beaux art and neoclassical features. Pick up the informative walking-tours brochure covering both trails at the visitor center, or visit exploreasheville.com. Listen to the audio commentary as you walk.

At the southwest corner of **Pack Square Park**, the glass-fronted **Asheville Museum of Art** is the cultural centerpiece of downtown. Across Patton Ave, say hello to several

WHERE TO EAT IN ASHEVILLE

Sunny Point Cafe
Perennial breakfast fave in West Asheville, where the the huevos rancheros and people-watching are top notch. **$**

Chai Pani
Get in line for saag paneer, sloppy jai sandwiches and Indian street food at this James Beard winner. **$**

Admiral
This low-key restaurant in a concrete bunker is one of the state's finest New American restaurants. **$$**

strutting bronze pigs and turkeys – this jaunty menagerie gives a nod to trade in the region in the early 1800s. The 1928 **Kress Building** is noted for its terracotta ornamentation while Pritchard Park just ahead hosts the **Friday Night Drum Circle** (April to December).

Follow Haywood St to **Malaprop's Bookstore & Cafe**, cherished locally for its expert staff, who maintain a carefully curated selection of regional fiction and nonfiction. A forged-metal rendering of **three busy shoppers** confirms Haywood's St's longtime shopping creds. Look for beaux art details on the wedged-shaped **Flat Iron Building** on Wall St. Follow Walnut St to shop-lined **Broadway**, continuing back to Pack Square. In summer, Pack Square hosts **Shindig on the Green**, a concert series celebrating mountain music. Conclude with a dessert flight at **French Broad Chocolate Lounge**.

West Asheville's Best Eats

GOOD FOOD AND GREAT PEOPLE

Some call it bohemian, but 'resourceful' might be the better term for West Asheville, an emerging neighborhood west of the River Arts District and the French Broad River. Here, a slew of innovative restaurants, breezy cafes, vintage shops, record stores and coffeehouses are breathing new life into old buildings. These newcomers coexist with auto repair joints, hair salons and a diner or two. Great restaurants are a hallmark of the neighborhood, as is the **Dolly Parton and RuPaul mural** (738 Haywood Rd).

Breakfast on the patio at **Sunny Point Cafe** is recommended – with a biscuit! – while creative tacos and hospitable service make **Taco Billy** a new local favorite at lunch. Recently reimagined, the appealingly divey **Tastee Diner** delivers comfort fare with personality – we're looking at you, fried chicken and grits brekkie bowl. Wine, small plates and amazing service join forces at breezy **Leo's House of Thirst**, where tap wine bottles are $25 on Tuesdays. **Nine Mile** serves decadent Caribbean dishes, while national powerhouse **New Belgium Brewing Co.** oversees a popular taproom and production facility beside the French Broad River.

MOUNTAIN MUSIC: WESTERN NORTH CAROLINA

For locally grown fiddle-and-banjo music, grab your dance partner and head deep into the North Carolina hills. Regional shows and music jams are listed on the **Blue Ridge Music Trails** (blueridgemusicnc.com) and **Blue Ridge Heritage Area** (blueridgeheritage.com) websites. Cities embrace the region's musical heritage, too. **Shindig on the Green** in Asheville hosts old-time and bluegrass bands most Saturday nights in summer in Pack Square.

One of the South's premier music festivals is **Merlefest**, held in April in Wilkesboro, about two hours north of Asheville. Created by legendary guitarist Doc Watson after his son Merle died in 1985, the festival has been showcasing the best in bluegrass, folk and Americana since 1988.

GETTING AROUND

For a short weekend trip to downtown and the South Slope Brewery District, there is no need to have a car. A quick rideshare or taxi ride will get you to neighborhoods within a mile or two of the city center, including the River Arts District and West Asheville. For trips to the Blue Ridge Parkway and the Biltmore Estate, you will need your own wheels. Asheville Rides Transit runs 18 bus routes across downtown and to outlying neighborhoods, but buses do not stop at the Biltmore Estate. For car-free travelers, a Gray Line hop-on hop-off trolley tour may be the best option during a short visit. The red trolleys stop at 10 attractions across town.

Beyond Asheville

The forests surrounding Asheville are a little feral, home to wild rivers, rugged trails, booming waterfalls and one crazy rock slide.

Rolling across western North Carolina and into the High Country, the contiguous Pisgah and Nantahala National Forests hold more than one million acres of dense hardwood trees and windswept mountain balds, some of the country's best white-water rapids, and sections of the Appalachian Trail and Blue Ridge Parkway. Breezy mountain towns are gateways for adventure and compelling destinations in their own right, with history, culture and good eats aplenty. Brevard, a haven for mountain bikers, is one of those charming mountain towns that set travelers daydreaming of putting down roots. Remote Bryson City may be small, but it welcomes paddlers, cyclists, hikers and steam-train fans with a big heart. We promise, regionwide, you won't get bored.

TOP TIP

The dining room at the popular Sierra Nevada Taproom & Restaurant is closed Tuesday and Wednesday – but you can still get beer, hot dogs and a few snacks on the back porch.

Museum of the Cherokee Indian

Chimney Rock

Relaxing on Chimney Rock

BIG CLIMB, BIGGER VIEW

The stupendous 315ft monolith known as **Chimney Rock** towers above the slender, forested valley of the Rocky Broad River on a gorgeous 28-mile drive southeast of Asheville. Protruding in naked splendor from soaring granite walls, its flat top bears a fluttering American flag and overlooks Lake Lure and Hickory Nut Gorge. You can climb to the top via the 499 steps of the **Outcropping Trail**, or simply ride the elevator deep inside the rock. Admission is charged.

Cherokee History & Culture

SEQUOYA AND TRAILS OF TEARS

An impressive 22ft-high wooden carving of Sequoya, who created the Cherokee writing system, marks the entrance to the **Museum of the Cherokee Indian**, about one hour west of Asheville. Three carved tears recall the forced relocation of the Cherokee and other indigenous tribes on the Trail of Tears (p152). Inside, the museum traces Cherokee history from the tribe's Paleo-Indian roots onward. Its villain is Andrew

SIERRA NEVADA TAPROOM & RESTAURANT

This monstrous restaurant and taproom in Mills River, the first East Coast venture from California-based **Sierra Nevada Brewing**, is a bustling pit stop for outdoor adventurers headed back to Asheville from Pisgah National Forest and Brevard. With great food, live music, an outdoor patio, 22 taps and a popular free tour, it's become a destination in its own right. You can catch live music in the outdoor amphitheater on Tuesday and Wednesday evenings and on Saturdays and Sundays in the afternoon.

The wide-ranging gift shop sells Sierra Nevada mustard, Hazy Little Thing bucket hats (named for its popular IPA) and, of course, beer. The brewery is 20 miles south of Asheville.

WHERE TO STAY BEYOND ASHEVILLE

Nantahala Outdoor Center
This fun place (p153) has a range of accommodations for those gearing up for rafting and other adventures. **$**

Everett Hotel
Stylish digs with a bistro in Bryson City, within walking distance of the scenic train rides. **$$$**

Pisgah Inn
Open more than 100 years, this small lodge comes with amazing views of the mountains. **$$$**

THE CHEROKEE & THE TRAIL OF TEARS

Under the Treaty of Holston, signed with the US government in 1791, the Cherokee were guaranteed the right to remain in perpetuity in northern Georgia and western North Carolina. Within 50 years, they had been rounded up at bayonet point and moved west of the Mississippi, on a forced march remembered as the Trail of Tears. Thousands died en route.

Cherokee today is the home of the Eastern Band of Cherokee Indians – the descendants of those who managed to hide in the mountains rather than be expelled. It is also the headquarters of the **Qualla Boundary**, an area of tribal-owned land that is not officially a reservation. The **Trail of Tears National Historic Trail** links the key sites (mnps.gov/tte).

Pisgah National Forest

Jackson, who made his name fighting alongside the Cherokee, but, as president, condemned them to the heartbreak of the Trail of Tears. One fascinating section follows the progress through 18th-century London of a Cherokee delegation that sailed to England in 1762. Authentic Cherokee craftwork is for sale at the **Qualla Arts & Crafts Mutual** across the street.

Rocking the Cradle of Foresty

WATERFALLS AND A ROCK SLIDE

Leafy trees form a deep-green tunnel around US 276 in late spring and summer, pressing in tight as the road rises from Brevard to the Blue Ridge Parkway. Traversing the southern end of the most spectacular section of **Pisgah National Forest**, this 15-mile stretch of highway is part of the **Forest Heritage Scenic Byway** – a staid name for a 76-mile loop that is a blast to explore, 30 miles south of Asheville. From Brevard, first up is **Davidson River Campground**. This riverside campground is in an idyllic wooded setting beside the wonderful **Art Loeb Trail**, a 30-mile peak jumper favored

WHERE TO EAT BEYOND ASHEVILLE

Meatballs Pizzeria
From the owners of Ilda, this wood-fired pizza joint serves Neapolitan and Roman-style pizzas. $

River's End Restaurant
Devour ribeyes, trout and fried chicken after hiking or river rafting in the Nantahala Gorge. $$

Square Root
Everyone in Brevard is here or on the way for delicious steaks, seafood and creative appetizers. $$

by backpackers. The informative **Pisgah Ranger Station Visitor Center** is across the highway.

Ahead, ooh and ahh at the glorious six-story **Looking Glass Falls**. For total exhilaration, don your bathing suit at popular **Sliding Rock Recreation Area**. Here, a natural 60ft slide of smooth, gently sloping granite – fed by 11,000 gallons of cool stream water per minute – propels bathers into a mountain pool. The **Cradle of Forestry** – an actual place! – marks the spot where the US first attempted scientific forestry management back in 1895.

Adventures at Nantahala Outdoor Center

BASE CAMP FOR WILD RIVER FUN

A true crossroads for adventure, the **Nantahala Outdoor Center** (NOC) sits at the junction of the state-crossing Appalachian Trail, the wild Nantahala River and scenic US 74. This huge and highly recommended outfitter specializes in wet 'n' wild rafting trips down the Nantahala. Its 500-acre main campus – it runs several adventure outposts regionally – also offers ziplining and mountain biking, and it has its own lodge, cabins, bunkhouses and campsites. You'll also find several dining options (some seasonal) and a beer joint (open May through September). Even if you're not adventuring, you can sit by the river and enjoy a beer while watching kayakers navigate the rapids. For sandwiches and pizza, try **Rivers End**, a wooden cabin (open year-round) that overlooks the Nantahala. You may see backpacks lined up by the entrance. NOC is 14 miles southwest of Bryson City and 75 miles southwest of Asheville.

Bryson City: Trains, Bikes & Rafts

MOUNTAIN AND RIVER SCENERY

Bryson City feels like a territorial outpost, a last bastion of civilization beside an untamed wilderness – known here as the **Nantahala Gorge**. To explore the gorge without driving, climb aboard the **Great Smoky Mountains Railroad** steam train, which chugs west from Bryson City into the wilds of the gorge with an indomitable, can-do spirit – game for whatever craziness Mother Nature throws its way. The trip is one of two scenic train excursions, each lasting around four hours, that leave the station on different routes – either east along the Tuckasegee River to Dillsboro, or southwest to the spectacular gorge. Up to four trains run daily on peak summer and

MT PISGAH

For an hour or two of scenic hiking that culminates in a panoramic view, pull into the parking lot beside the Mt Pisgah Trailhead (Mile 407). The 1.6-mile one-way trail climbs to the 5721ft summit of **Mt Pisgah**, topped by a TV tower. The going gets steep and rocky, but your reward is a view of the French Broad River Valley and **Cole Mountain**, made famous by Charles Frazier's novel, *Cold Mountain*. (Unhelpfully, the names 'Cold' and 'Cole' are often used interchangeably.)

One mile south is a campground, general store, a restaurant and the **Mt Pisgah Inn**, which also has fabulous mountain views. The inn and restaurant are open April though October.

WHERE TO DRINK CRAFT BEER BEYOND ASHEVILLE

Sierra Nevada Taproom & Restaurant
Twenty-two taps in the Mills River Taproom, with pub fare; 30 minutes from Asheville.

Innovation Brewing
The name fits for this welcoming brewery in Sylva with an appealing variety of choice across 25 taps.

Lazy Hiker Brewing Co
Get lazy with a helles-style beer inside its stonewalled digs on Main St in Sylva.

BLUE RIDGE SNORKEL TRAIL

Snorkeling? In the mountains? Yep, river snorkeling is a thing in the mountains of western North Carolina, where you can search for spotfin chub, eastern hellbenders and other colorful fish and amphibians in clear mountain waterways. Established in 2023, the **Blue Ridge Snorkel Trail** (ncfishes.com/blue-ridge-snorkel-trail) curates nine public-access destinations for snorkeling. Check the website for details about fish and amphibians to look for at each site. You might see tangerine darters in the Tuckaseegee River in Bryson City and saffron shiners in the Mills River south of Asheville. For a guided trip near Asheville and Brevard, consider **Oxbow River Snorkeling**.

fall weekends. There are five classes of seating, from open-air gondolas to all-adult first class with tables and large windows.

The train rides are the marquee activity in tiny Bryson City, which straddles the Tuckasegee River. It's a convenient base for exploring Great Smoky Mountains National Park, but it's an adventure destination in its own right: it's close to whitewater rafting and kayaking. For a pleasant respite after a day of adventuring, settle in on the patio at **Bryson City Outdoors**, an outdoor store with a bar. Try friendly **Bryson City Bicycles** for rentals, repair and expert advice about local trails.

Exploring Sylva
ENJOY OLD-SCHOOL CHARM

Tiny, downtown **Sylva** looks like it fell out of the sky, straight from the 1950s, its walkable, multi-block main drag cinematically capped by the magnificent **Jackson County Courthouse**, which is perched atop a hill. The delicious beers at **Innovation Brewing**, the wonderful **City Light Bookstore** and numerous good restaurants, not to mention the pervasive Southern hospitality, make Sylva a worthwhile detour from Great Smoky Mountains National Park, just 20 miles north. Recommended dining options include hearty Southern breakfasts at **Lucy in the Rye** and Italian–Appalachian fare at stylish **Ilda**. A perfect post-hike reward? Sitting creekside with an easy-drinking ale at **Innovation Brewing**. It will take just under an hour to drive to Sylva from Asheville.

Adventures in Nantahala National Forest
HIKING AND MOUNTAIN-BIKING A VAST REGIONS

The expansive **Nantahala National Forest** covers more than half a million acres of the state's westernmost portion, extending south from Great Smoky Mountains National Park all the way to the South Carolina and Georgia state lines. For hikers and mountain bikers, the most popular area of the forest is the **Tsali Recreation Area** in the Cheoah Ranger District. Tsali (pronounced SAH-lee) is about 20 minutes west of Bryson City.

GETTING AROUND

You will need a car to explore the mountain towns and national forests surrounding Asheville. Brevard and Bryson City have compact and walkable downtowns with lots of free parking. Cherokee is a bit more spread out, meaning you'll likely need a car to explore.

Highways around Asheville can get congested in late afternoon. If you're not in a rush, the Blue Ridge Parkway and US 276 may be a less stressful route from Asheville to Brevard. The best route to Sylva and Bryson City from Asheville is US 74 west. To get to Cherokee, you can follow US 74 west or US 19 south, which is a little twistier, from Asheville. Driving the Blue Ridge Parkway to Cherokee is also an option, but it is, again, slower going. Note that many roads just beyond Asheville are two-lane mountain roads, which may slow your estimated pace.

THE GUIDE

NORTH CAROLINA GATEWAYS & BLUE RIDGE PARKWAY ASHEVILLE

Jackson County Courthouse, Sylva

SHENANDOAH NATIONAL PARK

ADVENTURE BECKONS AT EVERY BEND

They built Shenandoah National Park with drivers in mind, unleashing a spectacular 105-mile scenic byway across the crest of the Blue Ridge Mountains.

A road trip through Shenandoah National Park is a drive with just the good bits left in. From the mountain-topping Skyline Drive, views of lonely farms, fertile valleys and mountain peaks intersperse the woodsy backdrop with perfect cinematic pacing. Seventy overlooks and a string of trailheads line the drive, which links Front Royal in the north with Waynesboro in the south. You'll likely see rabbits and white-tailed deer as your car eats up the miles. Seasonal charms – wildflowers in spring, colorful foliage in fall – keep the views engaging year-round.

The park was authorized in 1926, and the Civilian Conservations Corps built its trails and overlooks in subsequent years, primarily during the Great Depression. President Franklin Delano Roosevelt dedicated Shenandoah on July 3, 1936, during a ceremony in Big Meadows. This scrubby patch of wild grass is today one of the park's two hubs. The other is Skyland Resort, where the back terrace serves up mood-boosting sunsets. Today, the park draws hikers and backpackers with more than 500 miles of trails, including 101 miles of the Appalachian Trail, which blazes through on its 14-state journey between Georgia and Maine. Waterfalls are another draw, and leashed dogs are allowed on all but a handful of trails. Roosevelt said the park was a work of conservation built for 'enriching the character and happiness of our people.' That mission succeeds to this day.

THE MAIN AREA

SKYLAND & BIG MEADOWS
Waterfalls and lofty views. **p160**

Above: Skyline Drive (p163). Left: White-tailed deer

Find Your Way

Shenandoah National Park stretches 105 miles along the crest of the Blue Ridge Mountains in western Virginia. The park is divided into three districts: north, central and south. Mile markers border Skyline Drive, which rolls though all three districts.

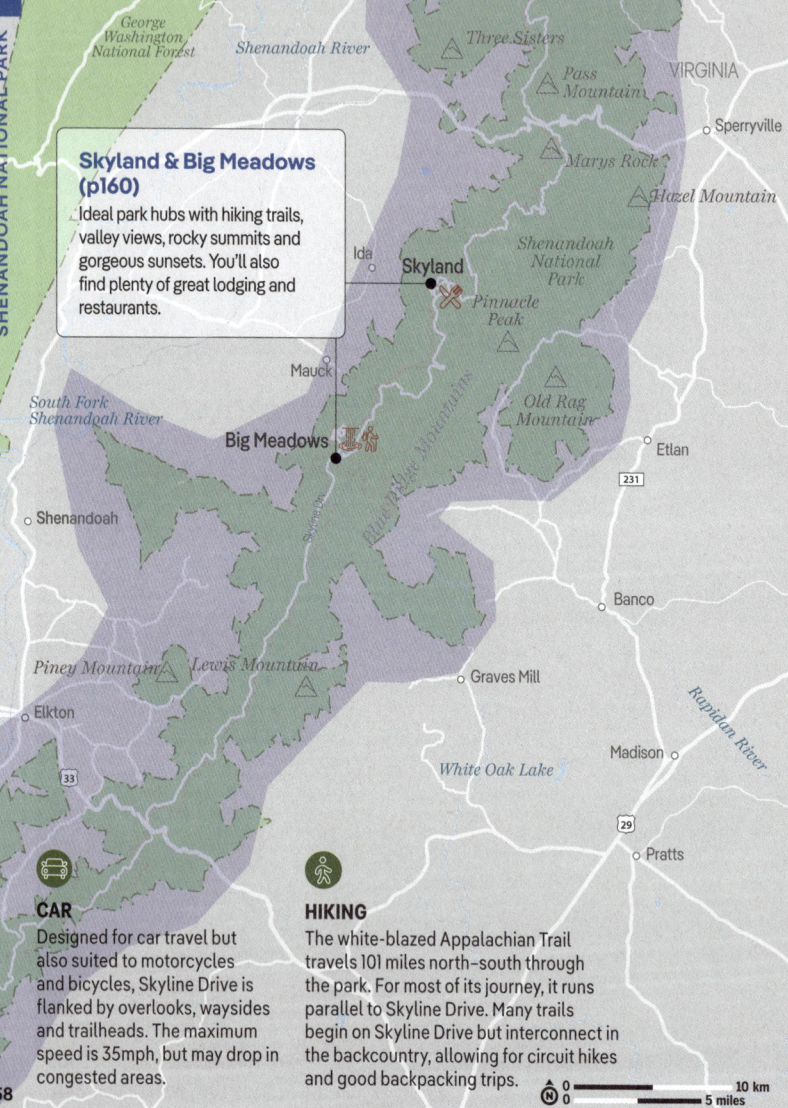

Skyland & Big Meadows (p160)

Ideal park hubs with hiking trails, valley views, rocky summits and gorgeous sunsets. You'll also find plenty of great lodging and restaurants.

CAR

Designed for car travel but also suited to motorcycles and bicycles, Skyline Drive is flanked by overlooks, waysides and trailheads. The maximum speed is 35mph, but may drop in congested areas.

HIKING

The white-blazed Appalachian Trail travels 101 miles north–south through the park. For most of its journey, it runs parallel to Skyline Drive. Many trails begin on Skyline Drive but interconnect in the backcountry, allowing for circuit hikes and good backpacking trips.

Dark Hollow Falls (p162)

Plan Your Time

Weekend travelers, Shenandoah is your happy place. City dwellers seeking a quick hit of inspiration can drive here in just a few hours from up and down the East Coast.

Pressed for Time

Base yourself centrally in **Big Meadows** (p160). Start by learning the history of park at the visitor center, then hike to the summit of **Hawksbill** (p161), or pack a picnic for a longer hike to **Rapidan Camp** (p162). Afterwards, dine at **Big Meadows Lodge** (p161), then attend an evening ranger talk followed by stargazing in the meadow – they say 2500 stars are visible. The next morning, admire the beauty of **Dark Hollow Falls** (p162).

Two Days to Explore

Savor a hearty Southern breakfast in **Winchester** (p165), then tour **Luray Caverns** (p165). Enter the national park at Thornton Gap to explore **Skyline Drive** (p163) and the roadside trails for the day. Enjoy the sunset at **Skyland Resort** (p163) before settling into your cabin. The next morning, drive south for a **waterfall hike** (p162). Grab lunch in Waynesboro before walking the **Blue Ridge Tunnel** (p167).

Seasonal Highlights

SPRING
It's wildflower season in the park, which hosts a wildflower weekend in early May. Bird-watching is also good.

SUMMER
With warm temperatures and traveling families, June, July and August constitute high season.

FALL
Colorful fall foliage draws large numbers of leaf peepers. Check the park's social media channels for updates on where to go when.

WINTER
Many facilities are closed November through February, but Skyline Drive remains open. Check online for alerts before visiting.

SKYLAND & BIG MEADOWS

With the western horizon aglow and a cold beverage in your hand, the terrace at Skyland is one of the most enchanting places in Virginia to kick back and appreciate the handiwork of Mother Nature. Perched on a ridge, this inviting resort is a place to pause after a day of driving and adventuring along Skyline Drive.

Just 10 miles south, Big Meadows is the epicenter of Shenandoah National Park, where nature, history and beauty join forces beside a charismatic mountain meadow. Trails drop to waterfalls, rangers explain the wonders of nature and a lifelike statue of a Civilian Conservation Corps worker reminds us that this bustling place is as a result of a lot of hard work. At night, you'll feel as if you can touch the stars from the wilds of the meadow, a haven for wildlife and mountain flora.

TOP TIP

The park and the Byrd Visitor Center are open year-round. Lodges, campgrounds, wayside stores and the Dickey Ridge Visitor Center are open, in most cases, from late March through mid-November. Skyline Drive may close occasionally due to snow or bad weather.

Hawksbill Summit

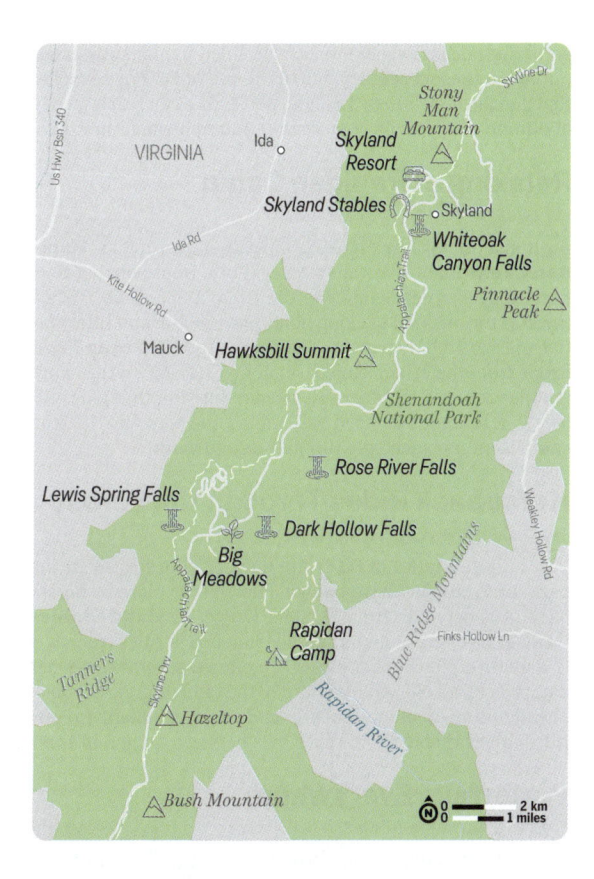

Top of the Park: Hawksbill Summit

LOOP HIKE TO BIG VIEWS

With a short climb on the Appalachian Trail, a fun scramble across boulder fields and a 360-degree view of farm-dotted valleys and rolling mountains, the 2.8-mile loop hike to the summit of **Hawksbill**, the highest point in the park at 4051ft, is a rewarding half-day adventure. Begin at the **Hawksbill Gap parking lot** (Mile 45.6), then link with the Appalachian Trail, the Salamander Trail and the Lower Hawksbill Trail along the way. Several other trails intersect in this area, so longer loop hikes are possible. The area below the summit's viewing platform has served as a protected nesting area for

GETTING STARTED IN SHENANDOAH NATIONAL PARK

Admission to the park is valid for seven consecutive days and costs $30 per vehicle, $25 per motorcycle and one passenger, and $15 per individual (16 years or older) arriving by foot, bicycle, bus or trail.

The primary road through the park is the 105-mile **Skyline Drive**. Lined with overlooks and trailheads, this scenic byway runs along the top of the Blue Ridge Mountains and bisects the park. There are four entrance stations. The **Front Royal** entrance is in the northern end of Skyline Drive, while the **Rockfish Gap** entrance is at the southern end. The **Thornton Gap** entrance is east of Luray, and **Swift Run Gap** is east of Elkton.

WHERE TO STAY IN SKYLAND & BIG MEADOWS

Skyland Resort
Enjoy grand views of the Shenandoah Valley from premium hotel-style rooms and small cabins (p163). $$

Big Meadows Lodge
Twenty-nine lodge rooms and cabins nestle in the woods near waterfalls, a visitor center and its namesake meadow. $

Lewis Mountain Cabins
Lewis Mountain has pleasant cabins with hot showers. Smaller cabins have bunk beds, but no linens or bathrooms. $

BEST FAMILY HIKES

Stony Man Trail (Mile 41)
An easy climb to a cool rock outcrop with views across the Shenandoah Valley; 1.6 miles round-trip.

Limberlost Trail (Mile 43)
This fully accessible 1.3-mile loop though mountain laurel is a kid-minded TRACK trail with nature brochures and one cool-looking rock formation.

Bearfence Mountain (Mile 56)
This 1.2-mile loop includes an adventurous rock scramble and a 360-degree view.

Blackrock Summit (Mile 84)
This short loop hike with views of Massanutten Mountain features an interactive TRACK trail with brochures and kiosk.

FOR MORE TRACK TRAILS

Read the Toolkit to find out more about **TRACK trails** (p174) in this region.

---

peregrine falcons, whose numbers declined significantly in the middle of the last century due to the use of DDT, a pesticide that damaged their eggs. In flight, peregrines can reach speeds of 60mph, and speeds of more than 150mph when they dive.

Relaxing at Rapidan Camp
EXPLORE A PRESIDENTIAL GETAWAY

Built in a thickly forested hollow between two creeks, **Rapidan Camp** doubled as the summer White House during Herbert Hoover's presidency and the Great Depression. Today, three of the original 13 camp buildings remain, and interpretive markers tell their story. The moderate **Mill Prong Trail** drops from the Milam Gap parking lot (Mile 52) to the camp (4 miles round-trip). There's a stream crossing that kids will love – across an oversized log – along the way. Visiting the camp is an unexpectedly fun half-day adventure.

Horseback Rides Through the Forest
SADDLE UP FOR A RIDE

Two hundred miles of trails are open to equestrians in the park, but you don't have to own a horse to explore by horseback. A short walk from Skyland Lodge, **Skyland Stables** (Mile 42.5) offers one-hour guided horseback rides from early May through October. Rides are offered several times per day, passing an old apple orchard in the Limberlost area. Book ahead online or simply walk up and check availability. Pony rides are available for younger kids between noon and 1pm.

Waterfalls Everywhere
PRETTY CASCADES NEAR SKYLINE DRIVE

Anticipation builds as you drop through the forest to **Dark Hollow Falls**, with slick rocks and thick moss slowly overtaking the scene, and the sound of splashing cascades becoming the soundtrack. Even with the inevitable crowds – the trail is near the **Byrd Visitor Center** – the pathway feels like a place of enchantment. And the creek-fed falls, dropping 70ft, are a beautiful sight.

For waterfall fans, the Central District holds an impressive collection of cascades, and you can view several on loop hikes along the district's interconnecting trails. In spring, wildflowers line the path to **Rose River Falls** (Mile 49; 2.6-miles round-trip), which expands into several parallel falls after rainstorms. This is a good alternative if crowds are heavy at Dark Hollow. A steep, rocky trail behind Big

---

WHERE TO CAMP IN SHENANDOAH NATIONAL PARK

Big Meadows Campground
This 217-site campground can feel crowded, but it has good facilities and is a great base for exploring. $

Lewis Mountain Campground
Smaller, secluded campground with 31 first-come, first-served spots, a camp store, bathroom and coin-operated showers. $

Backcountry Camping
Obtain a permit – currently free – then find the right secluded spot. The park website lists camping areas. $

Meadows Campground drops 1 mile to the 81ft-high **Lewis Spring Falls**. For solitude and a workout, head into the wilderness for a view of 34ft-tall **Cedar Run Falls** (Mile 45; 4 miles round-trip). A 2.3-mile trail descends to the 86ft-high **Whiteoak Canyon Falls** (Mile 42), the second highest in the park, and probably its most well-known.

Savoring the Scenery at Skyland

RIDGELINE RESORT WITH VALLEY VIEWS

Founded in 1888, the spectacularly located **Skyland Resort** commands views over the Shenandoah Valley countryside. The best place to appreciate the views is from the large patio between the restaurant and the lobby – particularly at sunset. You'll find a variety of room types across 28 buildings, including recently renovated premium rooms, rustic but comfy cabins, a taproom with a live entertainment program, and a full-service dining room. You can also arrange horseback rides from here. The resort opens a month or so before Big Meadows in the spring and stretches across 27 acres along mile markers 41 and 42.

Big Nature at Big Meadows

PARK HUB WITH NATURE APLENTY

While wandering the animal paths that crisscross the grasses of **Big Meadows**, you might pass a butterfly hunter carrying their best camera and looking for their next shot. Or a group of budding scientists taking an educational ranger walk. Or a lone hiker looking for, well, something. It's a unique, if not always gorgeous, place to explore.

Franklin Delano Roosevelt held the park's dedication ceremony here in 1936. An important habitat for wildlife, especially deer, this high-elevation wetland meadow, also known as a fen, is surrounded by forests. It's home to a diverse collection of plants, including 16% of the park's rarest plant species. Big Meadows is also the epicenter of the park, sitting in the middle of Skyline Drive at Mile 51. Here you'll find a visitor center, a gas station and a small wayside restaurant. There's also a camp store, where you can buy craft beer – Big Meadows IPA, Limberlost Lager – named after park attractions. A small museum delves into the creation of the park and traces park desegregation efforts from 1932 until 1950. A lodge and campground, plus a restaurant and taproom, are a short drive west of the visitor center.

FLYING ALONG SKYLINE DRIVE

A 105-mile road running down the spine of the Blue Ridge Mountains, Shenandoah National Park's **Skyline Drive** is one of the most scenic drives on the East Coast. You're constantly treated to an impressive view, but keep in mind the road is bendy, slow-going (35mph limit) and congested in peak season. It's best to start this drive just south of Front Royal, VA. From here, you'll snake over Virginia wine and hill country.

Numbered mileposts mark the way, and there are lots of pull-offs. One favorite is near Mile 51.2, where you can take a moderately difficult 3.6-mile-loop hike to Lewis Spring Falls.

GETTING AROUND

Driving your own car is the best way to reach Skyland and Big Meadows. From Washington, DC, it's a 95-mile drive west to the Thornton Gap entrance. From I-81, your best bet for reaching Skyland or Big Meadows is by entering the park at either Thornton Gap or Swift Run Gap – efficiency will depend on your location. There are no shuttles within the park, and trailheads and overlooks can be miles apart along Skyline Drive. There is one gas station, located at Big Meadows.

Beyond Skyland & Big Meadows

Fun awaits in every direction from Skyland and Big Meadows, from scenic drives and rocky hikes to a cavern tour and waterfalls.

Tucked between the Blue Ridge Mountains and the Allegheny Mountains, the 200-mile-long Shenandoah Valley is known for its picturesque small towns, farms, microbreweries, battlefields and caverns. Local lore says Shenandoah was named for a Native American word meaning 'Daughter of the Stars.' One of the most beautiful places in America, this was once the western border of Colonial America, settled by Scots-Irish and Germans, most traveling south on the Great Wagon Road, now Route 11. Outdoor activities such as hiking, cycling, camping, fishing, horseback riding and canoeing abound. Driving through the valley and the mountain foothills is unforgettable, particularly in the fall when the palette of the canopy ranges from russet red to copper-tinged orange.

TOP TIP

There is only one gas station in Shenandoah National Park, so fill up at one of the many gateway towns before entering.

Luray Caverns

The Music of Luray Caverns
UNDERGROUND WONDERLAND

The stalactites hanging above Dream Lake are mirrored with mesmerizing clarity in the still pool that lies beneath them. The reflection creates a tableau that resembles a window into another world. Thanks to this lovely scene, along with an impressive lineup of stalactites, stalagmites, columns, draperies and pools, **Luray Caverns** is your best bet of the regional cavern tours. The caverns are also home to the 'Stalacpipe Organ' – hyped as the largest musical instrument on Earth.

Tours can feel like a cattle call on busy weekends, but the stunning underground formations make up for all the elbow-bumping. To save time at the entrance, buy your ticket online ahead of time, then join the entry line. Also here, for an additional fee, is a **Rope Adventure Park** and a **Garden Maze**. The caverns are 25 miles south of Front Royal and 30 miles from Big Meadows.

Base Camp Winchester
APPLE BLOSSOMS AND SHENANDOAH HISTORY

It can be difficult to tell if locals are being sarcastic or on the level when they refer to their hometown as 'Funchester.' Plunked at the northern end of the Shenandoah Valley, 25 miles north of the park entrance, Winchester is a lovely, small city that embraces its history and beauty – and its abundant apple orchards.

The city goes all out for its annual **Shenandoah Apple Blossom Festival** in May. Gorgeous pink blooms complement 10 days of good food, live music, dancing and carnival rides. The city's **Museum of the Shenandoah Valley** comprises an 18th-century house filled with period furnishings, a six-acre garden and a multimedia museum that delves into the valley's history. Decorative arts are among the highlights of the museum, but don't miss the enormous moonshine still!

A few blocks away, the 250-year-old historic **Old Town** holds a pedestrian-friendly collection of shops, restaurants and museums. Kids can cool off in summer in the downtown **splash pad**. For an overnight stay, try the stately Georgian-revival **George Washington Hotel**, which celebrates its centennial in 2024.

SHENANDOAH BEERWERKS TRAIL

Craft beer comes with a mountain backdrop at many of the breweries along the **Shenandoah Beerwerks Trail** (beerwerkstrail.com), a collection of 17 breweries stretching through the Shenandoah Valley from Harrisonburg south to Lexington, a distance of about 80 miles. A handful have restaurants, but many rely on food trucks, and expect live music and convivial crowds on weekends.

After hiking in the south district of the park, stop for a pimento-slathered smashburger and an amber lager at **Stablecraft Brewing**, which sits on farmland with relaxing mountain-and-valley views just 12 miles north of Waynesboro.

In Rockbridge County near Lexington, you'll find bucolic settings and great beer at **Rockbridge Vineyard & Brewery** and **Great Valley Farm Brewery & Winery**.

WHERE TO EAT BEYOND SKYLAND & BIG MEADOWS

Bonnie Blue Southern Market & Bakery
Pastries, biscuits and creative breakfasts at this indoor-outdoor eatery in Winchester. **$**

Oak Stone Craft Pizza & Bar
Woodfired gourmet pizza with house-made dough on a sunny patio. Also serves Prohibition-era cocktails. In Winchester. **$$**

Jack Brown's Beer & Burger Joint
Try American Wagyu beef with decadent toppings at this regional burger empire. **$**

Hiking route on Old Rag Mountain

Scrambling up Old Rag

HIKE UP A MONADNOCK

Labeled 'very strenuous' by Shenandoah National Park, this 9.4-mile loop hike to the 3291ft summit of **Old Rag Mountain** is generally acknowledged to be the most challenging day hike in Virginia. It's also a ton of fun for hikers in reasonably good shape and up for a bit of adventure. The best part? A mile-long jumble of exposed granite boulders that must be navigated before reaching the top. Expect scrambling, climbing, leaping and the occasional tight squeeze.

A freestanding mountain on the eastern fringe of the national park, Old Rag is an erosion-resistant monadnock. It was formed more than one billion years ago from molten rock that crystallized after the collision of continents. Flat-ish boulders provide inviting picnic areas at the summit, and the best are backdropped by the rolling beauty of the forested Blue Ridge Mountains. To manage the crowds here, the park has implemented a day-use ticket requirement (March

---

DON'T MISS: VIEWS FROM THE RIDGE ROOM

You can gaze back at the Blue Ridge Mountains in style from the **Ridge Room**, a new rooftop bar and restaurant atop the **Hyatt Place** in Harrisonburg. (Pay no mind to the Home Depot and its parking lot, also on the horizon.) You'll find small plates spotlighting fare from regional gardens and farms plus wild-caught fish – try the blackened blue catfish tacos – along with an array of tempting craft cocktails.

Harrisonburg is an urban hub between Winchester and Staunton, about 20 miles from the Swift Run Gap entrance. Home to James Madison University, it also has plenty of midrange lodging and cheap eats.

WHERE TO EAT BEYOND SKYLAND & BIG MEADOWS

Hawksbill Diner
This country diner 6 miles south of Luray serves up consistently good breakfasts and great hospitality. $

Bar-B-Q Ranch
Since 1947 in Harrisonburg, this place has served no-fuss, delicious minced pork BBQ. Drive-in or dine inside. $

Valley Pike Farm Market
Step into this chic market in Weyers Cave for coffee, pastries, picnic sandwiches and food trucks. $

through November), and hikers must purchase the permit before they reach the park, either online or by phone. Visit nps.gov/shen for details. The trailhead is a one-hour drive from Big Meadows, and most hikers usually arrive from Charlottesville (p116).

Exploring Front Royal
CRAFT BEER & THE OUTDOORS

Downtown **Front Royal** can feel a little empty. But at lunch time, you'll find a lot of folks hanging out inside **Vbrissa Beer & Kitchen** on Main St, hunkered over the gourmet pub fare – sandwiches, smashburgers and pastas – and innovative beers. Front Royal is also a low-key launchpad for outdoor enthusiasts, with hiking, horseback riding, river rafting and canoeing opportunities aplenty. Stop here for gas and provisions before cruising **Skyline Drive**. The **Front Royal Visitor Center** is open daily on Main St, and the north entrance to Shenandoah National Park (p161) is a short drive from downtown. From mid-March through November, the **Dickey Ridge Visitor Center** (Mile 4.6; closed Tuesday and Wednesday mid-March though mid-May) is a good place to stop for information, ranger talks and books.

Swimming Hole & Waterfalls
LOOPS, CASCADES AND WADING

Anchored by the **Loft Mountain Wayside** (Mile 79.5) – and home to a campground, camp store, gift shop and grill – the low-key southern section of Shenandoah National Park is within 30 miles of both Charlottesville and Staunton and stretches from the Swift Run Gap entrance (Mile 65.7) to the southern entrance in Rockfish Gap (Mile 105). For a moderately strenuous day that takes in three waterfalls, numerous cascades, the Appalachian Trail and Doyles River, try the 7.8-mile **Doyles River Falls & Jones Run Falls** circuit hike, which begins at the Doyles River parking lot (Mile 81). You can shorten the loop – but still see all three falls – by hiking the Brown's Gap Fire Rd from the Browns Gap parking lot (Mile 83).

The **Riprap Trail** (Mile 90), about 15 miles north of the southern entrance to the park, is a 9.5-mile loop that passes a rocky overlooks with expansive views west over the Shenandoah Valley and swings past a swimming hole. The term 'riprap' refers to broken rocks covered in lichen – you will see plenty!

AN ABANDONED RAILROAD

The light at the end is about a mile away once you step into the **Blue Ridge Tunnel**, an abandoned railroad tunnel that bores through the mountains beneath Rockfish Gap.

Designed by engineer Claudius Crozet, the sloped structure was the longest railroad tunnel in North America when it was completed in 1858. Opened to hikers and cyclists in November 2020, it has no interior lighting, which makes for a unique but eerie walk.

Located between the southern entrance to Shenandoah National Park and the northern entrance of the Blue Ridge Parkway, the 2.25-mile one-way trail, which extends beyond the tunnel, is open sunrise to sunset. It's 90 minutes south of Big Meadows.

GETTING AROUND

The northern entrance to Shenandoah National Park is in Front Royal, which is 70 miles west of Washington, DC. The southern entrance at Rockfish Gap is a few miles from Waynesboro, and within a 30-minute drive of Charlottesville and Staunton. You will need your own vehicle to explore the region.

TOOLKIT

TOOLKIT

The chapters in this section cover the most important topics you'll need to know about in Great Smoky Mountains National Park. They're full of nuts-and-bolts information and valuable insights to help you understand and navigate the park, and get the most out of your trip.

Arriving p170

Getting Around p171

Money p172

Accommodations p173

Family Travel p174

Health & Safe Travel p175

Food, Drink & Nightlife p176

Responsible Travel p178

Accessible Travel p180

Nuts & Bolts p181

Gatlinburg Trolley (p171)

Arriving

The closest airports to Great Smoky Mountains National Park are McGhee Tyson Airport near Knoxville and Asheville Regional Airport. For Shenandoah National Park, Dulles International Airport is the closest. The Blue Ridge Parkway is 469 miles long, and there are many access points. To reach it in Virginia, fly into Charlottesville Albemarle Airport; in North Carolina, fly into Asheville.

Visas
Generally not required for stays of 90 days or less for citizens of Visa Waiver Program countries with ESTA approval (esta.cbp.dhs.gov). Apply online for ESTA approval at least 72 hours in advance.

Money
ATMs are widely available, but credit cards are required for car and hotel reservations. Tipping in the US is customary, not optional.

Cell Phones
Cell-phone coverage is generally unavailable in Great Smoky Mountains National Park. At some high points, you may get a signal, but don't count on it. Coverage comes and goes on Skyline Drive and the Blue Ridge Parkway.

Driving
Newfound Gap Rd is the only paved road that crosses the mountains within Great Smoky Mountains National Park. Watch for hikers and people looking at wildlife in Great Smoky Mountains and Shenandoah, and along the Blue Ridge Parkway.

ARRIVING BY CAR

The best way to reach Great Smoky Mountains National Park from McGhee Tyson Airport is to take Hwy 321 to Townsend, then the Laurel Creek Rd into the park, near Cades Cove. To reach Sugarlands Visitor Center and the start of the Newfound Gap Rd instead, stay on Hwy 321 past Townsend to Wear Valley, then turn south onto Line Springs Rd. This eventually turns into Little River Rd as it takes you straight into the park. The total driving time from Knoxville to either Cades Cove or Newfound Gap Rd is around 70 minutes. Both routes avoid Pigeon Forge traffic.

TRAVEL TIMES BY CAR
TO GREAT SMOKY MOUNTAINS NATIONAL PARK

FROM	DISTANCE	DRIVING TIME
ASHEVILLE	55 MILES	1HR 15MIN
KNOXVILLE	40 MILES	1HR
ATLANTA	170 MILES	3HR 15MIN

TO SHENANDOAH NATIONAL PARK

FROM	DISTANCE	DRIVING TIME
ROANOKE	110 MILES	2HR 30MIN
RICHMOND	105 MILES	1HR 30MIN
WASHINGTON, DC	170 MILES	1HR 30MIN

Getting Around

There are no public shuttles within Great Smoky Mountains National Park or Shenandoah National Park, or along the Blue Ridge Parkway. Unless you join a tour or use a private shuttle, you will need your own vehicle to explore.

TRAVEL COSTS

car rental **from €54/day**

gas **$3.20/gal**

EV charging **from $0**

mountain-bike rental **from $45/day**

Parking

Pursuant to the new Park It Forward Program, visitors to Great Smoky Mountains National Park must pay for a parking tag if they plan to stop for more than 15 minutes. Daily tags are $5. There is no parking fee in Shenandoah National Park or along the Blue Ridge Parkway.

Gatlinburg Trolley

This free trolley (gatlinburgtrolley.org) serves downtown Gatlinburg on various routes. The Red Line stops near the Gatlinburg Trail, which leads into Great Smoky Mountains National Park. The Pigeon Forge Trolley ($3 day pass) stops at the Gatlinburg Welcome Center, where you can pick up the Gatlinburg Trolley.

TIP
There are no gas stations in Great Smoky Mountains National Park, so fuel up in Gatlinburg, TN, or Cherokee, NC.

NO ADMISSION FEES

Great Smoky Mountains National Park is unique among its peers in that it has never charged an admission fee. The park's original deed contains a provision preventing the charging of a toll on two key roads to the park: Newfound Gap Rd and Little River Rd. The park began charging a parking fee in 2023 for extended stops in order to cover its maintenance and staffing needs.

Gatlinburg Trail

This pleasant hiking trail through the woods links downtown Gatlinburg with the Sugarlands Visitor Center. The 2-mile trail (one way) is open to hikers and cyclists and is pet-friendly. Pick it up on River Rd beside Hwy 441. It runs parallel to the West Prong of the Little Pigeon River.

Appalachian Trail

This trail runs along the spine of Great Smoky Mountains National Park for 71 miles. Shelters are spaced 3-8 miles apart. Check the park website for details about backpacking fees and permits for camping. The trail also runs the length of Shenandoah National Park and along the northern section of the Blue Ridge Parkway.

Private Shuttles

A handful of shuttle companies offer private transport to and from the trailheads inside Great Smoky Mountains National Park. Visit the park website for a list of approved companies. Reserve in advance. Visit the White Blaze website (whiteblaze.net) for an up-to-date list of shuttle providers along the entire AT.

DRIVING ESSENTIALS

Drive on the right

Speed limit is 35mph in Great Smoky Mountains National Park and 45mph along the Blue Ridge Parkway

A parking tag in Great Smoky Mountains National Park costs $5/day

Money

CURRENCY: US DOLLAR ($)

Credit Cards
Major credit cards are almost universally accepted. In fact, it is almost impossible to rent a car, book a hotel room or buy tickets over the phone without one. A credit card may also be vital in emergencies. Visa, Mastercard and American Express are the most widely accepted credit cards.

Debit Cards
When using debit cards to rent a car, be mindful of the fact that most major rental car companies will charge a hefty additional deposit. If the car is returned in good shape, this hold on the extra funds should be released within a day or two.

Taxes
There is a state sales tax of 7% in Tennessee, 4.75% in North Carolina and 5.3% in Virginia. Cities and counties may add an additional local sales tax. There is an additional hotel/occupancy tax of 2.5% in Pigeon Forge, 3% in Gatlinburg and 6% in Asheville.

HOW MUCH FOR...

national park entry
free–$30

museum admission
$12–15

Dollywood admission
$89

Asheville Drum Circle
free

HOW TO... Tip in the US

Hotel porters $2 to $3 per bag is standard; gratuity for cleaning staff is generally $2 to $5 per day.

Restaurants and bars 18% to 20% from the before-tax amount, unless a gratuity is included.

Bartenders 15% to 20% per round; minimum $1 tip per drink.

Guided trips It's customary to tip trip leader, at your discretion. Consider the length, party details and trip itinerary.

THE NEED FOR PARKING FEES

Great Smoky Mountains National Park is the most visited park in the national park system, but popularity does not mean the park receives more federal funding than its peers. In fact, its budget has seen only a slight increase over the last 10 years. Since the park's deed prevents it from charging admission fees, it has been forced to reduce services and staffing to balance its budget. In tough financial straits, the park began charging a parking fee in 2022, with 100% of the funds going back into the park for maintenance, staffing, preservation and safety.

LOCAL TIP
Emily Davis, national park ranger, advises to know your license plate number when paying for parking at the park. Your plate number is required for the parking tag, so if you know it, you won't hold up the line or lose your place by running back to check it.

Accommodations

Great Smokies Lodging

Great Smoky Mountains National Park provides varied camping options, but LeConte Lodge is the only place where you can get a room – and you have to hike to the top of a mountain to get there. Gatlinburg has the most sleeping options of any of the park's gateway towns, though prices are high. Pigeon Forge and Sevierville, further north, have cheaper options.

National Park Camping

There are 10 campgrounds in the Great Smokies, all with restrooms with cold water and toilets, but there are no showers, or electrical or water hookups, though some do have electricity for emergencies. Cades Cove and Smokemont campgrounds are open year-round. You must pay for and reserve all campsites online (recreation.gov). Shenandoah has five campgrounds, and there are eight along the Blue Ridge Parkway.

Backcountry Camping

Backcountry camping in Great Smoky Mountains National Park is an excellent option, and it's only chargeable for up to five nights ($8 per night, plus parking tag; after that, it's free). A permit is required, and you must stay at designated sites. Make reservations online (smokiespermits.nps.gov). A free permit is required for backcountry camping in Shenandoah National Park.

DreamMore Resort

The warm hospitality at Dollywood's DreamMore Resort in Pigeon Forge is a highlight, as are the impeccably clean rooms and the well-manicured grounds. The family-oriented rooms come with bunk beds, and you'll find a games room and playground on site. Guests can ride a free shuttle to the theme park and the waterpark. Cabins are now available, too.

HOW MUCH FOR A NIGHT IN...

a national park campground
$30

a hostel dorm
$32

the DreamMore Resort, Dollywood
$350

Budget Sleeps

There are hostels in Asheville, Hartford, TN, and near the AT in Virginia. For proximity to rafting and hiking, check out the hostel-style bunkhouses at the Nantahala Outdoor Center, west of Bryson City. You're more likely to find budget options in Pigeon Forge and Sevierville than in Gatlinburg, which borders Great Smoky Mountains National Park. Mom-and-pop motels in small towns may also be more budget-friendly.

APPALACHIAN TRAIL SHELTERS

There are 250 overnight shelters along the entire Appalachian Trail. These rustic structures have roofs and wooden floors. They usually have a simple privy nearby. In Great Smoky Mountains National Park, there are 12 shelters along the 71 miles of the trail. In spring, when the bubble of thru-hikers heads north, they can be lively places. Reservations and a backcountry permit are required for an overnight stay in the park's trail shelters. Backcountry permits are $8 per person per night. Note that thru-hikers must buy a $40 thru-hiker permit for the Appalachian Trail. Especially scenic is the Icewater Spring Shelter.

TOOLKIT

Family Travel

This region is a wonderland for young travelers. There are adventures aplenty, with mesmerizing wildflower-filled hikes, horseback rides, tubing trips and star-filled nights gathered around the campfire. In the Smokies, you can also go white-water rafting. Ripley's Museums, mountain coasters and putt-putt are hallmarks of Gatlinburg and Pigeon Forge.

National Park Junior Rangers

Great Smoky Mountains and Shenandoah have junior ranger programs geared to kids from ages five to 12. Pick up a junior ranger booklet at one of the visitor centers, then have the kids complete the activities in the book. Afterwards, present the book to a ranger at one of the visitor centers, and they'll be on their way to earning a junior ranger badge.

TRACK Trails

The Kids in Parks TRACK trails project (kidsinparks.com) designates trails near the Blue Ridge Parkway and in Shenandoah National Park that are family-friendly and loaded with opportunities to learn about plants and wildlife. Kiosks at the trailheads stock brochures describing what kids may see, and the kids can then register their discoveries online.

Food Deserts

Dining services are nonexistent in Great Smoky Mountains National Park, and infrequent in Shenandoah and along the Blue Ridge Parkway, so you'll need to load up on snacks and picnic fare beforehand. Bring plenty of water (or a filtration device), as there are no fountains at the trailheads.

Train Rides & Rafting

If you prefer to avoid the circus-like atmosphere of Gatlinburg, try Bryson City. It's the starting point for the Great Smoky Mountains Railroad, which offers scenic journeys aboard vintage steam- or diesel-powered trains. At the Nantahala Outdoor Center (p153), families can go rafting and zip-lining.

OUTDOOR ADVENTURES IN THE SMOKIES

Horseback Riding (p65)
Head off for a fun one-hour ride at Cades Cove, or at one of the park's other stables.

Cycling (p70)
Pedal bikes along the 11-mile Cades Cove Loop on car-free Wednesdays in summer.

White-Water Rafting (p81)
Feel the spray as you paddle along the churning rapids of the Pigeon River near Hartford, TN.

Camping (p65)
Roast marshmallows over a crackling fire as the sky fills with stars at Deep Creek Campground.

EMBRACE THE CHAOS

With their crowds and over-the-top distractions, Gatlinburg and Pigeon Forge are a wonderland for some (and hell on Earth for others). But the attractions can fill a day with wacky family fun. The roller coasters at Dollywood are renowned, and water slides swoop all across the adjacent Splash Country. In Pigeon Forge, try a few loops on the 200ft-tall Great Smoky Mountain Wheel and grimace at the horrors of crime at the Alcatraz East Crime Museum (older kids only). Mountain coasters are ubiquitous in Gatlinburg, as are the chairlifts, which rise from downtown to the mountains. In sum, there's something fun for just about every type of kid.

Health & Safe Travel

TRAIL SAFETY

Trails can become treacherous after heavy rain – you might encounter moss-covered rocks, wet leaves and slick roots. These can lead to bad falls, and consequences can be significant on trails that traverse steep, narrow cliffs. Wear ankle-supporting boots with good soles, and use crampons or spikes in icy conditions – which can persist into May on some trails. A good walking stick is also useful.

Waterfalls

Waterfalls are among the most outstanding attractions across the Blue Ridge and Great Smoky Mountains. But take care when visiting them, as slippery rocks can lead to bad falls. Don't try to climb up them either – while you might see rocky, muddy paths going up, it's never a good idea to try hike them, as there have been dozens of deaths on these paths over the years.

Rivers

Be cautious around mountain rivers and streams. Drowning is a leading cause of death in the Great Smokies, and hikers have suffered serious injuries from falls along riverbanks. Streams can become swollen after heavy rainfall, making passage dangerous, and the log bridges can be slippery. In general, if the water is flowing rapidly, and there isn't a bridge, don't cross if the water is above your knees.

TIP
Have a look around you before resting on the trail or setting up camp for the night. Move away from any trees or branches that might fall or pose a hazard.

APPALACHIAN TRAIL 'BLAZES'

White Blaze
A swath of white paint marking the route of the trail. Usually found on a tree or rock.

Double White Blaze
A double swath of white paint to show the trail is taking a sharp turn or that a trail junction is ahead.

Blue Blaze
A swath of blue paint along a spur trail leading off from the main trail.

Ticks

Ticks are present across all of the parks, so check yourself carefully after hiking and camping. Since some ticks can carry Lyme disease and other nasty things, you'll want to avoid them if possible. DEET repellent and appropriate dress (long pants, a hat) will minimize the risk of a tick being able to bite you.

BEAR AWARE

Black bears are active in this region and can be dangerous. Campers should keep all food in their cars or tied to cables. Hikers should never approach or feed bears. If a bear approaches, back away slowly. If the bear continues to approach, shout or wave your arms to intimidate it. As a last resort, throw rocks or other objects, or deter it with a large stick. Never run away.

Food, Drink & Nightlife

When to Eat

Breakfast (8am to 10am) Often a heavy meal, with the standard breakfast at diners consisting of eggs, bacon or sausage, hash browns, and toast or a biscuit.

Lunch (11:30am to 2pm) A midday affair with everything from takeout sandwiches to meals at food trucks, burger joints, cafes and restaurants.

Dinner (6pm to 8pm) Sometimes called 'supper' in the South. Often heavier than lunch, with burgers and pizzas popular near the parks.

Where to Eat

Diner Casual breakfast and lunch restaurant with booths and a long counter with stools.

Food truck Kitchen on wheels, parked where hungry pedestrians frequent. Orders are taken through a window, and you may be able to eat nearby, or just take it to go.

Brewery Many craft breweries offer a few snacks; you may find pub fare at larger ones.

Picnic area Designated spot with tables, trash cans and views are common in the parks. Bring your own food in most cases.

MENU DECODER

À la carte Choose anything you like from the menu; a side often must be ordered in addition to the main dishes.

Biscuits and gravy Homemade flaky yeast roll served warm and slathered with heavy sausage gravy.

Blue Plate Special of the day in a diner.

Grits Ground corn cooked to a cereal-like consistency. Best enjoyed with a pat of butter or with melted cheese.

Meat and three Usually in a 'choose your own adventure' restaurant where one meat and three sides are a fixed price.

Small plates Bigger than an appetizer but smaller than a main dish, these tapas-style dishes are often intended for sharing.

Sweet tea Pre-sweetened (and very sugary!) iced tea found on menus across the South.

HOW TO... Make S'mores

For purists, store-bought s'mores are a class-one felony. A s'more is not something pre-made that you pull out of a slick package, or combine with another cookie into a Frankenstein-like hybrid. No, a s'more is a sticky hot mess that you build and eat beside a campfire. There are five things you'll need to make one: a long stick plucked from the woods, marshmallows, thin chocolate bars, plain graham crackers and a campfire.

To begin: snap a graham cracker in two. Place a slab of chocolate on one half of the cracker and cover it with the other half. Hold in non-dominant hand. Place TWO marshmallows on the end of the stick, not one – one marshmallow is for those who are afraid to live. Warm the marshmallows over the campfire until mostly brown and gooey. Remove from the flame and smush them inside the graham-cracker sandwich, which softens the chocolate. Wait three seconds. Eat. Swear that you've got to do this more often. Continue eating.

HOW MUCH FOR A...

cup of drip coffee
$2.75

pint of craft beer
$6

diner breakfast
$10

gourmet burger
$15

wood-fired pizza
$20

scoop of homemade ice cream
$4

moonshine tasting
$5

HOW TO... Enjoy the Friday Night Jamboree

The Friday Night Jamboree (p135) is a highlight of any drive along the Crooked Road, a music heritage trail through southwest Virginia that celebrates Appalachian mountain music. Friday night shows at the Floyd Country Store fill up fast with a mix of locals, regional road-trippers and international travelers digging into Appalachian culture. With elbow-to-elbow attendance and limited seating, it's good to know the deal before arriving.

Shows, which have three sets, start at 6:30 pm. The gospel set is always first, followed by two sets of old-time dance tunes. Buy your $10 ticket at the door from 5:45pm, then mark your seat inside with a piece of paper. Forty-two seats can be reserved online ahead of time for $16 apiece.

Make your way to a local restaurant – we like Dogtown Pizza – for an early dinner, and then return to the store for the music, soaking up the soulful gospel before tapping your toes to the old-time dance tunes. When the dance band starts, listen for the click-clack of the buck dancers – they've got taps on the bottom of their dance shoes. And ladies, if you're not accompanied by a date, someone will likely ask you to dance. It's not gonna kill ya, and it might even be fun, so go on up for one twirl around the dance floor. On warm nights, slip outside at some point to enjoy the musicians playing on the sidewalk.

Granny's Rules

The Jamboree is a family-friendly event, and visitors must obey Granny's Rules during the Jamboree: no smoking, no alcohol, no cussing and no unbecoming conduct.

IT'S FRIDAY NIGHT IN ASHEVILLE

If you're rolling in from a hike and you're simultaneously pumped and exhausted – we know, it happens – but not too ripe, it's perfectly OK to celebrate with a beer on the patio at Burial (p148) before showering. And no, the mural of Sloth (from The Goonies) and Tom Selleck is not a reflection or a hallucination. But it is pretty awesome. If you haven't been hiking and have more time, spend an hour or two sampling craft beer at the many breweries in South Slope.

From here, a walk along Broadway toward downtown passes Mast General Store, where you can browse the retro candy or replace the sunglasses you lost on the trail. Back outside, sidewalk buskers – they're usually pretty good – fill the night with music.

A few blocks away, thumping beats drift from Pritchard Park, home of the Friday Night Drum Circle (p149) since 2002. Drumming begins around 6pm and lasts until 9:45pm. Next up is award-winning Indian food at Chai Pani (p148) – join the line, or try the innovative Spanish tapas at Cúrate (p148). If it's not too late, enjoy cocktails and the sunset from one of downtown's many new rooftops bars, which top the newer hotels. End with live music at the Orange Peel, Asheville's premier live-music venue and a showcase for big-name indie and punk bands since 2002.

TOOLKIT

Responsible Travel

Climate Change & Travel

It's impossible to ignore the impact we have when traveling, and the importance of making changes where we can. Lonely Planet urges all travelers to engage with their travel carbon footprint. There are many carbon calculators online that allow travelers to estimate the carbon emissions generated by their journey; try resurgence.org/resources/carbon-calculator.html. Many airlines and booking sites offer travelers the option of offsetting the impact of greenhouse gas emissions by contributing to climate-friendly initiatives around the world. We continue to offset the carbon footprint of all Lonely Planet staff travel, while recognizing this is a mitigation more than a solution.

Wildlife

Stay at least 50 yards away from all wildlife in the park. Never approach an animal, and if your presence changes the animal's behavior in any way, you're too close. Feeding wildlife is prohibited.

Food Storage

All food, and food preparation and storage items, must be kept sealed in a vehicle (preferably the trunk) when not in use. The following campgrounds have food-storage lockers: Balsam Mountain, Big Creek, Cades Cove, Cataloochee, Cosby, Deep Creek, Elkmont and Smokemont.

Farmers Markets

There's so much produce in the valleys and foothills of Appalachia. The Appalachian Sustainable Agriculture Program (appalachiangrown.org) lists farmers markets in western North Carolina. The North Asheville Market on the University of North Carolina's Asheville campus is lush with offerings every Saturday.

Appalachian Crafts

Created during the Depression to support craftspeople in Appalachia, the Southern Highland Craft Guild (southernhighlandguild.org) today promotes the sale of handmade crafts from makers across the southeast. Look for their shops on the Blue Ridge Parkway and in Asheville.

For high-quality jewelry, baskets, pottery and textiles made by Cherokee Indians, visit the Qualla Arts & Crafts Mutual (p152) in Cherokee, near the east entrance of Great Smoky Mountains National Park.

Defined as 'unexpected generosity,' Trail Magic is beloved by thru-hikers on the Appalachian Trail. Stashes of food. A ride into town. A snack from a tourist at an overlook. Those who provide the gifts are Trail Angels.

BUY PRE-OWNED GEAR

Second Gear in Asheville and Outdoor Gear Revival (p98) in Knoxville are consignment shops selling name-brand, secondhand outdoor gear – for hiking, biking, climbing, paddling and more – at affordable prices. At Second Gear, you'll find new products, too.

FARM CAFE

All guests, regardless of their ability to pay, can enjoy a nutritious, high-quality meal at this pay-what-you-can community cafe – FARM Cafe (p143) in Boone. Suggested donations are provided based on meal size. It's a welcoming place for all.

Stargazing

Urban light pollution diminishes the number of stars visible in the Great Smokies and Shenandoah, but stargazing is still pretty good. It's also a low-impact activity, with minimal detrimental effects on park infrastructure. One standout is Natural Bridge State Park (p194) in Lexington, VA, named an International Dark Sky Park in 2021.

Traveling with Fido

Great Smoky Mountains National Park does not allow dogs on it's trails, as they can disrupt wildlife. The exceptions are Gatlinburg and Oconaluftee River Trails (leash required). Shenandoah is more pet-friendly, and leashed dogs are allowed on most trails.

Greenways

In Roanoke, commuters pedal the greenway network to get to and from work while mountain bikers connect with mountain singletrack, and pedestrians enjoy river views. Asheville has scenic greenways along the French Broad River and the River Arts District.

Meditate and commune with nature on one of Great Smoky Mountains National Park's 14 short and scenic Quiet Walkway trails.

The solar panels and inverters at Innovation Brewing (p153) in Sylva provide more than half of the power for the business.

200m+

Founded by Dolly Parton, the Imagination Library gives books to qualifying children from birth up to age five on a monthly basis. So far, the Library has gifted more than 200 million books globally. Donate at imaginationlibrary.com.

RESOURCES

appalachiantrail.org
This nonprofit protects the Appalachian Trail, with volunteering opportunities.

gsmit.org
This institute offers courses and trips in the Smokies.

nps.gov/blri/getinvolved/volunteer.htm
Manages the annual Project Parkway event.

Accessible Travel

While all visitors can enjoy the park's scenic drives and auto tours, with overlooks along the way equipped with accessible parking, most hiking trails here are not wheelchair accessible. A few do accommodate travelers with disabilities.

Sugarland Valley Nature Trail

In Great Smoky Mountains National Park, the half-mile **Sugarlands Valley Nature Trail** is a smooth and level accessible trail, with a wide paved path that skirts along a pretty river and past remnants from the early 20th century.

Airport

Representatives in orange vests can provide wheelchair assistance (5am to 7pm) at McGhee Tyson near Knoxville. Wheelchairs are available for use at Asheville Regional. Both airports also have relief areas for service animals.

Accommodations

There are accessible accommodations in Shenandoah National Park, at both lodges and the Lewis Mountain Cabins; accessible sites are available at all of the campgrounds. There is none at Great Smoky Mountains National Park, but some campgrounds have accessible units.

RESOURCES

The websites for **Great Smoky Mountains** (nps.gov/grsm) and **Shenandoah National Park** (nps.goc/shen) have sections spotlighting accessibility, and they list all accessible facilities, trails and programs.

For details about accessibility on the Blue Ridge Parkway, visit blueridgeparkway.org.

CADES COVE

Cades Cove (p68) has hard-packed gravel paths running around the area. Most of the historic buildings on the Cades Cove Loop Rd are not wheelchair accessible and can only be viewed from the exterior.

High Points

The path to Clingmans Dome (p89) is paved but not approved by the Americans with Disabilities Act because of its steepness. However, with assistance, travelers with disabilities have made the trip. At Mt Mitchell (p147), there's an accessible trail to the summit and tower.

Limberlost Trail

A 1.3-mile path of crushed greenstone that loops through the woods, the Limberlost Trail (p162) in Shenandoah National Park is fully accessible and well-maintained. It passes through woods, with lots of spring wildflowers lining the way.

ASHEVILLE & BEYOND

There are several accessible places to enjoy nature in and around Asheville, including the Quilt and Bonsai Gardens at the North Carolina Arboretum, the Walled Gardens at the Biltmore Estate (p145), the French Broad River Greenway, and Looking Glass Falls on the Forest Heritage Scenic Byway (p152).

> There are a dozen wheelchair-accessible trails along the Blue Ridge Parkway. The 1-mile Abbott Loop Lake Trail at the Peaks of Otter (p127) is fully compliant with the Americans with Disabilities Act and is quite pretty.

Nuts & Bolts

OPENING HOURS

Typical opening hours are as follows:

Banks 8:30am to 4:30pm Monday to Friday

Bars 5pm to midnight Sunday to Thursday, to 2am Friday and Saturday

Post offices 9am to 5pm Monday to Friday

Shopping malls 9am to 9pm

Stores 9am to 6pm Monday to Saturday, noon to 5pm Sunday

Supermarkets 8am to 8pm (some 24 hours)

Internet Access

Wi-fi is generally available at visitor centers. Elsewhere in Great Smoky Mountains National Park, internet (and often cell-phone reception) is nonexistent.

Drones

Drones are not permitted in the Smokies or Shenandoah, or along the Blue Ridge Parkway.

Park Toilets

Public toilets are located at visitor centers, campgrounds and picnic areas.

GOOD TO KNOW

Time zone
US Eastern Standard Time

Country code
+1

Emergency number
911

US population
340 million

Electricity 120V/60Hz

Type A
120V/60Hz

Type B
120V/60Hz

PUBLIC HOLIDAYS

On the following national public holidays, banks, schools and government offices (including post offices) are closed, and transportation, museums and other services operate on a Sunday schedule. Holidays falling on a weekend are usually observed the following Monday.

New Year's Day January 1

Martin Luther King Jr Day Third Monday in January

Presidents' Day Third Monday in February

Memorial Day Last Monday in May

Juneteenth June 19

Independence Day July 4

Labor Day First Monday in September

Veterans' Day November 11

Thanksgiving Fourth Thursday in November

Christmas Day December 25

TOOLKIT

STORYBOOK

THE GREAT SMOKY MOUNTAINS NATIONAL PARK
STORYBOOK

Our writers delve deep into different aspects of life around the park.

A History of the Great Smokies & Beyond in 15 Places

There's history in these Appalachian hills, which were the longtime homeland of the Cherokee Nation before the arrival of European settlers.

Amy Balfour

p184

Meet the Ranger

A Q&A with Emily Davis, a ranger and public affairs specialist at Great Smoky Mountains National Park. She shares tips and ranger info, and tells us about the park's most famous residents: bears.

Amy Balfour

p188

Parks under Pressure

Overuse and underfunding have created unique challenges for southern Appalachia's national parks, but innovative initiatives hold promise for the future.

Gregor Clark

p190

Skyline Drive (p163), Shenandoah National Park

A HISTORY OF THE GREAT SMOKIES & BEYOND IN
15 PLACES

There's history in these Appalachian hills, which were the longtime homeland of the Cherokee Nation before the arrival of European settlers. These newcomers embraced family, church and farming, and maybe a little bit of moonshine. Created during the Great Depression, Great Smoky Mountains National Park and Shenandoah National Park preserved the mountain beauty for the entire nation.

THE STORY OF the Great Smoky Mountains and the Blue Ridge Mountains begins in primordial times, when supersized continents collided, creating a chain of mountains that are today among the oldest on the planet. Two of the most popular destinations today, Old Rag and Grandfather Mountain, are also home to the world's oldest rocks.

Humans have left their mark on these ancient Appalachian landscapes. Nomadic tribes were the first to the area, and they spent centuries hunting, trading and, in the case of the Cherokee, farming. In the mid-1700s, Scots-Irish and German settlers followed the Great Wagon Road south from Pennsylvania, establishing homesteads across fertile valleys and lush mountain slopes. In the 1900s, lumber companies arrived, nearly wiping out the forests in the process.

A few visionaries – and business promoters – soon fought for the creation of the national parks, which became a reality in the 1930s. Hundreds of families were displaced in the process. The ruins of cabins, churches and cemeteries are solitary markers of these once-thriving communities. In recent years, the story of the parks has been marked by environmental developments both good and bad. Today, Great Smoky Mountains National Park is the most visited national park in the country.

1. Old Rag Mountain
ANCIENT ROCKS ARE AN INSTAGRAM HIT

Formed more than one billion years ago from molten rock that crystallized after a grand collision of continents, the rocks comprising this popular hiking destination are among the oldest in the world. The granite here has survived the swells of grand oceans, a probable uplift event, another continental collision and flows of volcanic magma. Igneous rocks surrounding the granite eroded over millennia, leaving the older rocks exposed. A monadnock on the eastern fringe of Shenandoah National Park, Old Rag is famous today for its loop trail, which navigates a fun, mile-long stretch of boulders on its final summit push. Day-use reservations are currently required.

For more on Old Rag Mountain, see p166.

2. Cherokee
THE STORY OF THE CHEROKEE

One of America's largest indigenous groups, the Cherokee have roots in the Smoky Mountains that date back over 1000 years. Excellent farmers, they lived in fertile river valleys in small villages set with sturdy wooden houses and cornfields. Before the Trail of Tears exodus in 1838, a small group of Cherokee in western North Carolina received special permission to avoid being relocated. Around 1000 stayed behind and worked to buy back their lands. Today, the Eastern Cherokee number around 15,000, with most living outside the national park in the Qualla Boundary, which is anchored by the town of Cherokee, NC. Learn the full history at the Museum of the Cherokee Indian, also in Cherokee.

For more on Cherokee, see p151.

3. Monticello
THE MEANING OF LIBERTY

Designed and inhabited by Founding Father Thomas Jefferson, Monticello is the only home in America designated a Unesco World Heritage Site. Construction on the home, which sits on a mountain-top near Charlottesville, began in 1769. Jefferson moved into the house in 1770, but it wasn't fully completed for another 40 years or so. Built by white masons and enslaved apprentices, this architectural masterpiece has 43 rooms across the main home, its pavilions and terraces. Jefferson's extensive vegetable and flower gardens are also showcased. Tours spotlight the lives and significant contributions of the enslaved laborers who worked here over the decades.

For more on Monticello, see p118.

4. Cades Cove
A VIBRANT MOUNTAIN COMMUNITY REMEMBERED

A swath of mountain-flanked meadows in the western fringes of Great Smoky Mountains National Park, the lush Cades Cove was a hunting ground for the Cherokee before English, Scots-Irish and German settlers arrived in the 1820s. The newcomers built cabins and churches while clearing the valley's trees for farmland. Mills, forges and blacksmith shops followed. The population of Cades Cove peaked in the 1850s, when it had a thriving community of 685 residents, with farm sizes averaging between 150 and 300 acres. Today, an 11-mile loop road encircles the meadows and stops by a dozen or so historic buildings.

For more on Cades Cove, see p68.

5. Lexington
LEADERS OF THE LOST CAUSE

The Civil War lasted only four years (1861–65), but its impact reverberates across the South, with some Southerners still embracing nostalgic views of the Confederacy (the slavery-supporting states that seceded from the Union). This romantic view of the Old South perpetuates the Confederacy's racist origins. The city of Lexington, VA, is a cultural 'battleground' today, thanks to the impact of two Confederate generals: Robert E Lee, leader of the Confederate forces, and Thomas Jonathan 'Stonewall' Jackson. Both are buried in Lexington, with many statues and commercial establishments named for them. But these racist accolades are coming down, putting Lexington in the thick of cultural debates about racism and history.

For more on Lexington, see p122.

6. Tremont
A LOGGING BOOMTOWN

The logging industry emerged in the decades following the Civil War. At first, it started small, with selective timber cutting carried out by local landowners throughout the Smokies. By 1900, however, industrialists began buying old-growth properties

Monticello (p118)

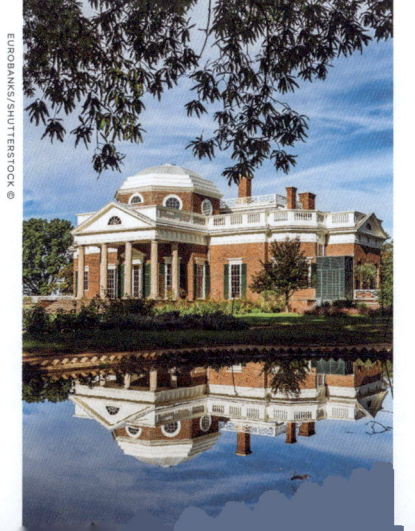

and commencing large-scale operations. Companies laid down railroad tracks, built large mills and created lumber towns and logging roads. Logging boomtowns arrived overnight, and the park still bears their place names: Smokemont, Proctor and Tremont. The Middle Prong Trail passes through Tremont, which existed from 1926 through 1938. No ruins remain, but the trail follows an old logging rail line. The *Tremont Logging History* auto tour booklet covers a section of Upper Tremont Rd.

For more on Tremont, see p74.

7. Carter Family Fold
KEEPING ON THE SUNNY SIDE

The Carter Family – AP Carter, his wife Sara and her cousin Maybelle – shot to fame after the songs they recorded during the 1927 Bristol Sessions hit the airwaves. Their harmonious singing, heartfelt mountain lyrics and memorable guitar licks sustained a major recording career that lasted until 1941. Dubbed 'the First Family of Country Music,' they performed 'Keep on the Sunny Side' and wrote many other classics of country music. To preserve the family legacy, Sara's daughter Janette built the Carter Family Fold, a performing space in Hiltons, VA, near the Tennessee state line. A welcoming spot, the fold hosts old-time musicians and dancers on Saturday nights.

For more on the Carter Family Fold, see p137.

8. Rapidan Camp
A PRESIDENTIAL RETREAT

The Marines built Rapidan Camp, a summer retreat for President Herbert Hoover, on the eastern slopes of the Blue Ridge Mountains between 1929 and 1932. Comprising 13 buildings at the headwaters of the Rapidan River, the camp was a place of rejuvenation for the president and his wife during the Depression, as well as a gathering spot for international policy discussions. One notable guest was UK Prime Minister Ramsay McDonald. Cabin-like buildings included a town hall, a mess hall and the Brown House – as opposed to the White House – where the president stayed. The camp became part of Shenandoah National Park in 1935.

For more on Rapidan Camp, see p162.

9. Skyline Drive
A ROAD BUILT BY THE CCC

As the Great Depression swept the nation in the early 1930s, President Roosevelt and Congress established the Civilian Conservation Corps (CCC). Part of the New Deal program, the CCC had two goals: to create jobs and to help the nation's reforestation by improving and developing national and state parks. CCC camps were set up across the country, with 12 in Shenandoah National Park and and 22 in the Great Smokies. During the program, which ran from 1933 to 1942, trees were planted, bridges, walls and footpaths were built, fire towers were erected, and fire roads cleared. In Shenandoah, the CCC built Skyline Drive, the 105-mile scenic byway that crosses the park.

For more on Skyline Drive, see p163.

10. Dolly Parton Statue
THE SMOKY MOUNTAIN SONGBIRD

Born in a one-room shack in the hamlet of Locust Ridge in East Tennessee in 1946, Dolly Parton was the fourth of 12 children. Immersed in church music and the ballads of her forebears, she started performing on Knoxville radio at 11 and moved to Nashville at 18 with all her belongings in a cardboard suitcase. She's made millions singing about her Smoky Mountains roots and remains a huge presence in her hometown, where she often donates money to local causes. Her theme park, Dollywood, opened in 1986. A statue of a young Dolly, smiling with her guitar

Lewis Mountain Cabins (p161)

in front the of Sevier County Courthouse, captures her charisma.

For more on Dolly Parton, see p107.

11. Lewis Mountain Cabins
DESEGREGATION IN THE PARK

Harold Ickes, Secretary of the Interior under Franklin Delano Roosevelt, supported integrated facilities at Shenandoah National Park. Unfortunately, the federal government's intentions clashed with Virginia's segregationist Jim Crow policies, so plans for separate facilities proceeded as the park developed. Lewis Mountain, a segregated lodge and cabin area south of Big Meadows, opened exclusively to Black visitors in 1939 while the Pinnacles Picnic Area welcomed all guests. Park facilities closed during World War II, but in 1946 Ickes directed park concessionaires to desegregate, although full integration wasn't achieved until 1950. An exhibit in the Byrd Visitor Center at Shenandoah spotlights the park's integration efforts.

For more on Big Meadows, see p161.

12. Cataloochee
WHERE ELK ROAM FREE

Great Smoky Mountains National Park released 25 elk into Cataloochee Valley in 2001. Another 27 were released the following year. Elk had once roamed the southern Appalachian Mountains, but overhunting and habitat loss caused their decline and eventual disappearance. Some have migrated from the valley, but a significant number still graze in the meadows and woods of Cataloochee. Adult males typically weigh 700lb to 800lb, while females clock in at 500lb. Reaching a height of 5ft, you'll likely see them grazing in the early morning and late afternoon along Cataloochee Rd. For safety, stay at least 50 yards from them.

For more on Cataloochee, see p76.

13. Ole Smoky Moonshine Distillery
SAMPLE MOONSHINE IN GATLINBURG

For decades, strict alcohol laws prevented the legal production of distilled spirits across much of southern Appalachia. A loosening of these laws by the Tennessee legislature in 2009 – plus the popularity of the Discovery Channel show *Moonshiners* – opened the door for mass production in the state, and the sale of 'legal' moonshine skyrocketed. Ole Smoky Moonshine was the first new distillery to open in Tennessee after the legislature voted to allow commercial distilling in 41 counties – an increase from only three. Tastings and tours are available at Ole Smoky Moonshine Holler in Gatlinburg. Apple Pie flavor is a crowd-pleaser.

For more on Ole Smoky Moonshine Distillery, see p108.

14. Chimney Tops
FIRE DEVASTATES THE PARK

On November 23, 2016, tragedy struck the Great Smokies when fire was reported on Chimney Tops, one of the national park's most popular trails. The combination of exceptional drought conditions, low humidity and wind gusts that topped 80mph caused the flames to spread over the next few weeks into what would soon become the deadliest wildfire in the eastern US since 1947. The park, Gatlinburg and Pigeon Forge suffered significant damage and 14 people died. Inside the park, Chimney Tops took the brunt of the blow, forcing its closure. It has since reopened, though the final quarter-mile of the trail to the peaks remains closed for safety reasons and resource preservation.

For more on Chimney Tops, see p88.

15. Newfound Gap
VIEWS, A DEDICATION AND PARKING KIOSKS

Pursuant to its original deed, which contained a provision prohibiting tolls on Newfound Gap and Little River Rds, Great Smoky Mountains National Park has never charged admission. With a recent explosion in visitation but no corresponding increase in federal funding, the park implemented a parking fee on March 1, 2023, for stops lasting more than 15 minutes. Daily parking tags are sold for $5 at kiosks, and you'll find one at Newfound Gap, an overlook at 5046ft with expansive mountain-and-valley views. Franklin Delano Roosevelt dedicated the park here in 1940, and it's a beautiful spot to admire the handiwork of Mother Nature and walk on the legendary Appalachian Trail.

For more on Newfound Gap, see p86.

MEET THE RANGER

Emily Davis is a ranger and public affairs specialist at Great Smoky Mountains National Park. In this Q&A, she shares some visiting tips and ranger info, and tells our writer Amy C Balfour about the park's most famous residents: bears.

What skills does someone need to become a park ranger?
The ranger 'field' is pretty wide. We have law-enforcement rangers, we have search and rescue rangers, and we also have education and interpretive rangers.

So are rangers specialized, or do they help out as needed across the park?
We are very fortunate at the Smokies that we have people who are experts in their fields, and we also have a number of staff who have collateral duties, or help out when needed. For instance, we have a number of members on our search and rescue team who are not full-time search and rescue rangers but who, if their daily duties allow and there's an emergency, will be released to go help.

Is there an interesting fact about the park that isn't well known?
One of the coolest things I learned recently is that this park is one of the most studied and researched of all the national parks.

Why is so much research going on here?
This place is beyond measure in terms of its biodiversity. We work closely with one of our partners, Discover Life in America (DLIA). The DLIA group and a lot of our researchers and park staff work to discover just how many plants, animals and living things are found in the park. They discovered many new species in the last 25 years – new to the park and some new to science as well.

Park Visitation

Great Smoky Mountains National Park recorded 12,937,633 visits in 2022 – it's second-busiest year, ever. But how does this compare with other parks? According to Emily, the park sees 'more people here every year than go to Grand Canyon, Yosemite and Yellowstone National Parks combined.'

Any recent discoveries that stand out?
Salamanders that bioluminesce under black light. It's just something that's come up very recently – in the last couple of years at most.

Any helpful tips for visitors that you can share?
A lot of our visitors tend to go to the 10 hot spots in the park, and those are all wonderful places, but...there are other places in this park that, even on the busiest day, visitors can go, that are equal or sometimes even better.

Any examples of hot spots?
Laurel Falls. It's great, it's easy to get to, but there are other waterfalls in the park and other hikes of equal distance and equal difficulty, or ease, that are really great places to discover.

What are good alternatives to hiking to Laurel Falls?
Middle Prong Trail is a really good one. Baskins Creek Trail is another.

Any other ways to avoid congestion and parking problems at popular trailheads?
We have been working a lot with some local businesses who have been offering shuttle services (nps.gov/grsm/planyourvisit/shuttles.htm) to some of those really popular spots in the park. To have that as an option to driving is really nice; it takes some of the pressure off visitors who don't want to try to find a place to park.

BEARS: WHAT YOU NEED TO KNOW

Just how many bears are there in Great Smoky Mountains National Park? And what should you do when you see one? Emily shares the scoop.

There are something like 1900 black bears in Great Smoky Mountains National Park. The best thing to do is observe from a distance. It's really a joy to see a bear in its natural habitat doing natural bear things. So if you see a bear, remain watchful. Don't approach it. Don't let it approach you. Just let it do its thing; 50 yards or greater is a safe distance.

Always make sure, especially if you're in a campground, to secure your food in a vehicle. In backcountry campsites, there is a set of cables where you put your food in a bin and put it up in the air to remove it from a bear's reach.

PARKS UNDER PRESSURE

Overuse and underfunding have created unique challenges for southern Appalachia's national parks, but innovative initiatives hold promise for the future. By Gregor Clark.

THE NATIONAL PARKLANDS of southern Appalachia are prone to overcrowding, a problem often exacerbated by underfunding. Roughly half of the population of the US lives within a day's drive of Shenandoah, the Smokies or the Blue Ridge Parkway, and National Park Service (NPS) statistics (irma.nps.gov/Stats/Reports/National) clearly illustrate the resulting impact. In 2022, the Blue Ridge Parkway received nearly 16 million visitors, more than any other NPS-administered entity. Meanwhile, Great Smoky Mountains National Park typically sees more annual visitors than the Grand Canyon, Yosemite and Yellowstone combined. In response to these pressures, the parks are taking measures to boost funding, control crowds, improve the visitor experience and protect the environment.

Great Smoky Mountains National Park is a paradox. It draws 2.5 times more visitors than any other American national park (Grand Canyon is second, with 4.7 million visitors in 2022 versus the Smokies' 12.9 million), yet it receives far less funding than other parks its size. The root of the problem lies in the park's legally mandated inability to collect entrance fees (p55). The result is a national treasure that often feels jarringly understaffed and ill-maintained.

Traffic heading into Great Smoky Mountains National Park

Among the challenges facing the park are deteriorating infrastructure, overcrowded parking areas and trailheads, and understaffing. The park's system of self-guided nature trails is a prime example. Try taking one of these short, easy loops, and you'll likely find poorly signposted trailheads, empty brochure boxes stuffed with trash and numbered trail markers buried in undergrowth or badly damaged. Elsewhere throughout the park, decades-old interpretive signs are sun-bleached, peeling or decayed to the point of illegibility.

Parking has become a serious issue on thoroughfares such as Newfound Gap Rd and the Roaring Fork Motor Nature Trail, and at the popular Laurel Falls and Alum Cave trailheads. Despite the construction of multiple paved lots, overuse has resulted in an epidemic of illegal parking along roadsides, prompting erosion and traffic snarls. On the staffing front, underfunding has forced the park to prioritize the hiring of traffic controlers over the interpretive and backcountry rangers that typically abound in a national park of this stature. Indeed, it can sometimes feel easier to spot a bear than a ranger here! Many visitor centers and campgrounds are staffed by non-NPS volunteers, and many NPS staff are seasonal only. As a result, interpretive ranger programs outside of peak summer times are few and far between.

So what to do? In March 2023, the park instituted a new system requiring all park visitors to purchase a daily, weekly or annual parking tag. At the time of research, this new system had already raised millions in revenue, promising better days ahead for the park. Visible improvements in infrastructure, such as posts and split-rail fencing erected to discourage illegal parking, were already in place by spring 2023, and new rangers were reportedly being hired. Park staff have also confirmed that plans are underway to revamp the self-guided nature trails by 2025.

GREAT SMOKY MOUNTAINS NATIONAL PARK DRAWS 2.5 TIMES MORE VISITORS THAN ANY OTHER AMERICAN NATIONAL PARK, YET IT RECEIVES FAR LESS FUNDING THAN OTHER PARKS ITS SIZE.

The takeaway? Be a good park citizen, and pay your parking fees – they really make a difference! Meanwhile, to reduce overcrowding, consider using a private shuttle service (p59) to reach popular trailheads, explore the park during off-peak hours or seek out some of the off-the-beaten-track experiences described in this guidebook.

Overcrowding has also recently become an issue at Shenandoah National Park. Starting in 2022, the park launched a pilot program requiring visitors to Old Rag Summit (p166) to pre-purchase a day-use pass. The new system limited visitor numbers to 800 per day to protect the natural environment and alleviate bottlenecks of up to an hour near the summit viewpoint. At the time of research, the day-pass requirement had been extended through 2023. Other Shenandoah trails affected by chronic overcrowding include Whiteoak Canyon and Dark Hollow Falls.

Like the Smokies, the Blue Ridge Parkway does not charge an entrance fee. Funding impacts here tend to be less severely felt than in the Smokies, though occasional budget shortfalls can result in slower repairs when roads must close due to weather damage or aging infrastructure.

Parking tag kiosks

INDEX

A

Abingdon 136, 138
accessible travel 180
accommodations 173
activities 14, 42-5, **44-5**, *see also individual activities*
admission fees 171
amusement parks
   Anakeesta 107
   Dollywood 102-5
   Gatlinburg Sky Park 107
   Ober Gatlinburg 107
animals 30-1, *see also individual animals*
   bears 30, 38-9, 56, 69, 175, 188-9
   birds 31
   elk 30-1, 82
   fireflies 55-6
   peregrine falcons 31
   salamanders 31
Antler Hill Village 145
Appalachian mountains 32-3
Appalachian people & culture 12-13
Appalachian Trail 39, 85, 138, 171, 175
   accommodations 173
aquariums 106
Arch Rock 88
Arrowmont School of Arts and Crafts 108
art galleries, *see also museums*
   Asheville Museum of Art 148
   Knoxville Museum of Art 98
   Taubman Museum of Art 133
Asheville 22, 35, 144-9, 177, **145**
   beyond Asheville 150-5
ATMs 170

B

bathrooms 181
BBQ 35
bears 30, 38-9, 56, 69, 175, 188-9
beer, *see breweries*
bicycle tours 70-1, **71**
Big Meadows 24, 160-3, **161**
   beyond Big Meadows 164-9
Biltmore Mansion 145
birds 31
bird-watching 58
Black history 121
blazes 175
Blowing Rock 22, 140-2
Blue Ridge Parkway 111-55, **112-13**
   itineraries 22-5, 114-15, **22**, **25**
   navigation 112-13
   planning 118
   travel seasons 114-15
Blue Ridge Tunnel 167
bluegrass 41
books 29
Boone 22, 142-3
breweries 11
   Blue Mountain Brewery 119-20
   Burial 148
   Damascus Brewery 138
   Funkatorium 147
   Great Valley Farm Brewery & Winery 125, 165
   Green Man 148
   HI-Wire 147-8
   Lost Province Brewing Co. 143
   Rockbridge Vineyard & Brewery 165
   Sierra Nevada Brewing 151
   South Slope Brewing District 147
   Stablecraft Brewing 165
   Wedge Brewing 146
bridges
   Linn Cove Viaduct 142
   Mile High Swinging Bridge 141
Bryson City 23, 153-4
business hours 181

C

Cable Mill 71
Cades Cove 20, 68-75, 185, **69**, **71**
Calloway Peak 141, 142
campgrounds
   Abrams Creek Campground 72
   Balsam Mountain Campground 66
   Big Creek Campground 81
   Cades Cove Campground 70, 72
   Cataloochee Campground 81
   Cosby Campground 21, 82
   Davidson River Campground 152
   Deep Creek Campground 65-6
   Look Rock Campground 73
   Peaks of Otter Lodge 127
camping 26, 39, 173
   Elkmont 58
   Great Smoky Mountains National Park 72-3
canoeing, *see kayaking & canoeing*
car travel 170, 171
Carter Family Fold 186
Cataloochee 76-83, 187, **77**, **79**
caves
   Alum Cave 88
   Luray Caverns 165
cell phones 170
cemeteries
   Hannah Cemetery 80
   Oak Grove Cemetery 127
   Palmer Chapel & Cemetery 78
Charlies Bunion 85
Charlottesville 25, 116-21, **117**
Cherokee, NC 23, 151-2, 184-5
Cherokee people 151-2, 184-5
Cherokee National Forest 81
children, travel with 43, 174
   Great Smoky Mountains National Park 61
   High Country (North Carolina) 140
   Knoxville 99
   Shenandoah National Park 162
Chimney Rock 151
Chimney Tops 88, 187
churches
   First Baptist Church 126
   Grace Episcopal Church 126
   Little Cataloochee Baptist Church 80
   Palmer Chapel & Cemetery 78
   Primitive Baptist Church 70-1
   University Chapel 124
cinema 29
Civil War 108
climate 26-7
climate change 178
climbing 143
Clingmans Dome 89

Map Pages **000**

192

INDEX

C–L

clothes 28
Cole Mountain 153
Cosby Campground 21, 82
country music 41
Cradle of Forestry 153
craft beer, *see* breweries
crafts 178
  Arrowmont School of Arts and Crafts 108
  Asheville 146
  Parkway Craft Center 140
credit cards 172
Crooked Road 137-8
cultural centers
  Beck Cultural Center 97
  Folk Art Center 146
culture 12-13
cycling, *see* bicycle tours, mountain biking

D

Daisy Town 59-60
Damascus 138
dangers, *see* safe travel
debit cards 172
Deep Creek 65-7
disabilities, travelers with 180
distilleries 187
dogs, travel with 179
Dollywood 102-5, 173, 174
Dragon's Tooth 131
DreamMore Resort 173
drinks 34-5, 176-7, *see also* breweries, distilleries, wineries
driving 170, 171, *see also* scenic drives
drones 181
Drum Circle 149

E

East Tennessee 90-109, **92**
  itineraries 20-1, 93, **21**
  navigation 92
  travel seasons 93
electricity 181
elk 30-1, 82
Elkmont 54-61, **54**
emergencies 181
etiquette 28
events, *see* festivals & events

F

family travel *see* children, travel with
festivals & events 27, *see also* individual locations
  arts & culture festivals 95
  food & drink festivals 35
  music festivals 41, 149
films 29
fireflies 55-6
firewood 57
fishing 63
flowers 26, 33, 65
Floyd 135-8
foliage 27, 85
food 34-7, 176-7
Forest Heritage Scenic Byway 23, 152-3
forests 33
  Cherokee National Forest 81
  Nantahala National Forest 154
  Pisgah National Forest 152-3
Friday Night Jamboree 177
Front Royal 167

G

gardens, *see* parks & gardens
Gatlinburg 21, 101-9, **101**
Gatlinburg Trail 171
Gatlinburg Trolley 171
geography 32-3
Grandfather Mountain 22, 141
Great Smoky Mountains Institute at Tremont 74
Great Smoky Mountains National Park 49-89, **50-1**,
  accommodations 173
  Cades Cove 68-75, **69**
  Cataloochee 76-83, **77, 79**
  Elkmont 54-61, **54**
  food 83
  High Country 84-9, **85**
  itineraries 52-3, 70-1, 78-9, 86-7, **71, 79, 87**
  navigation 50-1
  Oconaluftee 62-7, **62**
  parking 55
  shuttle buses 59, 171
  Sugarlands 54-6, **54**
  visitor information 58, 63, 71, 73
greenways 179
Gregory Bald 73
gristmills
  Cable Mill 71
  Mingus Mill 67
  Old Mill 108-9

H

Harrisonburg 166
Hartford 81
Hawksbill 161-2
health 175
High Country (Great Smoky Mountains National Park) 84-9, **85**
High Country (North Carolina) 139-43, **140**
highlights 8-17
hiking 8-9, 38-9, 42-3
  Asheville 147
  Big Creek 82-3
  Blue Ridge Parkway 152-3
  Cades Cove 72, 73
  Cataloochee 80
  Damascus 138
  Elkmont 60-1
  Gatlinburg 109
  Grandfather Mountain 142
  High Country (Great Smoky Mountains National Park) 85, 88
  High Country (North Carolina) 140-1
  Lexington 125
  Mt Pisgah 153
  Oconaluftee 64, 67
  Old Rag Mountain 166-7
  Roanoke 130
  Rock Castle Gorge 136-7
  Shenandoah National Park 161-2, 167
  Sugarlands 56-7
Hiltons 137-8
historic sites 15, 184-7
  Beech Grove School 78
  Biltmore Mansion 145
  Caldwell House 79
  Dan Cook Place 80
  Elijah Oliver Place 71
  John Jackson Hannah Cabin 80
  John Oliver Place 70
  Kress Building 148
  Lewis Mountain Cabins 187
  Rapidan Camp 162, 186
  Tipton Place 71
  Woody Place 79
history 108, 184-7
holidays 181
horseback riding 43
  Great Smoky Mountains National Park 65
  Shenandoah National Park 162
Humpback Rocks 121

I

Ijams River Trail 99-100
internet access 181
itineraries 20-5, **21**, **22-3**, **25**, *see also* individual locations

J

Jackson, Thomas Jonathan 'Stonewall' 127
James River 125
Jefferson, Thomas 118-19

K

kayaking & canoeing
  Knoxville 100
  Nantahala Gorge 154
Knoxville 20, 94-100, **95**

L

lakes
  Abbott Lake 127
  Fontana Lake 67
  Mead's Quarry Lake 100
language 29
LeConte Lodge 89
Lexington 25, 122-8, 185, **123, 126**
literature 29
Little Cataloochee 80
logging 75
lookouts 16-17
Luray Caverns 165

193

M

MacCrae Peak 142
markets 178
- Historic City Market 133
- Market Square Farmer's Market 95
- Marquee 147

McAfee Knob 131
Merlin 58
Mingus Mill 67
mobile phones 170
money 170, 172
Monticello 118, 185
Montpelier 118
monuments & statues
- Booker T Washington National Monument 121
- Doc Watson statue 142-3
- Dolly Parton statue 108, 186-7
- Tennessee Woman Suffrage Memorial 95

moonshine 34-5, 187
mountain biking
- Knoxville 100
- Roanoke 132-3

mountain music 40-1, 135-8, 149
movies 29
Mt Mitchell 147
Mt Pisgah 153
museums, see also art galleries
- Big Meadows 163
- Birthplace of Country Music Museum 135
- Carter Family Fold 138
- Center in the Square 133
- Great Smoky Mountains Heritage Center 73-4
- Harrison Museum of African American Culture 121
- Jackson House Museum 126
- Little River Railroad and Lumber Company Museum 75

Map Pages **000**

Mountain Farm Museum 63-4
- Museum of East Tennessee History 96-7
- Museum of the Cherokee Indian 151-2
- Museum of the Shenandoah Valley 165
- O Winston Link 131
- Ripley's Believe It or Not Museum 106
- Virginia Museum of Transportation 133
- VMI Museum 124
- Women's Basketball Hall of Fame 97

music 29, 40-1, 135-8
festivals 41, 149

N

Nantahala Gorge 153-4
national parks, see Great Smoky Mountains National Park, Shenandoah National Park
Native American history 152, see also Cherokee people
Native American sites 73-4
Newfound Gap 86-7, 187, **87**
nightlife 176-7
North Carolina 111-55, **112-13**
- itineraries 22-3, 114-15, **22-3**
- navigation 112-13
- travel seasons 114-15

O

Oconaluftee 62-7, **62**
Old Mill 108-9
Old Rag Mountain 119, 166-7, 184
opening hours 181

P

parking 171, 172, 191
parks & gardens
- Azalea Garden 145
- Julian Price Memorial Park 140
- Mill Mountain Park 130

Moses H. Cone Memorial Park 140
- Pack Square Park 148
Parton, Dolly 102-5, 107, 108, 179
peregrine falcons 31
Pigeon Forge 21, 101-9, **101**
Pigeon River 81
planning
- basics 28-9
- clothes 28
- etiquette 28
- hiking 38-9
- itineraries 20-5
- travel seasons 26-7
plants 33
population 181
public holidays 181

R

rafting, see white-water rafting
ranger 188-9
Rapidan Camp 162, 186
responsible travel 178-9
Roanoke 129-33, **130**
- beyond Roanoke 134-8
Roanoke Star 130
Rocky Knob Recreation Area 136
roller coasters 142, 174, see also amusement parks

S

safari parks 124
safe travel 175
- bears 38-9, 175
- hiking 8, 38-9, 175
- waterfalls 175
salamanders 31
scenic drives
- Forest Heritage Scenic Byway 23, 152-3
- Newfound Gap 86-7, **87**
- Road to Nowhere 66
- Roaring Fork Motor Nature Trail 57
- Rte 11 124
- Skyline Drive 163, 186
scenic railways 153-4
Sharp Top 127
shelters 89, 173
Shenandoah National Park 156-67, **158**
- itineraries 159

- navigation 158
- visitor information 161
- shuttle transport 171
Skyland 24, 160-3, **161**
- beyond Skyland 164-7
Skyline Drive 24-5, 161, 163, **25**
snorkeling 154
stargazing 179
state parks
- Grandfather Mountain State Park 141-2
- Natural Bridge State Park 124-5
statues, see monuments & statues
Staunton 25, 122-8, **123**
Sugarlands 54-61, **54**
sustainability 190-1
swimming
- East Tennessee 127-8
- Knoxville 100
- Sliding Rock Recreation Area 153
Sylva 23, 154

T

taxes 172
Tennessee, see East Tennessee
theaters
- Abingdon 138
- Charlottesville 121
- Knoxville 97
- Staunton 124
theme parks, see amusement parks
ticks 175
time 181
Tinker Cliffs 131
tipping 172
toilets 181
Townsend 20, 73
TRACK trails 174
traffic 191
Trail of Tears 151
trains 153-4
travel seasons 26-7
Tremont 74-5, 185-6
tubing 65

U

universities
- University of Virginia 118-19

Virginia Military Institute 124
Washington and Lee University 124
Urban Wilderness 98-9

V

viewpoints 16-17
Virginia Military Institute 124
Virginia Triple Crown 131
visas 170

W

walking, see hiking
walks

Cataloochee 78-9, **79**
Lexington 126, **126**
Washington and Lee University 124
waterfalls 10, 26, 175
  Abrams Falls 69
  Baskins Creek Falls 60
  Cedar Run Falls 163
  Chasteen Creek Waterfall 65
  Dark Hollow Falls 162
  Doyles River Falls 167
  Grotto Falls 56
  Hebron Falls 140
  Indian Creek Falls 67
  Jones Run Falls 167
  Juney Whank Falls 67
  Laurel Falls 57
  Lewis Spring Falls 163
  Linville Falls 143
  Looking Glass Falls 153
  Lynn Camp Prong Falls 75
  Midnight Hole 82-3
  Panther Falls 127
  Rainbow Falls 56-7
  Ramsey Cascades 60, 61
  Rose River Falls 162
  Three Waterfalls Loop 60, 67
  Tom Branch Falls 67
  Whiteoak Canyon Falls 163
weather 26-7
white-water rafting
  Great Smoky Mountains National Park 81
  Nantahala Gorge 153, 154
wildflowers 26, 33, 65
wildlife 30-1, 178
Winchester 24, 165
wineries
  12 Ridges Vineyard 127
  Antler Hill Village 145
  Blenheim Vineyards 121
  Great Valley Farm Brewery & Winery 125, 165
  King Family Vineyards 121
  Pippin Hill Farm & Vineyards 121
  Rockbridge Vineyard & Brewery 165

Z

zoos 130

NOTES

Grandfather Mountain (p141) is the highest of the Blue Ridge Mountains. It attracts hikers, wildlife spotters and visitors to its Mile High Swinging Bridge.

Home to an interesting museum, an apple blossom festival and an Old Town with shops and restaurants, Winchester (p165) is a perfect base camp for exploring the Shenandoah Valley.

All rights reserved. No part of this publication may be copied, stored in a retrieval system, or transmitted in any form by any means, electronic, mechanical, recording or otherwise, except brief extracts for the purpose of review, and no part of this publication may be sold or hired, without the written permission of the publisher. Lonely Planet and the Lonely Planet logo are trademarks of Lonely Planet and are registered in the US Patent and Trademark Office and in other countries. Lonely Planet does not allow its name or logo to be appropriated by commercial establishments, such as retailers, restaurants or hotels. Please let know of any misuses: lonelyplanet.com/legal/intellectual-property.

pping data sources:
nely Planet
enStreetMap http://openstreetmap.org/copyright

LEFT: SEAN PAVONE/SHUTTERSTOCK ©. RIGHT: KOSOFF/SHUTTERSTOCK ©

Cartographer
Bohumil Ptáček

Assisting Cartographer
Eve Kelly

Assisting Editors
Peter Cruttenden,
Shauna Daly,
Kate James

Cover Researcher
Kat Marsh

Thanks
Ronan Abayawickrema,
Fergal Condon,
Alex Conroy, Karen
Henderson, Alison
Killilea, Darren
O'Connor, Katerina
Pavkova

Paper in this book is certified against the Forest Stewardship Council™ standards. FSC™ promotes environmentally responsible, socially beneficial and economically viable management of the world's forests.

Published by Lonely Planet Global Limited
CRN 554153
3rd edition – Feb 2024
ISBN 978 1 83869 792 1
© Lonely Planet 2024 Photographs © as indicated 2024
10 9 8 7 6 5 4 3 2 1
Printed in China